HERALDRY IN THE VATICAN
A historical walk with the Prefect of the Pontifical
Household through the treasures of papal heraldry

L'ARALDICA IN VATICANO
Passeggiate storiche con il Prefetto della Casa Pontificia
tra gli stemmi pontifici in Vaticano

HERALDIK IM VATIKAN
Ein historischer Spaziergang mit dem Präfekten des
päpstlichen Haushalts durch die heraldischen Schätze
der Päpste

HERALDRY IN THE VATICAN
L'ARALDICA IN VATICANO
HERALDIK IM VATIKAN

JACQUES MARTIN

**Edited and introduced
by
Peter Bander van Duren**

VAN DUREN

British Library Cataloguing in Publication Data

Martin, Jacques
    Heraldry in the Vatican = L'Araldica in
Vaticano = Heraldik im Vatikan.
    1. Heraldry — Vatican City
    I. Title II. Bander van Duren, Peter
    929.6′ 0945′ 634   CR/978.V3

ISBN 0-905715-25-X

Produced in Great Britain
Phototypeset by Grove Graphics, Tring, Hertfordshire,
Colour and Monochrome Origination by
Vorberry Graphics Limited, Aylesbury, Buckinghamshire
and printed and bound by
Billing & Sons Limited, Worcester

CONTENTS

9

LIST OF COLOUR ILLUSTRATIONS

PLATES WITH FOUR ILLUSTRATIONS ARE DESCRIBED TOP, LEFT TO RIGHT, BOTTOM, LEFT TO RIGHT.

Between pages 96 and 97

13

15

AUTHOR'S PREFACE

Nowhere more than in the Vatican can the observer see so clearly how much heraldry is a complementary science to history. Visitors to the Vatican, and particularly those who live there, cannot help noticing the abundance of armorial blazons everywhere: here an eagle, there a dragon, a *fleur-de-lis* or a lion; they are all the 'signatures' of past reigning pontiffs.

Thus, thanks to Borgia Bull or a Lion rampant, or the Barbarini bees, one can state immediately and with certainty that, for example, such a tower belongs to the fifteenth century, this chapel to the sixteenth century and that staircase to the seventeenth century.

There is more: to those who understand the language of heraldry, ancient walls come alive, and the coats of arms, heraldic charges or *imprese* of the popes are like eyes that look at us while revealing much of the past.

The *rovere*, the uprooted oak tree of Julius II, reminds us of Michelangelo on his scaffolding while painting the ceiling of the Sistine Chapel; the Medici roundles of the unfortunate Clement VII bring back the horrors of the sacking of Rome in 1527; the bends in the arms of Pope St. Pius V remind us of the victory of the papal fleet at Lepanto in 1571 and, indeed, the institution of the Feast of the Rosary; the Moor's heads of Pius VII bring back to mind the tragic hours of the captive Pontiff at Savona and the sad event at Fontainbleau. This is the history of the papacy, sometimes glorious, at other times tragic; it is all called to mind because heraldry is a window on history.

I have lived in the Vatican for more than half a century. In my early days I was intrigued by the many armorial representations I saw when I crossed the courtyards, walked along the corridors or entered the many rooms of the Vatican buildings; later I became more and more interested, until in the end I had become expert in reading and translating the innumerable blazons.

The enjoyment I deprived from the heraldic explorations made me decide to share my discoveries with everyone who is interested, and in 1969 I was invited to write a number of illustrated articles for *L'Osservatore della Domenica*. Thanks to the encouragement of many good friends, the assistance of some excellent photographers and particularly the tireless and diligent work of Dr. Peter Bander van Duren, who edited the articles and the many addenda for publication here, I am now in a position to present a more comprehensive study, not only of heraldry in the Vatican, but by making use of heraldry, take my readers on twenty excursions, during which I shall endeavour to bring alive the events of five and a half centuries and fifty-eight pontificates, from Eugene IV (1431) to John Paul II, who ascended the See of St. Peter in 1978.

During the last three years, Peter Bander van Duren and I have collaborated very closely on this project. Naturally, on one or two points our views differed slightly, and, on occasion, I felt that I had to yield to his greater experience in publishing. However,

I always told him of any apprehensions I had, especially if he suggested something which I considered might invite criticism.

For example, there was the question of the introduction: he asked me to allow my writings on the Prefecture of the Pontifical Household to be combined with statements about the person of the Prefect. He made a strong case for not separating the Prefect from the Prefecture and convinced many experts in this field, who in turn, persuaded me to agree to the Introduction in its present form.

The interest shown in the heraldry of the Apostolic Palace by many of the visitors I have had the pleasure of meeting there, and the unexpected questions and well-informed comments confirmed that many coats of arms, heraldic charges or *imprese* of former Pontiffs had often a significance far beyond the small Vatican City State.

On the other hand, heraldry is not without its mysteries: for example, among the *imprese* on the coffered ceiling in the *Sala dei Chiaroscuri*, placed there by Pope Leo X (1513–1521), are three ostrich feathers which are very much like the heraldic badge of the Prince of Wales, derived from the ostrich feathers of the Black Prince (d. 1376). But to Leo X they symbolised the three theological virtues which adorn the human soul in which God lives. The papal *imprese* and the royal badge have different origins and meanings, and yet a casual observer might wonder what the feathers of the Prince of Wales are doing on the ceiling of Pope Leo X, the first Medici Pope.

Somewhat embarrassing to me was the importance attached to the changes in my own armorial bearings which I had adopted when I was consecrated bishop.

With my appointment as Prefect of the Pontifical Household, I enjoyed the unique privilege of impaling my own arms with those of the sovereign Pontiff whom I served.

If I have made a contribution to the history of pontifical heraldry, it was by the Grace of God and the trust that three successive Pontiffs, Paul VI, John Paul I and John Paul II, placed in me when they appointed me Prefect of the Pontifical Household.

I must give an explanation about the 'Author's Acknowledgement' which I have placed at the end of the book so that readers have a deeper understanding and appreciation of my gratitude and endebtedness to many friends and acquaintances who have helped me and Peter Bander van Duren during the production of the book. It is very difficult to acknowledge kindnesses and help received by listing persons in a manner which makes allowances for their eminent status or the significance of their assistance. I have endeavoured to group together various kinds of assistance, but every help has been deeply appreciated.

However, I must make two exceptions and express my very special gratitude here: to Mr. Pierre Blanchard of the Administration of the Patrimony of the Holy See, who often acted in a liaison capacity between me and Dr. Bander van Duren, and who has given much of his free time when the pressures of my office made it impossible to undertake certain tasks myself. Secondly, I wish to place on record my gratitude to Mr. Leslie Hayward, who has worked so hard and with such enthusiasm on preparing the entire artwork for this book.

The reason I have not given greater prominence to the work of my collaborator, Peter Bander van Duren, whose tenacity and determination made this book possible and who wrote the introduction, is his express wish that I should not do so. But I know that he is aware of my sentiments.

Palazzo Apostolico
Città del Vaticano
April 1987

+ Jacques Martin

AUTHOR'S ACKNOWLEDGEMENT

It is difficult to compile a list of acknowledgements which does justice to the many friends and acquaintances who have so freely given assistance and advice and deserve to be mentioned here. I am very grateful to many, and I acknowledge their kindnesses with deep gratitude.

I am endebted to the renowned heraldic expert and artist, Archbishop Bruno Heim, who has painted the three impaled coats of arms to which the author has been entitled as Prefect of the Pontifical Household of the late Popes Paul VI and John Paul I, and Our Holy Father John Paul II, *gloriosamente regnate*. Archbishop Heim has also made freely available all the heraldic artwork and photographs we had asked for, as well as some correspondence from the time he was secretary to the Nuncio in France, Archbishop Angelo Giuseppe Roncalli, the late and much beloved Pope John XXIII, a fellow heraldist.

My editor and I are very grateful to those who have given their time and assistance with some of the translation: Archbishop Cesare Zacchi, the members of the Apostolic Nunciature in London, notably Mons. Rino Passigato and Mons. Kieran Conry, and Sig. Tullio Turchi, an Italian student, who worked part-time for Dr. Bander van Duren, assisting with the basic preparation for translating much of the material which had appeared in *L'Osservatore della Domenica* in 1969.

This book owes much to the skill and generosity of several photographers. First, I must mention Sig. Enrico Zuppi, who took the photographs for my articles. The original photographs have been lost, but thanks to the latest technology employed by the publishers in reproducing some photographs from the magazine with the use of laser scanning, Mr. John Adams and Mr. Ray Howson were even able to improve on the quality of the pictures that had been printed in 1969.

Special gratitude goes to Sig. Arturo Mari, the photographer of *L'Osservatore Romano*, who has taken innumerable pictures in colour and in black and white specially for this book, and who has placed them so generously at our disposal; his excellent work will help many to appreciate much that is hidden from the eyes of the visitors to the Vatican. I wish to thank also the pontifical photographer Sig. Felici for allowing me to use some photographs taken on solemn occasions in the Vatican. I am endebted to Count Andrzej Ciechanowiecki for placing at our disposal photographs of paintings and busts of popes from his art gallery. My thanks to the late Mr. Peter Dean for assisting with architectural terminology, and to his son Richard, for the photographs of the coats of arms on the book jacket.

The great number of illustrations in this book have helped me to do what I set out to achieve: to bring alive not just the heraldry in the Vatican but five and a half centuries and fifty-eight pontificates. My collaborator and I decided at the beginning of our work on this project that if the captions to the illustrations could be multi-lingual, more people could join me on my exploratory walks. For technical reasons, we were restricted to three languages, and we chose English, Italian and German. The typesetting of tri-lingual captions demands great skill and concentration, and I wish to thank the brothers Keith and Ian Lawrence for their excellent work.

Last but by no means least, I must thank the publishers, especially the Managing Director, Mr. Colin Smythe, for sparing no effort and resources to produce this work. It has truly been a labour of love. I have already paid tribute in my Preface to Mr. Leslie Hayward, another Director of Van Duren Publishers Ltd.

On a personal note, it has been particularly gratifying and enjoyable to have been so closely involved with all the stages of the production of this book and to see what has grown from the small seeds which I planted in 1969 in the original articles in *L'Osservatore della Domenica*.

Palazzo di S. Carlo
Città del Vaticano
April 1987

+ Jacques Martin
Tit. Archbishop of Neapoli in Palaestina
Prefect emeritus of the Pontifical Household

INTRODUCTION

by

Peter Bander van Duren

THE PREFECTURE OF THE PONTIFICAL HOUSEHOLD

In preparing this work for publication, I have always worked in close collaboration with the author, His Excellency the Most Reverend Monsignore Jacques Martin, Prefect of the Pontifical Household. There was only one occasion when some persuasion was needed to obtain Mons. Martin's permission to allow me to modify his text; it was the section on the Prefecture of the Pontifical Household. As editor of this work I have often used my discretion concerning interpretations and additions, and I have always had the unstinting support of the author. However, the Introduction needed more than mere revision of the text. I felt it needed substantial additional material.

It had soon become clear to me that it was impossible to separate the Prefect from the institution and historic buildings of the Prefecture. The Prefect, our host and guide on the heraldic walks we are about to embark on, has himself made heraldic history, and much of the knowledge we shall gain is the fruit of his personal scholarship and particularly the love for his home in which he has lived for over fifty years. Monsignore Martin has lived in the Vatican since the days when he joined the French Section of the Secretariat of State of His Holiness in 1936, and after he had been consecrated Titular Bishop of Neapolis in Palaestina in 1964, during the pontificate of Paul VI, first as Prefect of the Apostolic Palace and then as Prefect of the Pontifical Household.

Those privileged to know Monsignore Martin personally, have experienced his natural kindness, his unassuming simplicity and his courtesy to all who meet him. These qualities are deeply cherished by his many friends. Few people have enriched my life as much as has Monsignore Martin, but I was facing a dilemma: should I present the Prefecture of the Pontifical Household and its fascinating history based only on the text I had received from the author? It contained only very little information about the present incumbent of the Prefect's office. Had I done so, I would have failed in my duty to present a comprehensive view; had I written about the Prefect of the Pontifical Household in a separate section, I would have presented many historical facts, and especially the uniqueness of the historic and heraldic rôle of Monsignore Martin, out of context, and the significance of many points would have been lost on the reader.

25

(Opposite)
His Excellency Most Reverend Mons. Jacques Martin, Prefect of the Pontifical Household, the first dignitary in the history of the papacy to hold this high office under three pontiffs, leaving the Prefecture on the first floor of the Apostolic Palace on his way to a meeting with the Holy Father. The Prefecture of the Pontifical Household combines the functions formerly carried out by the Congregation for Ceremonies, the Majordomo and the Chamberlain of his Holiness. The Prefecture prepares audiences and papal ceremonies (except for the strictly liturgical part), makes arrangements for the Pope's visits inside Rome and Italy and collaborates with the Secretariat of State in preparing the Pope's journeys abroad.

(Lato Opposto)
Sua Eccellenza Reverendissima Mons. Jacques Martin, Prefetto della Casa Pontificia (è il primo dignitario nella storia del papato ad occupare questo alto ufficio sotto tre Pontefici) mentre lascia la Prefettura al primo piano del Palazzo Apostolico per recarsi dal Santo Padre. La Prefettura della Casa Pontificia, riunendo le attribuzioni già un tempo della Congregazione Cerimoniale, del Maggiordomo e del Maestro di Camera di Sua Santità, prepara le udienze e le cerimonie pontificie (esclusa la parte strettamente liturgica), dispone quanto necessario per gli spostamenti del Papa in Roma e in Italia, e collabora con la Segreteria di Stato per i viaggi del Sommo Pontefice fuori d'Italia.

(Gegenüber)
Seine Exzellenz der Hochwürdigste Mons. Jacques Martin, Präfekt des päpstlichen Haushalts, der erste Würdenträger in der Geschichte des Papsttums, dieses hohe Amt unter drei Päpsten zu halten, verlässt die Präfektur auf der ersten Etage des Apostolischen Palastes, um sich zum Heiligen Vater zu begeben. Die Präfektur des päpstlichen Haushalts vereinigt in sich die Pflichten der ehemaligen Zeremonienkongregation, des Haushofmeisters und des Kammerherrn Seiner Heiligkeit. Sie bereitet die Audienzen und päpstlichen Zeremonien vor (mit Ausnahme des liturgischen Teils), organisiert die Besuche des Papstes innerhalb der Stadt Rome und Italien und bereitet gemeinsam mit dem Staatssekretariat die Reisen des Papstes ins Ausland vor.

The painting of Pope John Paul II in the entrance lobby of the Prefecture; it is a life-size picture and the first sight the visitor to the Apostolic Palace has of the Pontiff.

Il dipinto di Papa Giovanni Paolo II nell'atrio della Prefettura. È in grandezza naturale e costituisce la prima immagine che il visitatore del Palazzo Apostolico ha del Pontifice.

Das Gemälde des Papstes Johannes Paulus II in der Vorhalle der Präfektur; es ist ein lebensgrosses Bild und gibt dem Besucher zum Apostolischen Palast den ersten Blick auf den Papst.

With the agreement of Monsignore Martin, I have made full use of the narrative he provided and I have inserted relevant references to the author and his unique position in heraldry and in the history of the papacy.

I must now explain therefore that this introduction is not jointly written by author and editor. I have used my prerogative as editor and inserted material about the author where I believe it complements his information about the Prefecture and the Prefect of the Pontifical Household.

Throughout my work, which was sometimes far more difficult than it should appear to the reader, I have had the unstinting support and trust of the author. The difficulties I found were in the interpretation of individual words or phrases. Both the author and I worked towards the greatest possible perfection in bringing out the right nuances of meaning which were so eloquently expressed by the author in his Italian language articles in L'OSSERVATORE DELLA DOMENICA. Bishop Martin often questioned a sentence in this context, not to criticise but make sure that the right nuance had been obtained.

It was Mons. Martin's masterly and original personal style, his use of words and nuances, and the manner in which he used the Italian language to speak diplomatically yet plainly, for all to understand and for none to take offence, which had so deeply impressed me and which I wanted to preserve.

Sadly, the subtle differences between the Latin and the Anglo-Germanic languages have forced me on occasion to change the structure of a sentence or the vocabulary in order to bring out more clearly a nuance the author wanted to communicate. The Anglo-Germanic languages, especially English, lend themselves to plain or scientific speaking, but they also allow coherent verbosity which uses many words and say nothing. But what worried me most was that a certain honest bluntness of the English language would appear harsh or sharp when translated back into Italian. Nowhere in his original text has Monsignore Martin been harsh or sharp, let alone hurtful, to anyone.

If I cannot reproduce the Author's style precisely, I owe it to him and to the readers of this work to give the assurance that I have tried to the best of my ability to render an accurate interpretation.

Prefect Martin has been host on heraldic walks to countless visitors to the Vatican. When greeting visiting Heads of State or official visitors to the Pope, he leads them through the halls and rooms full of heraldic treasures, and sometimes he can point out a direct link with the visitor's predecessors or country.

A very much reduced reproduction of the ceiling in one of the rooms of the Pontifical Prefecture (taken with a wide-angle lens). At both ends of this long ceiling, which has the arms of Julius III as its centre point, and where the ceiling begins to curve into decorative mouldings, are the semi-circular paintings with the heraldic 'mobili' of Cardinal Ricci.

Una piccolissima riduzione dell'intero soffitto in una delle stanze della Prefettura Pontificia (presa con grandangolare). Agli estremi di questo lungo soffitto, che ha come suo punto centrale lo stemma di Giulio III e dove il soffitto comincia a piegarsi in cornici decorative, ci sono i dipinti semicircolari con i mobili araldici del Cardinal Ricci.

Eine sehr verkleinerte Reproduktion einer der Decken in den Räumen der Pontifikalen Präfektur (mit Weitwinkellinse aufgenommen). An beiden Enden der langen Decke, die als Mittelpunkt das Wappen des Julius III hat, und wo die Decke sich zu wölben beginnt und in dekorative Stuccoarbeit übergeht, sieht man die halbkreisförmigen Gemälde mit den heraldischen 'mobili' des Kardinals Ricci.

The outside of the Prefecture.

La parte esterna della Prefettura.

Die Aussenseite der Präfektur.

But our heraldic excursions with Monsignore Martin are far more extensive and comprehensive; sometimes they will take us briefly outside the Vatican City State. It was not easy for our host to guide us through fifty-eight pontificates, from Eugene IV (1431–1447), the second Pope who took up residence in the Vatican Palace, to John Paul II (1978–) now gloriously reigning.

Such a chronological exploration means that on occasion we may have to go to and fro several times, passing through the same room or hall time and time again. One soon becomes familiar with the lay-out of the Apostolic Palace and the Vatican City.

We start our first heraldic excursion at the Prefecture of the Pontifical Household on the first floor in the Apostolic Palace, where we meet our host. He will explore with us the history of fifty-eight pontificates, using heraldry as one of the most reliable scientific aids to history.

The Prefecture of the Pontifical Household (*Prefettura della Casa Pontificia*) is not a Congregation, nor is it a Tribunal or a Secretariat as are all the other administrative departments of the Roman Curia. Anybody who searches for its entry in the 2,000 odd pages of the *Annuario Pontificio* will find the Prefecture listed after the Administration of the Patrimony of the Apostolic See and before the Office of the Almoner to His Holiness in the section *Uffici*.

The Prefecture of the Pontifical Household is an organism somewhat apart from all the others; it is solely dependent on the person of the sovereign pontiff. This 'organism' is headed by a Prefect who has as his deputy a Regent, and a staff of attachés who are responsible for protocol, audiences, ceremonies, papal visits, travel arrangements and other matters.

Over the centuries the Prefect has been known by several different titles, such as 'Chamberlain to His Holiness' or' *Maestro di Camera*', and he has always been endowed with extraordinary and unique privileges. For example,he is the only prelate of the Roman Curia who may enter the Pope's library unannounced at any time: he is at the Pope's side at audiences that are not strictly private, and he accompanies the Holy Father on all his travels in and outside Rome.

The most unusual and remarkable privilege is the right to impale his personal coat of arms with that of the Pontiff whom he serves as Prefect. In fact, he shares the reigning Pontiff's armorial bearings.

The Prefect resides, of course, in the Vatican, and the Prefecture, which houses his offices and official reception rooms, was built on an inclined plane of the ancient wall that surrounded the Vatican and which dated from the pontificate of Nicholas V (1447–1455). The Prefecture itself was built in the pontificate of Julius III (1550–1555), the former Cardinal Del Monte who had played such an outstanding part in the first phase of the Council of Trent.

Bernini's colonnade partly conceals the exterior view of the Prefecture when seen from St. Peter's Square. The interior is a vast construction, and its most striking feature is a suite of three large rooms with ceilings profusely · decorated by Stefano Veltroni da Bologna. Veltroni was a pupil of Giorgio Vasari, who was working at the time on the decorations in the Sala Regia. Other contemporary artists who worked in the Prefecture were Pietro da Imola, also known as

Apostolic Palace: on the second floor is the 'noble apartment', used for papal audiences. It is a sequence of fine rooms, restored in 1964, which begins with the Clementine Hall and finishes with the Library where the Pope receives important public figures.

Palazzo Apostolico: al secondo piano l'appartamento nobile, utilizzato per le udienze pontificie. È una fuga di saloni, restaurati nel 1964, che inizia colla Sala Clementina e si conclude colla Biblioteca, dove il Santo Padre riceve personaggi di particolare rilievo.

Apostolischer Palast: auf der zweiten Etage ist das 'Appartamento Nobile', in dem päpstliche Audienzen stattfinden. Die in 1964 restaurierte Flucht von Salons beginnt mit dem Sala Clementina und endet mit der Bibliothek, wo der Papst offizielle Würdenträger zur Audienz empfängt.

31

COLOUR PLATES

I

FULL CIRCLE

The simplicity and elegance of the heraldic display of the first known armorial bearings in the Apostolic Palace which belong to Eugene IV (1431–1447); the opulent armorial ceilings of the sixteenth century, here the arms of Clement VIII (1592–1605); the less attractive heraldic designs of the nineteenth century, showing, as in the arms of Gregory XVI (1831–1846), complicated charges in the shield and unnecessary additions, such as wreaths and scrolls, and the heavy pontifical insignia – the keys are completely out of proportion to the coat of arms –, and finally, the extremely simple and almost abstract armorial bearings of Paul VI (1963–1978), cover 550 years of heraldry in the Vatican.

RICORRENZA CICLICA

La semplicità e l'eleganza della rappresentazione araldica del primo stemma conosciuto nel Palazzo Apostolico: appartiene a Eugenio IV (1431–1447); gli opulenti soffitti araldici del XVI secolo [qui é quello con lo stemma di Clemente VIII (1592–1605)]; i meno attraenti disegni araldici del XIX secolo che mostrano, come nel caso dello stemma di Gregorio XVI (1831–1846), complicati mobili nello scudo e superflue aggiunte, come le chiavi che sono proporzionalmente sbagliate; ed infine il semplicissimo e quasi astratto stemma di Paolo VI (1963–1978), costituiscono 550 anni di araldica nel Vaticano.

EINE VOLLE WENDUNG

Die Schlichtheit und Eleganz des ersten bekannten Wappens im Apostolischen Palast, das dem Eugen IV (1431–1447) gehörte; die reiche heraldische Decke des 16. Jahrhunderts, hier mit dem Wappen des Klemens VIII (1592–1605); die weniger schönen heraldischen Entwürfe des 19. Jahrhunderts, die, wie hier, im Wappen des Gregorius XVI (1831–1846), ein kompliziertes und überladenes Schield haben mit unnötigen Zusatzen, wie Kränze und Schnörkel, und mit Würdenzeichen wie die Schlüssel, die gänzlich unproportional das ganze Wappen überwältigen; und zuletzt das ausserordentlich einfache und nahezu abstrakte Wappen des Paulus VI (1963–1978). Zusammen zeigen sie die Entwicklung der päpstlichen Heraldik im Vatikan in den letzten 550 Jahren.

II & III

His Excellency Bishop Jacques Martin holds the unique distinction in the history of the papacy of having served three successive pontiffs as Prefect of the Pontifical Household: Popes Paul VI, John Paul I and John Paul II.

He is the only Prelate to have impaled his personal arms with those of the three Popes.*

Sua Eccellenza il Vescovo Jacques Martin detiene la distinzione, unica nelle storia del papato, di aver servito tre consecutivi pontefici in qualità di Prefetto della Casa Pontificia: Paolo VI, Giovanni Paolo I e Giovanni Paolo II.
É l'unico dignitario ad avere il proprio stemma impalato con quelli di tre Papi.*

Seine Exzellenz Bischof Jacques Martin ist der einzige Prälat in der Geschichte des Papsttums, der drei Päpsten als Präfekt des päpstlichen Haushalts gedient hat: den Päpsten Paulus VI, Johannes Paulus I und Johannes Paulus II.

COLOUR PLATES

Er ist auch der einzige Würdenträger, der sein persönliches Wappen mit dem Wappen der drei Päpste gespalten führen darf.

* Design of the three coats of arms:
Disegno dei tre stemmi:
Entwurf der drei Wappen: Mons. B. B. Heim

IV

The Prefect of the Pontifical Household greets all heads of state and official visitors on arrival in the Vatican. He then leads them through the historic rooms, adorned with heraldic treasures, to meet the Pope, (Top): Her Majesty Queen Elizabeth II of the United Kingdom. (Below): Their Royal Highnesses The Prince and Princess of Wales.

Il Prefetto della Casa Pontificia riceve tutti i Capi di Stato e visitatori ufficiali al loro arrivo nel Vaticano, li conduce poi attraverso le storiche stanze ornate da tesori araldici per incontrare il Papa. (In alto): Sua Maesta la Regina del Regno Unito Elisabetta II. (In basso): le Loro Altezze Reali il Principe e la Principessa di Galles.

Der Präfekt des päpstlichen Haushalts begrüsst alle Staatsoberhäupte und offiziellen Besucher bei ihrer Ankunft im Vatikan. Er führt sie dann durch die historischen, mit heraldischen Kunstwerken geschmückten Säle zum Papst. (Oben): Ihre Majestät Königin Elizabeth II des Vereinigten Königreiches. (Unten): Ihre Königlichen Hoheiten der Prinz und die Prinzessin von Wales.

V

(Top): President Mr. Ronald Reagan of the United States of America. (Below: President Herr Karl Carstens of the Federal Republic of Germany.

(In alto): Il Presidente degli Stati Uniti Mr Ronald Reagan. (In basso): Il Presidente della Repubblica Federale Tedesca Herr Karl Carstens.

(Oben): Der Präsident der Vereinigten Staaten von Amerika Mr Ronald Reagan. (Unten): Der Bundespräsident von Deutschland Herr Karl Carsten.

VI

(Top): The President of the Italian Republic Sig. Francesco Cossiga. (Below): Mons. Martin receives His Majesty King Juan Carlos I of Spain.

(In alto) Il Presidente della Repubblica Italiana Sig. Francesco Cossiga. (In basso); Mons. Martin riceve Sua Maestà Juan Carlos I, Re di Spagna.

(Oben): Der Präsident der italienischen Republik Sig. Francesco Cossiga. (Unten): Mons. Martin empfängt Seine Majestät Juan Carlos I, König von Spanien.

COLOUR PLATES

VII

The Prefect of the Pontifical Household locks the door of the second conclave in 1978, and later he introduces the newly elected Pope to the pontifical apartments.

Il Prefetto della Casa Pontificia mentre chiude la porta del secondo conclave nel 1978 e mentre introduce il nuovo Papa negli appartamenti Pontifici.

Der Präfekt des päpstlichen Haushalts schliesst die Tür zum zweiten Konklave in 1978 ab, und später führt den neugewählten Papst in die pontifikalen Apartments.

VIII

One of the most beautiful ceilings is in the Antechamber of the Prefecture of the Papal Household. Two thirds of the centre are occupied by the arms of Pope Julius III and the lower third by the arms of Cardinal Ricci di Montepulciano, who like the present Prefect had the privilege of impaling his personal arms with those of the Pope whom he served.

Uno dei più bei soffitti è nell'Anticamera della Prefettura della Casa Pontificia. Due terzi del centro sono occupati dalle armi di Giulio III; il restante, dalle armi del cardinale Ricci di Montepulciano che, come l'attuale Prefetto, aveva il privilegio di impalare le sue armi personali con quelle del Papa del quale era al servizio.

Eine der schönsten Decken im Apostolischen Palast ist in dem Vorzimmer der Präfektur des päpstlichen Haushalts. Zwei Drittel in der Mitte der Decke sind vom Wappen des Papstes Julius III eingenommen; im unteren Drittel ist das Wappen des Kardinals Ricci di Montepulciano, der, wie der augenblickliche Präfekt, das Recht hatte, sein persönliches Wappen mit dem des regierenden Papstes zu verbinden.

This painting of the heraldic 'mobile' of Cardinal Ricci di Montepulciano does not only show one of the many heraldic symbols in every room of his apartment, but the photograph itself, taken by Sig. Arturo Mari, the pontifical photographer, is a masterpiece of the modern art form of photography, bearing in mind that the hedgehog looking at the sun (part of the arms of Cardinal Ricci) is painted very small and on a curved ceilings.

Questo dipinto del mobile araldico del Cardinal Ricci di Montepulciano non solo mostra la moltitudine di simboli araldici in ogni stanza del suo appartamento, ma la foto stessa, presa dal Sig. Arturo Mari, il fotografo pontificio, è un capolavoro di forma artistica moderna, se si tiene conto che il riccio rivolto verso il sole (parte dello stemma del Cardinal Ricci) è dipinto molto piccolo e su un soffitto curvato.

Dieses Gemälde eines heraldischen 'mobile', das aus dem Wappen des Kardinals Ricci di Montepulciano stammt, gibt nicht nur einen Eindruck von den vielen heraldischen Symbolen, die in allen Räumen seines Apartments gefunden werden können, sondern es ist auch ein Beispiel der modernen Kunstform der Fotografie. Das Bild ist von Sig. Arturo Mari, dem päpstlichen Hof-Fotografen, aufgenommen worden, und man muss bedenken, dass das Gemälde sehr klein ist auf einer sehr grossen und kurvierten Decke.

Julius III (1550–1555)
Giulio III (1550–1555)
Julius III (1550–1555)
G.M.CIOCCHI DEL MONTE

Pietro Venale, and Lelio di Montepulciano. The architect was Nanni di Baccio Bigio. One must remember that this is still the century of Raphael and Michelangelo, so the style is derived from the *grotteschi* of the Raphael *Logge* and inspired by the decoration of Nero's *Domus Aurea* which had been restored in the first years of the sixteenth century.

It is possible to date the elaborate decorations not only because of surviving documents which give details of payments made to the artists and architect, but in a far more direct way: the papal coat of arms that adorns the ceilings is that of the contemporary pope, Julius III. So the Prefecture was obviously built in his reign.

Here as elsewhere, heraldry is a good guide. This complementary science to history can, apart from its chronological function, help us to identify the name of the reigning Pontiff because Julius III had adopted canting (or 'speaking') arms. The three mountains, also reproduced in the four corners of one of the ceilings, tell us clearly that he was Cardinal Del Monte.

Examples of canting arms are quite common in the Vatican; Pope Benedict XV, Giacomo della Chiesa, had a church in his coat of arms, and the mountains reappeared again in the pontificate of Paul VI, Giovanni Battista Montini. Paul VI had the interior of the Prefecture renovated by the Milanese architect Bellini.

Heraldry has yet another surprise for us; it helps us to discover who was the important person for whom all this work was done during the pontificate of Julius III. The observer will note a second coat of arms on the ceiling, half of which reproduces the arms of the reigning pope, the other half depicts under *fleurs-de-lis*

36

a little animal curled up in a corner and looking diagonally at the sun. (See Colour Plate VIII). The animal is a hedgehog (in Italian *riccio*, plural: *ricci*). These too are canting arms because we are in the apartment of Monsignore Giovanni Ricci, a personal friend of Pope Julius III and *Praefectus Aerarii Sanctae Romanae Ecclesiae*, (Treasurer of the Holy Roman Church). He had overseen much of the pontiff's administration, and later became a cardinal who was himself a candidate for the tiara in the conclave of 1565, when he received thirty of the thirty-four votes needed to become pope. However, the conclave elected Antonio Michele Ghisleri, who took the name Pius V.

Monsignore Giovanni Ricci from Montepulciano in Tuscany, an eminent prelate of the Renaissancce, was an extraordinary personality; he was a great traveller in the service of the popes, a famous collector of *objets d'art*, and especially a great builder. He commissioned the building of the Villa Medici and the Sacchetti Palace, originally known as Villa Ricci and the Ricci Palace. Even before he was elevated to the cardinalate, he had built for himself, with the consent of his friend Julius III, "a modest residence" in the Vatican: the very one which bears today his coat of arms impaled with that of Julius III.

Monsignore Ricci was not *Maestro di Camera* or Prefect of the Papal Household as the impaled coat of arms might suggest. Heraldic discipline in the days of Julius III was less rigid than today, and some other members of the *famiglia pontificia* had been given permission to impale their personal arms with those of the reigning pontiff.

Many a coat of arms, canting or otherwise, contains information about family legends or refers to specific patronage or notable historical

Giovanni Cardinal Ricci di Montepulciano (1497–1574). (Palazzo Ricci-Paracciani, Roma).

Exceptionally beautiful three-dimensional heraldic 'mobili' are on the ceilings of most rooms in the Pontifical Prefecture.

Here the hedgehog looking at the sun is moulded and gilded on the white ceiling in a garland of fruit, also in exquisite stucco work.

All over the rooms are little gilt 'monti' (heraldic mountains) in stucco, (Julius III, Giammaria M. Ciocchi Del Monte).

The age of Julius III was in every respect one of the highlights in the evolution of heraldry, and the apartments on the first floor of the Apostolic Palace hold countless heraldic treasures and curiosities. Sadly, most of them are in rooms not open to the public.

Nei soffitti della maggior parte delle stanze della Prefettura Pontificia ci sono mobili araldici tridimensionali eccezionalmente belli.

Qui il riccio rivolto verso il sole è plasmato sul soffitto bianco, in una corona di frutti, anch'essa in squisito lavoro di stucco.

Per tutte le stanze ci sono piccoli monti dorati in stucco (Giulio III, Giammaria M. Ciocchi Del Monte). Il periodo di Giulio III era sotto ogni aspetto uno dei migliori nell'evoluzione dell'araldica, e gli appartamenti nel primo piano del Palazzo Apostolico presentano innumerevoli tesori araldici e curiosità. Sfortunatamente la maggior parte di essi si trovano in stanze non aperte al pubblico.

Aussergewöhnlich schöne drei-dimensionale heraldische 'mobili' kann man in allen Räumen der Pontifikalen Präfektur an den Decken finden.

Hier sieht man den Igel, der an die Sonne schaut, modelliert in einer äusserst feinen Girlande von Früchten, ebenfalls in Stucco.

In allen Räumen findet man ebenfalls kleine, manchmal vergoldete 'monti', heraldische Berge, (Julius III, Giammaria M. Ciocchi Del Monte).

Das Pontifikat von Julius III war in jeder Hinsicht ein Höhepunkt der heraldischen Entwicklung, und die Apartments der ersten Etage des Apostolischen Palastes geben Zeugnis davon mit unzähligen heraldischen Schätzen und Kuriositäten. Leider sind die meisten Räume nicht der öffentlichkeit zugängig.

The impaled arms of Cardinal Ricci di Montepulciano.
Lo stemma impalato del Cardinale Ricci di Montepulciano.
Das gespaltene Wappen des Kardinals Ricci di Montepulciano.

events in which ancestors of the bearer had been involved, Monsignore Ricci's sun-gazing hedgehog is no exception. The eminent prelate had an ancestor in the twelfth century whom one might compare to one of today's weather forecasters; he announced to all and sundry what the weather would be like with such certainty that his fellow citizens soon accused him of witchcraft and threatened to burn him alive. To escape certain death, the man revealed his secret; he kept a hedgehog on his terrace, and depending whether the animal came out of his nook or quickly went back into it, the weather infallibly turned out fine or bad the next day. Monsignore Ricci's ancestor soon gained the nickname *Riccio*, which passed on to his descendants in its shortened form *Ricci*.

The origin of the name Ricci may be judged legendary, but the animal faithfully accompanied the prelate wherever he built or had a room decorated. Hedgehogs can be found in the Sacchetti Palace and in the Villa Medici. A hedgehog even accompanied our prelate in death, for it can be seen on the beautiful monument over his tomb in San Pietro in Montorio.

In his lifetime, Monsignore Ricci was often called after the town of his origin: Cardinal Montepulciano, and his Vatican residence inherited the name 'Montepulciano Apartment'.

Under the successors of Julius III, especially under Gregory XIII and Sixtus V, the buildings inside the Vatican expanded considerably. In view of the proximity of the Montepulciano Apartment to the private apartments of the pontiffs, it was desirable and practical that it should be reserved for the prelate who had to work most often and most intimately with the reigning pontiff; the Chamberlain of His Holiness.

40

The title Chamberlain has been changed twice recently; first in 1967 when Paul VI reformed the Roman Curia and added to the duties of Chamberlain those of *Maggiordomo* and *Maestro di Casa*, giving him the new title *Prefetto del Palazzo Apostolico*. Later, the Pope wishing to revive the ancient name and concept of *Domus Pontificalis*, changed the prelate's title to *Prefetto della Casa Pontificia*.

Sadly the days have gone when eminent servants of the reigning pontiff, such as the author's predecessor, Monsignore Ricci, would commission some building or monument for posterity to remember them by. Future scholars of heraldry and of history of the papacy will regret the passing of those days because the author, who at the time of writing this work is the Prefect of the Pontifical Household, has set a precedent in the history of heraldry and of the papacy: Monsignore Jacques Martin has been the first prelate who has served as Prefect of the Pontifical Household under three Popes, Paul VI, John Paul I and John Paul II. On each appointment he was given the special privilege of impaling his personal episcopal coat of arms with that of the pontiff he was to serve.

Following heraldic precedent and hitherto usual practice, a prelate thus honoured by his pontiff may bear the impaled coat of arms for life, Monsignore Martin has received this honour three times. While serving the reigning pontiff as Prefect of the Pontifical Household, he naturally impales his arms with those of John Paul II.

An interesting question which had been raised by some heraldic scholars concerned the armorial bearings Mons. Martin might adopt should he retire from office of Prefect, though the Prefecture with him seemed unthinkable.

I never raised this question with him because he would have considered even a theoretical

Above: the arms of Popes Paul VI, John Paul I and II.
Below: the impaled arms of Prefect Martin.

In alto: gli stemmi dei Papi Paolo VI, Giovanni Paolo I e II. In basso: gli stemmi impalati del Prefetto Martin.

Oben: die Wappen der Päpste Paulus VI, Johannes Paulus I und II. Unten: die gespaltenen Wappen des Präfekten Martin.

41

The episcopal coat of arms of His Excellency Most Reverend Bishop Jacques Martin, (1964).

Lo stemma episcopale di Sua Eccellenza Reverendissima il Vescovo Jacques Martin (1964).

Das Bischofswappen Seiner Hochwürdigsten Excellenz Herrn Bischof Jacques Martin, (1964).

discussion of this subject inappropriate. I always felt that he would disappoint those heraldists who expected some armorial novelty. On 18 December 1986, His Holiness Pope John Paul II accepted his resignation and appointed Mons. Martin Tit. Archbishop of Neapolis in Palestina and Prefect emeritus. Although his heraldic achievement would now be a hat with ten tassels either side, he reverted to his original episcopal coat of arms and impaled the arms of the three Pontiffs whom he had served as Prefect of the Pontifical Household, on his heart and not on his shield.

However, I thought it essential to preserve this unique case in pontifical heraldry for future scholars to study, and with the permission of Mons. Martin I approached Archbishop Bruno Heim, then Apostolic Pro-Nuncio in London, and regarded as one of the finest heraldic artists and experts on ecclesiastical heraldry. He had worked as a young secretary for almost five years with another heraldist, Archbishop Angelo Giuseppe Roncalli, the future Pope John XXIII; the author has given a most valuable insight in the heraldic work of Pope John in Chapter XIX. Mons. Heim was delighted to design the three impaled coats of arms Mons. Martin has been entitled to bear, and they are reproduced on Colour Plate III.

In the course of my preparing the Introduction and Mons. Heim designing and painting the three coats of arms, an interesting and quite understandable dispute arose between two groups of heraldic scholars, though the principal in the event, Mons. Martin, was for a long time not even aware of any differences of opinion. The dispute arose over the "heraldic achievement of dignity", the ecclesiastical hat which should be placed above the shield.

This is not an arbitrary adornment; in a manner of speaking it takes the place of a coronet or crown in secular heraldry, though ecclesiastical coats of arms never have a crest.

When Mons. Heim's designs for the three coats of arms were completed, they showed the shield surmounted by a single traversed cross of a bishop and a green bishop's hat with six tassels either side. Several heraldists protested that Mons. Martin, being the Prefect of the Pontifical Household, was not only entitled to ten tassels either side, but former holders of his position had borne the splendid "achievement" of a *Prelato di Fiocchetto*, a deep red hat with ten scarlet tassels pending either side.

Many prelates have occupied the position of *Maestro di Camera*, *Maggiordomo* or *Prefetto del Palazzo Apostolico*. They were Superior Prelates holding the rank of a *Prelato di Fiocchetto*. On relinquishing their position in the papal household, they were usually raised to the dignity of a bishop and became cardinal.

Mons. Martin had been consecrated bishop in 1964, before being appointed the Prefect of the Papal Household. As Titular Bishop of Neapolis in Palaestina, was therefore entitled to bear the episcopal 'achievement of dignity' above his coat of arms: the single traversed cross and a green ecclesiastical hat with six tassels pending on either side.*

Of course, Mons. Martin is a Superior Prelate, but that title, like the designation *Monsignore*, is a collective grouping, similar to

Mons. Calori di Vignale, *Prelato di Fiocchetto* and *Major-domo* of Pope Pius XII, impaled his family arms with the arms of the Pope.

Mons. Calori di Vignale, *Prelato di Fiocchetto* e *maggiordomo* del Papa Pio XII, unì le sue armi di famiglia con quelle del Papa.

Mons. Calori di Vignale, *Prelato di Fiocchetto* und Oberhofmeister von Papst Pius XII, teilte sein Familienwappen mit dem des Papstes.

* Some heraldists suggested that Mons. Martin's hat, though episcopal green, should have ten tassels pending on either side. Ten tassels and a double traversed cross are the 'achievement' of an archbishop.

A rather unexpected and unusual walk.

Una passeggiata inaspettata e un pò straordinaria.

Ein ganz unerwarteter und ziemlich ungewöhnlicher Spaziergang.

the one in the army, where 'Officer' embraces the ranks from Lieutenant to Captain, Major and Lieutenant Colonel are 'Field Officers', and Brigadier and above are 'General Officers'.

In spite of the glamorous appearance of the heraldic 'achievement' of a *Prelato di Fiocchetto*, the red hat with twenty scarlet tassels, the heraldic achievement of a bishop takes priority. †

The unique privilege of impaling the coats of arms of three Popes with his personal episcopal arms, sets both a precedent in the history of ecclesiastical heraldry and of the papacy. As such it is an important part of any work that deals with either subject, especially Heraldry in the Vatican.

Personally, but also voicing the view of many heraldic scholars, it would be an invaluable contribution to heraldry in general if this unique event would not only be placed on record in this book but if, as in the past, such a memorable and historic event could be artistically preserved somewhere in the Vatican, where visitors on an heraldic excursion, long after Mons. Martin has ceased being the host and guide, could see and study this unique event which enriched heraldry in the latter half of the twentieth century.

Many things have changed in the course of the last few centuries: in the entourage of the popes, in the style and frequency of pontifical audiences and ceremonies, and even in the department of the Chamberlain of yesterday who has become the Prefect of today.

† For all hierarchical heraldic achievements see: *Heraldry in the Catholic Church – its origin, customs and laws –* by Bruno B. Heim, Van Duren, Gerrards Cross, England.

44

His Excellency Monsignore Martin considers that of all the privileges conferred on the Prefect by his office, the most precious are those unchanged by history's vicissitudes, of approaching the person of the Vicar of Christ more closely than others and without being announced, of occasionally receiving his confidences and, in the words of an eminent Belgian prelate of the last century, Monsignore de Mérode, that are deeply treasured by Bishop Martin, "of experiencing daily the immense consolation of approaching this rock on which the Church is built".

The most precious privilege of the Prefect is that of experiencing daily the immense comfort of approaching the person of the Vicar of Christ, the rock on which the Church is built.

Il privilegio più grande del Prefetto è quello di provare ogni giorno l'immensa gioia si avvicinare la Persona del Vicaro di Cristo, la roccia su cui è costruita la Chiesa.

Das kostbarste Privileg des Präfekten is der unermessliche Trost, der Person des Stellvertreters Christi, dem Felsen auf dem die Kirche gebaut ist, so nahe sein zu dürfen.

The papal arms of Paul II. Above: Cortile del Maresciallo; right: Palazzetto di Venezia.

Lo stemma ponteficio di Paolo II. In alto: Cortile del Maresciallo; a destra: Palazzetto di Venezia.

Das Papstwappen von Paulus II. Oben: Cortile del Maresciallo; rechts: Palazzetto di Venezia.

46

I

FROM EUGENE IV

TO

INNOCENT VIII

EUGENE IV (1431–1447) NICHOLAS V (1447–1455)
CALIXTUS III (1455–1458) PIUS II (1458–1464)
PAUL II (1464–1471) SIXTUS IV (1471–1484)
INNOCENT VIII (1484–1492)

Our first heraldic excursion begins with the coat of arms of Eugene IV, Gabriele Condulmer, (1431–1447), on the third floor of the Apostolic Palace. These arms were discovered during the extensive building and restoration work in the apartments of the Secretariat of State of His Holiness during the Second World War. It seems to be the oldest coat of arms in the Apostolic Palace and, in fact, the entire Vatican City.*

This should not surprise us because during the Middle Ages the popes lived mainly in the Lateran Palace, and most of the pontiffs were

* From this statement we must exclude a few coats of arms which we find in the Grotto of the Vatican Basilica, mainly on tombs which belong to popes earlier than Eugene IV. Among these are the arms of Boniface VIII, Benedetto Caetani, (1294–1303), and Urban VI, Bartolomeo Prignano, (1378–1389), but we must also bear in mind that the arms of Boniface VIII in the mosaic, for example, are of a far more recent date. Near the tomb of Nicholas III, Giovanni Gaetano Orsini, (1277–1280), we can see two stone blocks with the Orsini arms carved on them. We shall return to those when we reach the pontificate of another Orsini Pope, Benedict XIII, (1724–1730).

The arms of Eugene IV, carved in stone, were discovered during restoration work in the apartments of the Papal Secretariat of State.

Lo Stemma di Eugenio IV in pietra ritrovato durante dei lavori nella Segreteria di Stato.

Das Wappen von Eugen IV in Stein gemeisselt, wurde während der Renovierung des päpstlichen Staatssekretariats gefunden.

47

Pope Eugene IV receives the symbolic keys from St. Peter. Bronze door by Filarete, Vatican Basilica.

Papa Eugenio IV riceve da S. Pietro le simboliche chiavi. La Porta del Filarete della Basilica Vaticana.

Papst Eugen IV nimmt von St. Petrus die symbolischen Schlüssel entegegen. Die Porta del Filarete in der Vatikanischen Basilika.

buried there. They resided in the Vatican Palace only for short periods; the Lateran Palace was the permanent papal residence. At the time of Eugene IV, the third floor of the Apostolic Palace had not even been built; it was then an open air terrace as can be seen on old prints, which also show that there was a chapel on the terrace. It is very probable that the coat of arms of Eugene IV was originally in that chapel.

Let us first look at the marvellous simplicity of these armorial bearings: *"d'azzurro alla banda di argento"*; azure a bend argent. In heraldry simplicity is synonymous with beauty. In the entire city of Rome we find only two more representations of the arms of Eugene IV: on the Palazzo Senatorio and on the tomb which holds the pontiff's mortal remains. The tomb is in the refectory of the ancient convent San Salvatore in Lauro; however, this is one of those facts which seems to be known to very few scholars of heraldry.

This was a very sad time in the history of the papacy which had only just recovered from the severe blows it had suffered during the Great Schism in the West (1378–1417). Martin V, Oddone Colonna, who had been elected Pope at the Council of Constance, could only enter the desolate capital of Christianity in 1420.

Eugene IV, Gabriele Condulmer, who succeeded to the papacy in 1431, had to flee from Rome only three years after becoming Pope. On that tragic morning in 1434, dressed in the habit of a Benedictine monk, he went to the river Tiber where a boat was waiting for him. But less fortunate than Pius IX, who fled Rome in 1848, Pope Eugene was recognised by the mob whilst trying to board the boat. He came under a hail of stones, but managed to get up river and then on to Florence, where he joined the Seventeenth Oecumenical Council. He was forced to spend ten of his sixteen years as pontiff in exile. It is for that reason that only very few traces of this Pope and his coat of arms can be found on Roman buildings, and they are of great importance to heraldry because they are so rare.

There is, however, one memorial to Eugene IV which everybody can admire on entering St. Peter's Basilica. It was Eugene IV who commissioned the famous bronze door from Filarete; in 1445 it was located in the porch of the old Constantinian Basilica. It was later put into St. Peter's Basilica. On the two bottom panels of the door one can see Eugene IV crowning the Emperor Sigismund in Rome and also the reception of the Eastern prelates who had come to Florence for the short-lived union with the Latin Church.

However, Eugene IV did not return to Rome empty-handed; he had brought with him from Florence the most famous of the pioneers of the Renaissance which was to flourish under his successors: Frà Giovanni da Fiesole, a humble friar, better known as Beato Angelico. We can admire his work when we come to the successors of Eugene IV on the floor below us.

Through a secret door on the second floor we enter the Stanze di Raffaello, the rooms of Raphael. Here the decorations are much later but on the key-stone on the arch are the arms of Nicholas V, Tommaso Parentucelli (1447–1455), the great humanist pope, who founded the Biblioteca Vaticana, the world-famous Vatican Library. But these armorial bearings are very difficult to see from here, and there are other places where they can be seen more easily.

Through a small door we enter a square room which is completely covered with frescos; the

Nicholas V (1447–1455);
Niccolò V (1447–1455);
Nikolaus V (1447–1455);
TOMMASO PARENTUCELLI.

The humble Pope Nicholas V did not want a personal coat of arms but adopted the armorial bearings of the Roman Church.

L'umile Pontifice Niccolò V non volle altro stemma che quello della Chiesa romana.

Der bescheidene Papst Nikolaus V weigerte sich ein persönliches Wappen anzunehmen; er begnügte sich mit dem Wappen der römischen Kirche.

49

The Constantinian Basilica was completed in the fourth century. Nicholas V restored it before it was demolished under Julius II.

La Basilica Constantiniana fu terminata nel IV secolo. Niccolò V la restaurò prima che fosse demolita sotto Giulio II.

Die konstantinische Basilika wurde im vierten Jahrhundert vollendet. Nicholaus V hatte sie wieder herstellen lassen, bevor der Abbruch unter Julius II begann.

inscription on the floor gives us a clue to the date of the frescos: «NICOLAUS P. P. QUINTUS». In fact, we are standing in the private chapel of Pope Nicholas V, and his coat of arms appears time and time again on the walls of the room. The simplicity of the Pope's armorial bearings reflects his humility. Nicholas V just adopted those of the papacy without adding any charges or personal *mobili*. The blazon of his arms reads: *"di porpora a due chiavi decussate e legate di rosso"*; purple, two crossed keys interlaced at the bows with a cord *gules*.

Frà Beato Angelico worked in this chapel from 1447 until 1455, throughout the pontificate of Nicholas V. When he painted Pope Sixtus II, he gave him the features of Nicholas V. In spite of the very troubled times – Constantinople had fallen to the Turks in 1453 – Nicholas V had the Vatican transformed into a large building site and artist's studio.

50

An old print of the first Fontana di Trevi which was built under Pope Nicholas V.

Antica stampa raffigurante la prima Fontana di Trevi fatta costruire sotto Papa Niccolò V.

Ein alter Kupferstich des ersten Fontana di Trevi, der unter Papst Nicholaus V gebaut wurde.

Nevertheless, they also had to think of defending themselves against possible aggressors, and if one goes into the Vatican Gardens one can see the Leonine Tower, named after Leo IV (847–855) who had it built. However, one can also see on it the crossed keys of Nicholas V who had strengethened the walls.

Before going through the Porta di S. Anna, we can also see the Torrione, the embattled tower. Unfortunately, none of the armorial bearings or *mobili* of its founder have been preserved, but we know that the same Pope also built four smaller towers surrounding the Castel S. Angelo. It is worth the effort looking at the only one that has survived, as it still bears the crossed keys and the abbreviated inscription:

51

Callistus III (1455–1458);
Callisto III (1455–1458);
Calixtus III (1455–1458);
ALFONSO BORGIA.

«N.P.P.V. – NICHOLAS PAPA QUINTUS». For more than five centuries the river Tiber has been flowing past the tower.

The scholarly Pope has been laid to rest in the Grotto of the Vatican near the tomb of Boniface VIII. The Pope's coat of arms has been carved on the side of his tomb. It is partly obscured and so missed by visitors unless they are looking for it.

In order not to miss any link in the succession of the pontiffs, we must make a quick excursion upstream as far as the Ponte Milvio to the North of the City. It is here that Constantine defeated Maxentius in A. D. 312, and where we find one of the rarest coats of arms belonging to a Pope, that of Calixtus III, Alfonso Borgia (1455–1458): *"d'oro al toro di*

S.MARIA IN MONSERRATO:

The Borgia tomb of Callistus III and Alexander VI.

Monumento funebre ai papi Borgia, Callisto III e Alessandro VI.

Grabmal der Borgia Päpste Calixtus III und Alexander VI.

rosso passante su una terrazza di verde, alla bordura di rosso caricata da otto fiamme d'oro''; on a field of gold a bull passant *gules* on a field of ground *vert* surrounded by a border *gules* decorated with eight golden flames. Only one other example exists. It is in the Church of S. Prisca on the Aventine Hill, where the coat of arms can be found on the left wall of the choir. Calixtus III dedicated his brief pontificate, which lasted only three years, to preparing the crusade against the Turks, not to the enrichment of the arts or architecture.

Inside the tower of the Ponte Milvio are carved in stone next to each other the armorial bearings of two Borgia Popes: in the centre that of Callistus III, on the left, that of the future Alexander VI, then still a cardinal, and a nephew of Callistus III.

Nell'interno della torre di Ponte Milvio sono affiancati gli stemmi dei due Papi Borgia: al centro quello di Callisto III; a sinistra quello del nipote, ancora Cardinale, il futuro Alessandro VI.

Im Turm der Ponte Milvio sieht man in Stein gemeisselt, nebeneinander, die Wappen von zwei Borgia Päpsten: in der Mitte das Wappen von Calixtus III, und links, das Kardinalswappen seines Neffen, dem zukünftigen Alexander VI.

Pius II (1458–1464);
Pio II (1458–1464);
Pius II (1458–1464);
ENEA SILVIO PICCOLOMINI.

From the Ponte Milvio we return to the Vatican and go on the second floor into the Cortile di S. Damaso; from there we continue through a small passage to the Cortile del Maresciallo, the quadrangle of the Marshal of the Conclave. Today this courtyard is an additional car park for special visitors and those who work in the Vatican.

One cannot help wondering what the good Pope Pius II, Enea Silvio Piccolomini (1458–1464) would say if he saw the spectacle of one car after the other driving through the archway which he had built in 1460, and which was made particularly attractive by the bas-relief attributed to Giovanni Dalmata. It depicts two kneeling angels holding the drapery of the pontifical coat of arms: *"d'argento alla croce patente d'azzurro caricata di cinque crescenti d'oro, 1, 3, 1."*; on a silver field a blue cross with five golden crescents, arranged 1, 3, 1.

Like Calixtus III before him, Pius II was totally committed to the crusade against the Turks. Indeed, he paid for his commitment to this cause with his own life because he died at Ancona as he was about to leave for the East. Among the few mementoes he left behind in Rome is a small shrine commemorating the place where in 1462 he took possession of that precious relic, the head of St. Andrew. The shrine is on the Via Flaminia near the Ponte Milvio. The relic was returned to the Orthodox Church in 1964 by Paul VI, and the author had the privilege to be appointed a member of the Papal Mission which returned this precious relic.

The mortal remains of Pius II are buried in S. Andrea della Valle. His tomb stands in the nave near the North transept, on the right, facing the tomb of his nephew, the future Pius III (1503). Both tombs were transferred here from St. Peter's Basilica in 1614.

Above: the arms of Pius II in the former Hall of the Synod of Bishops, and below: on the outer wall of S. Stefano degli Abissini.

In alto: lo stemma di Pio II nella antiche stanze del Sinodo dei Vescovi, e in basso: sulla parete esterna di S. Stefano degli Abissini.

Oben: das Wappen von Pius II im ehemaligen Saal der Bischofssynode, und unten: and der Aussenmauer von S. Stefano degli Abissini.

Paul II (1464–1471);
Paolo II (1464–1471);
Paulus II (1464–1471);
PIETRO BARBO.

Leaving this beautiful Teatime Church, we go as far as the Palazzo Venezia where we can admire the richly decorated residence of the successor of Pius II, Pope Paul II, Pietro Barbo (1464–1471). There is little left in the Vatican itself to remind us of this great Venecian Noble, except a few fragments of his tomb and one arch in the Cortile del Maresciallo which survived by a miracle, considering the structural changes which have been made in this place. Besides, Paul II preferred to live in his regal palace in the Piazza Venezia at the entrance of which one can see his coat of arms: *"d'azzurro al leone d'argento dalla cotissa d'oro attraversante"*; *azure*, a silver lion rampant and a gold bend overall.

The heraldic scholar is more fortunate with Pope Paul's successor, Sixtus IV, the

The armorial bearings of Paul II, surmounted by a cardinal's hat, outside the main entrance of the Palazzo Venezia.

Lo stemma di Papa Paolo II, ancora Cardinale, porta principale del Palazzo Venezia.

Das Wappen von Paulus II mit dem Kardinalshut am Haupteingang des Palazzo Venezia.

Only a few examples of the coat of arms of Paul II exist in the Vatican. These arms are on the façade of the Basilica di S. Marco, part of the Palazzo Venezia where Paul II preferred to live.

In Vaticano rimangono soltano pochi esemplari dello stemma di Paolo II. Quello che qui riproduciamo è murato sulla facciata della Basilica di San Marco, incorporata nel Palazzo Venezia dove Paolo II preferì abitare.

Im Vatikan gibt es nur wenige Beispiele des Wappens von Paulus II. Das hier illustrierte Wappen ist an der Fassade der Basilica di S. Marco, die zum Palazzo Venezia gehört, wo Paulus II es vorzog, seinen Wohnsitz zu haben.

TEMPLA DOMVM EXPOSITIS VICOS FORA MOENIA PONTES
VIRGINEAM TRIVII QVOD REPARARIS AQVAM
PRISCA LICET NAVTIS STATVAS DARE COMMODA PORTVS
ET VATICANVM CINGERE SIXTE IVGVM
PLVS TAMEN VRBS DEBET NAM QVAE SQVALORE LATEBAT
CERNITVR IN CELEBRI BIBLIOTHECA LOCO

Franciscan Friar Francesco Della Rovere (1471–1484), who has left many important heraldic reminders of his pontificate in the Vatican. His gigantic bronze tomb, scrulpted by Pollaiolo, takes up a large area in the Vatican Grotto.

From the Cortile del Maresciallo we walk to the Cortile dei Pappagalli; here we immediately see a door with the inscription: «SIXTUS P. P. IIII». This was the place where the Floreria Apostolica* was situated for a long time.

Five hundred years later, Paul VI had the building changed into one of the assembly halls for the Synod of Bishops. At the time of Sixtus IV, it accommodated the Biblioteca Vaticana. Platina, the librarian and one of the greatest humanists of his century lived there.

Sixtus IV endowed the library with thousands of precious manuscripts, and he was the first Pope to allow access to the Vatican Library to scholars from all over the world. The coat of arms which can be seen in the second room, the old Greek Library, is not that of Sixtus IV as one might expect, but that of Nicholas V, which Sixtus IV had placed there to honour the founder of the Library.

* The *Floreria Apostolica* is an enormous warehouse where surplus thrones, armchairs, benches, *prie-dieu*, carpets, unwanted paintings and all manner of *objets d'art* are stored.

The arms of Sixtus IV.
Lo stemma di Sisto IV.
Das Wappen von Sixtus IV.

Investiture of Platina as Prefect of the Library by Sixtus IV in 1477. The Cardinal standing in front of the Pope is Giuliano della Rovere, his nephew and future Pope Julius II.

Sisto IV mentre nomina Platina Prefetto della Biblioteca nel 1477. Il cardinale in piedi di fronte al Papa è Giuliano della Rovere, suo nipote e, più tardi, successore col nome di Giulio II.

Sixtus IV ernennt Platina zum Präfekten der Bibliothek in 1477. Der Kardinal, der vor dem Papst steht, ist Giuliano della Rovere, sein Neffe und zukünftige Papst Julius II.

Sixtus IV (1471–1484);
Sisto IV (1471–1484);
Sixtus IV (1471–1484);
FRANCESCO DELLA ROVERE

Turning to the left, we enter the Cortile Borgia and then the Cortile della Sentinella, so called because of the Security Corps which mounted guard in the Apostolic Palace.

These strong medieval walls give a claustrophobic feeling, and we are constantly under the impression that those sentinels are still watching every move we make.

Looking up, we can see the *"rovere"*, the old, uprooted oaktree of the Della Rovere family. Pope Sixtus IV is, of course the 'father' of the Sistine Chapel. Here we stand in front of the greatest achievement in the history of Italian art, perhaps even the greatest artistic creation in the world.

It is well known that only the frescos on the walls were painted in the pontificate of Sixtus IV. The most famous frescos, those by Michelangelo, were painted much later; when Sixtus IV died in 1484, Michelangelo was only nine years old.

One finds the armorial bearings and the name of Sixtus IV, the first Pope of the Della Rovere family, in many districts of Rome. The blazon is: *"d'azzurro alla rovere sradicata d'oro"*; *azure*, a golden, unrooted oaktree with crossing branches. We find his coat of arms in the windows and on the walls of the Hospital di Santo Spirito in Sassia, in the stained glass windows and they are on the Porta del Popolo and in the nearby church S. Maria del Popolo in the sanctuary which the Pope loved so much. The sanctuary had been a small chapel which Sixtus IV had enlarged to build this church. The Pope's coat of arms is also on the bridge which he had built to celebrate the Holy year of 1475 and which has been named after him.

Melozzo da Forlì painted the great Franciscan Pope in a famous fresco which is today in the

60

The large tomb of Pope Sixtus IV in the Vatican Grotto is dominated by his coat of arms which was later borne by his nephew Julius II.

La monumentale tomba del Pontifice Sisto IV nel tesoro di S. Pietro è dominata dal suo stemma, che sarà anche quello del nipote Giulio II.

Das grosse Grabmal von Papst Sixtus IV in der Vatikanischen Grotte ist überragt bei seinem Wappen, das später von seinem Neffen Julius II auch geführt wurde.

The Sistine Chapel, named after Sixtus IV, was built between 1475 and 1483. It is the private chapel of the popes and the seat of the conclaves for their election.

La cappella Sistina (di Sisto IV) completata negli anni 1475–1483). È la cappella privata dei Pontifici e vi si tengono i conclavi per l'elezione del Papa.

Die in den Jahren 1475–1483 vervollständigte Sixtinische Kapelle (benannt nach Sixtus IV), ist die Privatkapelle der Päpste. Hier wird bei der Papstwahl das Konklave abgehaltem.

The Monument to Innocent VIII by the Pollaiolo brothers is the only tomb which was transferred from the old basilica to the new one.

Tomba di Innocenzo VIII dei frateli Pollaiolo. È l'unico monumento transferito dall'antica basilica nella nuova.

Das Monument Innozenz VIII der Brüder Pollaiolo ist das einzige Grabmal, das von der alten Basilika stammt.

Pinatoteca Vaticana; it shows him with his nephew, the future Pope Julius II, and with Platina, the librarian.

To see the arms of the next Pope, Innocent VIII, (1484–1492), Giovanni Battista Cibo, the Genoan, who added the Lance of Longinus to the treasures of the reliquary of St. Peter's Basilica, we must take a slightly longer walk until we almost reach the entrance of what are today the Museums in the Belvedere. At that time, Bramante had not yet built the interlinking galleries, and all around us we would have seen the beautifully open countryside stretching out before our eyes.

In this imposing building, founded by Innocent VIII, the frescos by Mantegna are sadly missing, and only a few angels by Pinturicchio have been left on the crescent-shaped vault, but the coat of arms of Innocent VIII can be seen everywhere. It is on all the inner doors and also on the facade in front of Monte Mario. The blazon of the Pope's arms was *"di rosso alla banda scaccata di tre file d'argento e d'azzurro. Al capo di Genova che è d'argento alla croce patente di rosso"*; *gules*, a bend checky silver and *azure* and a chief of Genova, silver and a cross *gules*.

There is a superb example of the Pope's arms in multi-coloured majolica in the Borgia apartments. The ancient tower in the Vatican gardens looks quite ageless, but the bend checky decoration tells us that it dates from the pontificate of Innocent VIII.

Finally, let us turn towards St. Peter's Basilica, where Pope Innocent VIII is immortalised by his magnificent tomb which is on the left side of the nave. It was cast in bronze by the sculptor Pollaiolo. This is the only papal tomb which was originally in the old

64

Constantinian Basilica before being placed in St. Peter's. The Pope, who holds a lance in his right hand, and whose coat of arms is in colour on the side of the tomb, is honoured and commenorated with the inscription «NOVI ORBIS SUO AEVO INVENTI GLORIA». Those who wrote this tribute must have used some poetic licence because the Pope died in July 1492, and only in August of that year did Christopher Columbus land in the New World. Poets who exalt the dead often give themselves such liberties.

So far we have covered half a century of papal history. We continue with Alexander VI and the opening half of an era which has become known as 'the Golden Century'.

The arms of Innocent VIII on his tomb in St. Peter's Basilica.

Lo Stemma di Innocenzo VIII sul suo monumento funebre nella Basilica di S. Pietro.

Das Wappen von Innozenz VIII auf seinem Grabmal in der St. Peter Basilika.

Innocent VIII (1484–1492);
Innocenzo VIII (1484–1492);
Innozenz VIII (1484–1492);
GIOVANNI BATTISTA CIBO.

65

A portrait of Alexander VI in the Sala dei Misteri.

Un ritratto di Alessandro VI nella Sala die Misteri.

Ein Gemälde von Alexander VI im Sala dei Misteri.

II

FROM ALEXANDER VI
TO
CLEMENT VII

ALEXANDER VI (1492–1503)   PIUS III (1503)
JULIUS II (1503–1513)   LEO X (1513–1521)
ADRIAN VI (1522–1523)   CLEMENT VII (1523–1534)

We begin our second excursion on the first floor of the Appostolic Palace in the apartments above the old Vatican Library of Sixtus IV and below Raphael's Stanze. These were the apartments of Alexander VI, Rodrigo Borgia (1492–1503), whose coat of arms is clearly visible on the ceiling and walls which were adorned with the famous frescos by Pinturicchio.

In the veins of Alexander VI flowed not only the blood of the Borgias, but through his mother he was also descended from the noble family of Oms. For that reason his armorial bearings are blazoned: *"Partito. Al primo d'oro al toro di rosso passante su una terrazza di verde alla bordura di rosso caricata da otto fiamme d'oro [Borgia]; al secondo fasciato d'oro e di nero [Oms]; – or* a bull passant *gules* on a piece of ground *vert* and on a border *gules* eight flames *or'* Borgia] impaled with *or* three bars *sable* [Oms]. The coat of arms of Alexander VI differed from that of his uncle Calixtus III because he had added a simplified version of the Oms arms to that of the Borgias.

The arms of Alexander VI can also be seen in the Basilica di S. Maria Maggiore on the wooden ceiling which was gilded with the first

Gate in the courtyard of the Swiss Guard, surmounted by the coat of arms of Alexander VI and a commemorative plaque dating from 1492.

La porta che dà sul Cortile della Guardia Svizzera sormontato dallo stemma di Alessandro VI, ed una placca commemoritiva datata 1492.

Über dem Torweg im Hofe der Schweizer Garde findet man das Wappen von Alexander VI und eine steingemetzte Tafel von 1492.

67

Many 'mobili' of the Borgia Pope Alexander VI decorate ceilings and marble friezes. This is part of the ceiling decorations in gilded stucco work on a blue background in the Sala delle Arti Liberali.

Molti 'mobili' di Papa Borgia Alessandro VI decorano soffitti e fregi marmorei. Questa è una parte delle decorazioni del soffitto in stucco d'oro su sfondo azzurro nella Sala delle Arti Liberali.

Viele heraldische 'mobili' des Borgia Papstes Alexander VI schmücken Decken und Marmor Friesen. Dies ist ein Teil der Decke in goldener Stuccoarbeit auf einem blauen Hintergrund im Sala delle Arti Liberali.

gold that had been brought from the New World. Another example of his arms can be seen on the old High Altar in S.Maria del Popolo, one of the masterpieces by Andrea Bregno, which was later moved to the sacristy. His coat of arms is on the fountain in the Largo

68

dei Cavalleggeri. There are also many examples of the Pope's armorial bearings in the Vatican: on the Torre Borgia, the Borgia Tower, in the Cortile interno della Guardia Svizzera, the inner quadrangle of the Swiss Guard. They are displayed where the Passetto di Borgo begins which Alexander VI had covered up in the first year of his pontificate, to make the corridor safer and to serve as a secure passageway between the Apostolic Palace and the Castel S.Angelo.

At the castle one can also see what is left of the Borgia-Oms armorial bearings which had been carved in stone but which have been almost completely obliterated not only to remove any memory of Alexander VI who had been responsible for many beautiful buildings and works of art, but mainly to wipe out any memory of the temporal power of the papacy. This act of vandalism was carried out by the Roman Republic in 1798 with the complicity of General Berthier's Militia.

France comes to mind again when we look at the fortifications Alexander VI had prepared

Alexander VI (1492–1503)
Alessandro VI (1492–1503)
Alexander VI (1492–1503)
RODRIGO BORGIA.

69

The arms of Alexander VI under the Loggia of the Castel Sant'Angelo.

Blasone di Alessandro VI sotto la loggia di Castel Sant'Angelo.

Das Wappen von Alexander VI unter der Loggia im Castel Sant'Angelo.

70

and at the elegant decorations in the Borgia apartments. The fortifications were built with great enthusiasm when in autumn 1494 word reached Alexander of the imminent arrival of the army of Charles VIII, the young King who, it was reported, had summoned a Council to depose Alexander VI. The young King entered Rome on the last day of the year and set up his general headquarters in the Palazzo Venezia, and he directed his mighty artillery on the Castel S.Angelo where the Pope and some of his cardinals had taken refuge. Fortunately, diplomacy prevailed, and a treaty was signed on 16 January 1495, to be followed afterwards by a sumptuous banquet in the Borgia apartments here in the Vatican. These apartments were then known as 'the new apartments', and Pinturicchio had just finished painting them.

Charles VIII, in whose honour the Borgia apartment was used for the first time, was as overwhelmed by the beauty of the frescos, as are the visitors who look at them today.

From an artistic point of view, we have now reached the beginning of the peak of the Golden Age: in the following year, 1496, Michelangelo arrived in Rome, and Bramante followed three years later. The famous Pietà was created by Michelangelo in 1500.

After a very short pontificate of only twenty-six days, Pius III, Francesco Piccolomini (September to October 1503), a nephew of Pius II, died. His armorial bearings were identical to those of his uncle and can be seen on his tomb in S.Andrea della Valle.

Opposite: the arms of the second Borgia Pope, Alexander VI, inside the Courtyard of the Swiss Guard. Above: the arms in the Borgia Courtyard.

Lato opposto: lo stemma del secondo Papa Borgia, Alessandro VI, nel cortile della Guardia Svizzera. In alto: lo stemma nel cortile Borgia.

Gegenüber: Das Wappen des zweiten Borgia Papstes, Alexander VI, im Hof der Schweizer Garde. Oben: das Wappen im Borgia Hof.

It was therefore really the warrior-Pope Julius II, Giuliano Della Rovere (1503–1513), who succeeded the Borgia Pope, and who gave a new impetus to the artistic activities in the capital city of Christianity.

Julius II, a nephew of the founder of the Sistine Chapel, Sixtus IV, and who bore the same Della Rovere arms as had his uncle, lies buried with Sixtus IV in a simple tomb in the passage between the apse of the Vatican Basilica and the Chapel of S.Petronilla, and not in the planned, rather ostentatious sepulchral monument for which Michelangelo had already sculpted the famous statue of Moses.

Julius II had to be satisfied with the simple Latin inscription: « SIXTI IV IULII II ROMM. PONTT. NATIONE LIGUR. PATRIA SAONEN. GENTE ROBOREA GALEOTTI DI RUVERE CARD. S. PETRI AD VINCULA IULII II SORORIS FILII ET FATII SANCTORI CARD. S. SABINAE ET EPISCOP. CAESENATEN. LIPSANE HUC TRANSLATA E SACELLO SS. SACRAMENTI IDIBUS DECEMBRIS MCMXXVI ».

Pius III (1503) and his coat of arms.
Pio III (1503) e suo stemma.
Pius III (1503) und sein Wappen.
FRANCESCO PICCOLOMINI.

Julius II, a life-long enemy of Alexander VI, had no wish to take up residence in the Borgia Apartments; instead he occupied the rooms on the floor above, and he commissioned Raphael, a young painter from Urbino, to paint the rooms which have become known as the Stanze di Raffaello. Going up to the apartments of Julius II and passing such famous masterpieces as 'The Dispute over the Holy Sacrament' and 'The School of Athens', one notices everywhere the *'rovere'*, the oak tree which has become the signature of a great patron of the arts at the start of the sixteenth century.

The oak tree can be seen above the door of the Chapel of Nicholas V and also on the two beautiful doors of the Sala dei Chiaroscuri, the Hall of Light and Shade, which is not open to visitors to the Vatican Museums because the rooms are next to the private apartments of high officials of the Papal Household, such as, the *Sostituto*, the Deputy Secretary of the Papal Secretariat of State.

Above the doors, the acorns which branch off from the oak tree create the most beautiful heraldic frame.

While Raphael worked in the Loggia, Michelangelo was painting the ceiling of the Sistine Chapel, and Bramante was quite happily demolishing the old Vatican Basilica. The two grand galleries which run parallel to each other and which link the Vatican with the Belvedere are attributed to Bramante, "Maestro Ruinante" – the Grand Master of Demolition.

Entering through the Porta di S. Anna, one cannot help noticing the name of Julius II which is displayed on yet another building by Bramante and where one finds the Cortile del Belvedere: « IULIUS II PONT.MAX. LIGURUM VI PATRIA SAONENSIS SIXTI QUARTI NEPOS VIAM HANC STRUXIT PONT. COMMODITATI ».

Bramante drew up the plans for the Loggias, the building of which was continued during the pontificates of Pius IV, Gregory XIII and Sixtus V, and which ultimately formed the cortile di S.Damaso. Going along the Loggia of Raphael, one can see the Cortile di S. Damaso through very large windows. These were put there to protect the Loggia from the effects of bad weather, surprisingly only in the nineteenth century.

Joachim Murat, the King of Naples, was responsible for the idea of this wise precaution during the very short period of his annexation of Rome in 1814; however, it took another forty

Julius II (1503–1513) and his coat of arms.
Giulio II (1503–1513) e suo stemma.
Julius II (1503–1513) und sein Wappen.
GIULIANO DELLA ROVERE.

73

The Second Loggia of Raphael is the second story of the building by Julius II. Begun by Bramante (1508) and completed under Leo X by Raphael (1519).

La Seconda Loggia di Raffaelo è il secondo piano della fabbrica voluta da Giulio II. Iniziata da Donato Bramante (1508) e completata (1519), sotto Leone X, da Raffaello.

Die zweite Loggia Raffaels ist das zweite Geschoss des unter Julius II von Bramante (1508) begonnenen und unter Leo X von Raffael (1519) beendeten Bauwerks.

years for Murat's plans to be implemented, as can be seen from the inscription which says: « Pius P.P.IX ANN.VIII. PIUS P.P.IX ANN. IX : 1854 E 1855 ». It is really a miracle that the wind and rain of three centuries have left the frescos by Raphael almost entirely undamaged.

A new coat of arms, one with the roundels of the Medici family, can be seen in the Loggia of Raphael. The Medici arms can be found everywhere because they were also the arms of several successors of Julius II: Leo X, Giovanni

The oak-tree above the entrance to the Chapel of Nicholas V belongs to Julius II, who retained the arms of his uncle Sixtus IV.

La rovere sulla porta che immette alla cappella di Niccolò V, è di Giulio II, il quale adottò il medesimo stemma dello zio Sisto IV.

Der Eichenbaum über dem Portal der Kapelle des Nikolaus V ist das Wappen des Julius II, der das Wappen seines Onkels Sixtus IV beibehalten hat.

IS·MORTIFICATIONEM·IN·SVO CORPORE·PORTAVIT

Leo X (1513–1521) and his coat of arms.
Leone X (1513–1521) e suo stemma.
Leo X (1513–1521) und sein Wappen.
GIOVANNI DI MEDICI.

de'Medici (1513–1521), followed Julius II, and Giulio de'Medici, a cousin of Leo X, reigned as Clement VII (1523–1534). The Medici coat of arms is carved on their tomb, which can be seen in the choir of the church S. Maria sopra Minerva. The same coat of arms was borne by Pius IV, Giovan Angelo de'Medici (1559–1565), the Pope from Milan who commissioned Michelangelo to build the Porta Pia, a town gate in the Aurelian Walls, and finally it was borne for the last time at the dawn of the seventeenth century by Leo XI, Alessandro Ottaviano de' Medici (1605), who died twenty-seven days after his election to the papacy. He had earlier built the Villa del Pincio. Both in the Loggia of Raphael and in the apartments of Pius IV on the upper floor, the same coat of arms can be found time and time again, either carved in relief or painted in colour: "*d'oro a sei palle poste in cinta, la prima d'azzurro caricata di tre gigli maleordinati d'oro, le altre cinque di rosso*"; or six roundles in orle *gules* that one in the middle chief debruised by a hurt of larger dimensions *azure*, charged with three *fleurs-de-lis or*.

The *fleurs-de-lis* in the armorial bearings do not refer to the city of the red *fleur-de-lis*, Florence, as the heraldic scholar might assume; they found their way into the Medici arms as a direct result of the good relations which existed between France and the House of de'Medici.

Cosimo de'Medici the Elder, (for whom Beato Angelico worked for such a long time, which accounts for the great number of paintings recalling the lives of SS.Cosmos and Damien), was the father of a very sickly son, Piero il Gottoso – Peter the Gouty –, who in turn, was the father of Lorenzo the Magnificent, who only reigned for a short while. King Louis XI of France gave to Piero de'Medici in 1465 the privilege of augmenting

76

The coffered ceiling in the Sala dei Chiaroscuri with the *'imprese'* of Leo X.
Il soffitto a cassettoni della Sala dei Chiaroscuri con le *'imprese'* di Leone X.
Das quadriert Deckenfeld im Sala sei Chiaroscuri mit den *'imprese'* von Leo X.

The Loggia on the first floor of the Apostolic Palace was commissioned by Leo X. The arms of the Medici Pope can be seen on the door frame and in the arch.

La loggia del primo piano del Palazzo Apostolico, voluta dal Pontefice Leone X. Si notino gli stemmi del papa mediceo sull'architrave della porta e sull'arco.

Die Loggia auf der ersten Etage im Apostolischen Palast wurde von Leo X. gebaut. Sein Wappen kann man auf dem Türramen und im Gewölbe sehen.

his armorial bearings with the golden *fleur-de-lis* in a blue field, the heraldic charges of the House of Capet, replacing the roundel in the middle chief by one of *azure*, charged with the three *fleurs-de-lis*.

Relations between France and the illustrious family of Florence continued to be excellent, and Francis I signed a Concordat with the nephew of Piero il Gottoso, Leo X (1513–1521), the first of the Medici Popes.

The Concordat abolished the "PRAMMATICA SANZIONE DI BOURGES", and France chose from the House of de'Medici two of her Queens: Catherine, wife of Henry II and mother of Francis II, Charles IX and Henry III, and Maria, the wife of Henry IV and the mother of Louis XIII. But all this was still in the distant future when Raphael was painting his biblical scenes on the ceiling of the Loggia.

Leo X not only used his coat of arms as his armorial device: on the coffered ceiling in the Sala dei Chiaroscuri one can see two of his personal *imprese*. The meaning of such devices can be found in the original sense of the word: the heraldic device bears a symbol, *il corpo*, (the body), and a motto, *massima, l'anima* (the soul). There is, for example, a yoke with the inscription «SUAVE», meaning light, not heavy; and there are three ostrich feathers held together by a ring, jewelled with a diamond, and with the inscription «SEMPER». All these are abbreviations and a play on words, both in Latin and Italian, on «SEMPER ADAMAS IN POENIS», *penne* meaning feather. The yoke is an allusion to the yoke Cardinal Giovanni de'Medici, the future Leo X, wanted to place *"soavemente"*, gently, on the shoulders of Florence, which had opened its gates to him after eighteen years in exile. The three feathers originated in the imagination of Cosimo the

78

Elder, who believed that they symbolised the three theological virtues which adorn the human soul in which God lives; the play on words is on DIO, *il diamante*.

Many popes have used similar symbolism and *imprese* over the years. Those of Gregory XIII (1572–1585) are on the floor in the Sala Regia.

Leo X commissioned Raphael and his pupils to decorate the Loggia and also the rooms which bear the artist's name today. At the time less building work was carried out because of lack of funds. Examples of the arms of Leo X and of his *imprese* can be seen in the Church of S. Maria in Domnica, which had been his titular church when he was a cardinal. There are two coats of arms on the façade which frame the armorial bearings of Innocent VIII, the Pope who in 1489 made a cardinal of this thirteen-year-old boy who went on to become Pope Leo X. On the ceiling of the porch are the yoke and the feathers held by a diamond ring, one superimposed on the other. It was during the pontificate of Leo X that the beautiful fountain of Navicella was discovered and placed outside the church. The arms of Leo X were sculpted on the base of the fountain.

This is the time when the 'Golden Age' draws to a close. Bramante died in 1514 and Raphael in 1520. Pietro Bembo or Antonio Tebaldo remembered Raphael in the beautiful inscription on his tomb in the Pantheon: «ILLE HIC EST RAPHAEL, TIMUIT QUO SOSPITE VINCI RERUM MAGNA PARENS, ET MORIENTE MORI». Leo X died in 1521.

His successor, the Fleming Adrian VI, Adriano Florensz (1521–1523), was not interested in the Renaissance, nor in the arts or architecture. The only coat of arms

Loggia of Raphael on the second floor of the Apostolic Palace; the arms of Leo X.

Loggia di Raffaello, secondo piano del Palazzo Apostolico; lo stemma di Leone X.

Die Loggia von Raffael auf der zweiten Etage im Apostolischen Palast; das Wappen von Leo X.

commemorating his pontificate is on his tomb in Santa Maria dell'Anima: *"In quartato 1° e al 4° d'oro a tre rocci, di scacchiere, di nero, poste 2 e 1 in pala; al 2° e al 3° d'argento al leone di nero, armato lampassato e incoronato dello stesso"*. Galbreath's *"Papal Heraldry"* gives a different blazon from the official one: Quarterly, 1 and 2 gold three wolfhooks *vert*, 2 and 3 silver a lion *sable* crowned *or*. According to the official record Adrian VI featured three rooks or castles *sable* from a chess board in the first and fourth quarter and not three green wolfhooks. Adrian VI, the last non-Italian Pope until John Paul II ascended to the papacy in 1978, was buried in Santa Maria dell'Anima in 1523.

Adrian VI (1522–1523) and his tomb by Peruzzi.

Adriano VI (1522–1523) e suo monumento sepolcrale del Peruzzi.

Hadrian VI (1522–1523) und sein Grabmal von Peruzzi.
ADRIANO FLORENSZ.

With Clement VII, Giulio de'Medici (1523–1534), we go back once again to the Medici arms. Several of the Medici arms in Castel S. Angelo belong to his pontificate; some are on doors and others on the fire places. We find Clement's arms more publicly displayed on the bridgehead at the Lungotevere of the Tor di Nona. That coat of arms on the bridge rather reminds us of that tragic morning of 6 May 1527, when the unfortunate Pope had just about time to reach the fortress of Castel S. Angelo through the corridor built by Alexander VI, to take refuge from the advancing lancers of that 'most pious of Emperors', Charles V, who had chosen 'to pay a visit' in such a fashion to the Capital of the Holy Roman Church.

Clement showed his sorrow and dismay by not shaving, and he grew a beard to show his grief publicly. The terrible sacking of Rome was the beginning of a long interval during which no new buildings were erected or new pictures painted. Only one coat of arms of Clement VII is to be seen in the Vatican itself; it is a very beautiful one in the corner of the Loggia.

As a patron of the arts, his greatest claim to
fame is that he commissioned Michelangelo to
paint the Last Judgement on the altar wall in
the Sistine Chapel. This incomparably beautiful fresco was completed in the pontificate of
his successor, Paul III, Alessandro Farnese
(1534–1549), whose splendid golden arms with
the six *fleurs-de-lis azure* awaits us in the Sala
Regia where our next excursion will begin.

Castel Sant'Angelo. Clement VII erected on the
bridgehead facing the Tor di Nona statues of the Apostles
Peter and Paul; one bears his Medici coat of arms.

Castel Sant'Angelo. Sulla testata del ponte che guarda Tor
di Nona Clemente VII innalzò le statue degli Apostoli
Pietro e Paolo; una reca il suo stemma mediceo.

Castel Sant'Angelo. Klemens VII errichtete auf dem
Brückenkopf gegenüber dem Tor di Nona die Statuen der
Apostel Peter und Paul; auf einer Plinthe kann man sein
Medici Wappen sehen.

Clement VII (1523–1534).
Clemente VII (1523–1534).
Klemens VII (1523–1534).
GIULIO DE'MEDICI.

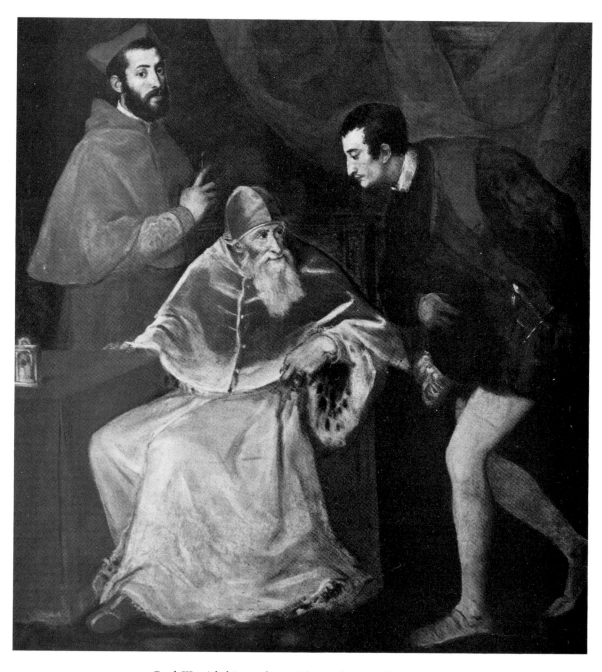

Paul III with his nephews Alessandro and Ottavio.
Paoli III con i suoi nipoti Alessandro ed Ottavio.
Paulus III mit seinen Neffen Alessandro und Ottavio.

III

FROM PAUL III (1534–1549)
TO
ST. PIUS V (1566–1572)

**PAUL III (1534–1549)   JULIUS III (1550–1555)
MARCELLUS II (1555)   PAUL IV (1555–1559)
PIUS IV (1560–1565)   S.PIUS V (1566–1572)**

With the advent of Paul III, Alessandro Farnese (1534–1549), whom Titian has immortalised in a famous painting, the Golden Age of the Renaissance had come to an end, though the arts were enjoying a short 'Indian Summer', or St. Martin's Summer as the people called it because St. Martin's day on 11 November is said to be always fine. But one of the leading figures of the Golden Age, perhaps the most important one of them all, Michelangelo, was still alive, and though he was now more than sixty years old, he was still up on his scaffolding in the Sistine Chapel painting the Last Judgement. The work took him from 1536 to 1541, more than four years, to complete the painting in this famous chapel, where Daniele da Volterra would one day cover up some of the nudity.

Coat of arms of the Farnese Pope Paul III above the entrance to the Pauline Chapel.

Lo stemma di Papa Farnese Paolo III all'ingresso della Cappella Paolina.

Das Wappen des Farnese Papstes Paulus III über dem Eingang der Paulinischen Kapelle.

On the near left of the majestic Sala Regia is the passage which leads to the Sala Ducale. On the far left is the doorway leading to the Scala Regia.

Nel lato sinistro dell'ampia Sala Regia si trovano prima il passagio alla Sala Ducale, poi la porta che dà sulla Scala Regia.

Auf der linken Seite des majestätischen Sala Regia ist der Eingang der zum Sala Ducale führt. Am fernen Ende ist der Durchgang zur Scala Regia.

No coat of arms bears witness to the fact that the gigantic fresco was completed in the pontificate of Paul III. The Pope would have liked to have seen his armorial bearings prominently displayed like those of Julius II above the entrance door, but Michelangelo refused to comply with the Pope's wishes, saying that the idea for the fresco had come from the Pope's immediate predecessor, the Medici Pope Clement VII, and Paul III respected the Master's view.

If one wants to see the *fleurs-de-lis* of the Farnese family, one has to go into the adjoining chapel, called the Pauline Chapel after Paul III, who commissioned it to be built between 1542 and 1549 in honour of his Patron Saint. There too are the last two frescos by Michelangelo, which seem to baffle the visitor at first sight: the Crucifixion of St. Peter and the Conversion of St. Paul.

The Sistine Chapel and the Pauline Chapel are linked by the grandiose and majestic Sala Regia, where one can admire the splendid coffered ceiling and where in the centre are the pontifical armorial bearings: *"d'oro a sei fiori di giglio azzurri 3,2,1,"*; – gold, six *fleurs-de-lis azure*, placed 3,2, and 1.

This beautiful hall, perhaps the most splendid of all the halls in the Apostolic Palace, was also built by Paul III. It is very sad that building the Sala Regia meant destroying the Chapel of St. Nicholas, which had been built at the beginning of the fourteenth century, and where Beato Angelico had painted his beautiful frescos in the fifteenth century. Judging by the splendour of the Chapel of Nicolas V, which we have already visited, the demolished Chapel of St. Nicholas must have been a perfect jewel.

84

It is difficult to explain such a paradox in attitudes; Paul III was certainly no barbarian. One has only to look at his Palace in the Piazza Farnese, where today the French Ambassador to the Quirinal has taken up residence. The great crowning cornice is by Michelangelo. One can also look at the sumptuous and richly decorated apartments he had built in the Castel S. Angelo, commissioning for this work those artists who had fled Rome at the time of the sacking of the city in 1527. Furthermore, it was Paul III who wanted Michelangelo to become the architect of St. Peter's Basilica, and he commissioned from Vasari the famous Sala dei Cento Giorni in the Palace of the Apostolic Chancery. It is really incomprehensible why those who lived in the sixteenth century showed so little regard for the artists of earlier centuries. They were perhaps quite convinced that they themselves had reached the pinnacle of artistic achievement which could never be surpassed, the *nec plus ultra*. It is very sad that not even Beato Angelico was able to change their ideas.

It would be premature to speak of the frescos in the Sala Regia now because they were painted in the pontificate of successors of Paul III. Instead, we move to the adjoining Hall, the Sala Ducale, which the Pope has to cross when he goes into the Sistine Chapel or the Vatican Basilica.

This is the oldest part of the Apostolic Palace. According to historians, the Sala Ducale was built on top of the buildings which had been erected there by Innocent III (1198–1216) and Nicholas III (1277–1280). Before then, the popes took up residence in the Vatican only very occasionally. It would be too optimistic to expect coats of arms from such a distant past to have survived to this day; all we see in the Sala Ducale today are the arms of two

At the far end of Sala Regia is the Pauline Chapel; on the right is the Pope's entrance to the Sistine Chapel.

Al termine della Sala Regia è la Cappella Paolina. A destra, l'ingresso del Papa alla Cappella Sistina.

Im Hintergrund des Sala Regia sieht man die Cappella Paolina; rechts ist der Eingang des Papstes zur Sixtinischen Kapelle.

From the Sala Regia we enter the Sala Ducale, which was also commissioned during the pontificate of Paul III. Here the Supreme Pontiff received sovereign dukes and their ambassadors.

Dalla Sala Regia si entra nella Sala Ducale, essa pure commissionata durante Pontificato di Paolo III. Qui, il Sommo Pontefice riceve sovrani duchi, ed i loro ambasciatori.

Von dem Sala Regia entern wir den Sala Ducale, der ebenfalls während des Pontifikats von Paul III beauftragt wurde. Hier empfing der Papst die regierenden Herzöge und deren Botschafter.

successors of Paul III: those or Paul IV, Gian Pietro Carafa (1555–1559), *"di rosso a tre fasce d'argento"*, and the arms of the Medici Pope Pius IV, Giovan Angelo de'Medici (1560–1565), with the six roundels.

If we want to find the immediate successor to Paul III, Pope Julius III, Giovannni Maria Ciocchi del Monte (1550–1555), we must go the upper floor. These rooms used to be the headquarters of the Guardia Nobile Pontificia, the Pontifical Noble Guard; on the floor one can see, beautifully displayed, the quite original armorial bearings of this Pope: *"d'azzurro alla banda di rosso filettata d'oro, caricata di tre monti d'oro, due al capo e due in punta dalle impugnature decussate al naturale"*. They are *arme parlanti*, canting arms, because of the mountains. The family name of Julius III was Del Monte. The trained eye can easily discern those mountains high up on the wall; many angels seem to dance along the cornices, holding those letters which make up the inscription ≪IULIUS III PONTIFEX OPTIMUS MAXIMUS≫.

There is another apartment in the Vatican Palace where the arms of Del Monte are prominently displayed: it is in the offices of the Prefect of the Pontifical Household, the Prelate whose title used to be *Maestro di Camera di Sua Santità*. The offices of the Prefect are just off the Cortile di San Damasco. Walking down from the upper floor of the Palace to the offices of the Prefect, I explain to my visitors that this Renaissance Pope was not only preoccupied with the Vatican, he also thought a great deal about his vineyard, and his mind was very much on the villa which was in the process of being built for him by Vignola just outside the Porta del Popolo. This Villa Giulia is well known to tourists and artists, and it has become a museum. The Pope used to go there by boat on the Tiber in order to take a rest from the fatiguing task of governing the Church. There is an amusing anecdote about the Pope's preoccupation with his vineyard; when once some prelates asked him the question: *"Eritne cras Consistorium, Beatissime Pater?"*, "will there be a Consistorium tomorrow, Holy Father?", he answered with a smile: *"Cras erit vinea!"*, "tomorrow there will certainly be the vineyard".

In the offices of the Prefect of the Pontifical Household are some splendid ceilings where *monti* (mountains) alternate with *ricci* (hedgehogs). The monti remind us of the Del Monte Pope Julius, and the hedgehogs refer to Cardinal Ricci di Montepulciano, who was the Treasurer General of the Holy Roman Church and also responsible for these buildings.

The armorial bearings in these apartments are of particular interest to scholars of heraldry: Cardinal Ricci, a friend of the Pope, had obtained the privilege of impaling his personal coat of arms with that of the reigning Pontiff, and on one of the ceilings the impaled coat of

The canting arms of Julius III (del Monte); hence the mountains in the blazon, which appear again with Paul VI (Montini).

Lo stemma 'parlante' di Giulio III (del Monte); Da ciò i monti del blasone, come nello stemma del Pontefice Paolo VI (Montini).

Das 'sprechende' Wappen von Julius III (del Monte); daher die Berge im Wappen, die wieder erscheinen im Pontifikat von Paulus VI (Montini).

The Monument to Marcellus II (1555) and his coat of arms in the Grotto of St. Peter's Basilica.

Il Monumento di Marcello II (1555) e suo stemma nelle grotte di San Pietro.

Das Grabmal von Marcellus II (1555) und sein Wappen in der Grotte der St. Peter Basilika.

arms shows on the sinister side the hedgehog (*il riccio*) looking at the sun, and on the dexter side the mountains and wreaths (*monti e coroni*) of Julius III.

The successor of Pope Julius, the pious Pope Marcellus II, Marcello Cervini (1555) left nothing behind, as far as armorial bearings are concerned. Marcellus II and Adrian VI (1521–1523) are the only pontiffs in the more recent past who retained their baptismal names when they became popes.

Marcellus II died only twenty-two days after his elevation to the papacy in April 1555. He had canting arms like those of Julius III with his *monti* and Cardinal Ricci with his *riccio*. The arms of Marcellus II were most elegantly designed, and displayed a *cervino*, a small deer, which was based on the Pope's family name Cervini. The full blazon was: "*d'azzurro al cervo d'oro posante su una pianura terrazzata al naturale e accollato a nove spighe di grano d'oro poste in ventaglio*".

Galbreath gives the papal arms as : *azure* nine wheat-stalks gold in groups of three, growing from a base *vert* and fawn (*cervino*, not a stag) gold at rest before them".

Similarly, there is nothing left to remind us of that meddlesome Pope Paul IV, Gian Pietro Carafa, (1555–1559) from Naples, whose coat of arms can be seen in the Sala Ducale. The Counter-Reformation had begun and Pope Carafa, whose pontificate was a great disappointment, had no inclination towards the arts either. He who, at the beginning of his pontificate was honoured by a public statue, lived to see it torn down and mutilated by the hostile population in Rome.

With Pius IV, Giovan Angelo de'Medici (1560–1565), a Medici from Milan whose great

88

ambition was to emulate the Medicis of Florence, began a pontificate rich in public works. His coat of arms has already been mentioned in the Corridore di Borgo, about twenty examples exist on the walls which surround the Città Leonina.

He also commissioned the Porta Pia and the ancient street which had the same name and is today known as Via Venti Settembre. Pius IV built the Borgo Pio and the Porta Angelica, so called after the Pope's baptismal name Angelo. He is also responsible for the elegant house which was built by Pirro Ligorio in the Vatican Gardens, and for the completion of the Belvedere.

Let us leave the Sala Ducale where the arms of Pius IV are on the ceiling next to those of Paul IV and let us move to the Loggia on the third floor. Here are the offices of the Papal Secretariat of State. The large windows offer a magnificent panorama of Rome.

In the past the Loggia was known as the Loggia della Cosmographia because the frescos are all geographical maps. Here too one can see on the ceiling the coat of arms of Pius IV which is, of course, identical to that of Leo X.

Did the Medicis of Florence and those of Milan have more in common than their name?

The two families were related, though rather distantly. In the beginning they had different armorial bearings. The arms of the Medicis of Milan consisted of a single *bezant* on a field *gules*. When in 1594 the future Pius IV was created a cardinal by Paul III, the Grand Duke of Toscana, Cosimo I, who was his protector, persuaded him to add the other roundels to his coat of arms to show publicly that he was a real Medici. He retained the Medici coat of arms

Ceiling of the Sala Ducale in the Apostolic Palace with the coat of arms of Paul IV (1555–1559).

Soffitto della Sala Ducale nel Palazzo Apostolico con stemma di Paolo IV (1555–1559).

Die Decke im Sala Ducale im Apostolischen Palast mit dem Wappen von Paulus IV (1555–1559).

89

The arms of Pius IV (1560–1565).
Lo stemma di Pio IV (1560–1565).
Das Wappen von Pius IV (1560–1565).
GIOVAN ANGELO DE'MEDICI.

when he became pope. This is why it is rather difficult to state with absolute certainty to whom a particular Medici coat of arms belongs unless one has additional information. There is no doubt that the arms in this Loggia belong to Pius IV; the inscription which runs along the top of the windows tells in detail what Pius IV has done to enhance the beauty of Rome and of the Vatican Palace.

The geographical maps in the Loggia della Cosmographia are magnificent masterpieces. The Holy Land is painted in gold, and one can see in many of the scenes the Hebrews, who had crossed the Red Sea and lived in tents in the desert, arriving in the Holy Land. These are real geography lessons, made even clearer by the legends which are inscribed on the frescos. On the map of France, for example, it says '*Gallia post Evangelium receptum Ecclesiae Romanae periclanti saepe auxilio fuit,*' and we can just about make out '. . . *solum ita foecundum ut nulla in re cedat florentissimae Italiae*'. The last one, the *fiorentissima Italia* deserves our special attention: first of all, it is painted in gold, like the Holy Land; but the inscription is fascinating. It says that in this age of universal corruption, Italy is the last line of defence and a fortress of virtue: '*unicum fere virtutis perfugium*'.

After this brief distraction from heraldry, we must now return to the pontificate of Pope St. Pius V, Antonio Michele Ghislieri (1566–1572), the Pope of the Battle of Lepanto, which was recaptured by Giorgio Vasari in one of the famous frescos in the Sala Regia.

To see this fresco one has to go back to the starting point of our heraldic excursion in the Apostolic Palace. Going down two floors to the Sala Regia, I always point out to my guests that reforming popes have always placed great masterpieces of art in serious jeopardy. To give

The Gallery of Maps. The wall decoration (forty 'maps' of the regions of Italy) was carried out (1580–1583) by the cosmographer Ignazio Danti.
La Galleria delle Carte Geografiche. La decorazione parietale (quaranta 'carte' delle regioni d'Italia) fu eseguita nel 1580–1583 dal cosmografo Ignazio Danti.
Galleria delle Carte Geografiche. Die Wanddekoration (vierzig 'Landkarten' der Regionen Italiens) wurde zwischen 1580–1583 von dem Kosmographen Ignazio Danti ausgeführt.

but one example: Pius V started giving away the beautiful Pagan statues which belonged to the Villa Giulia and the Casina di Pio IV because he considered them unsuitable for the collection of the Vicar of Christ. Fortunately, true holiness is not incompatible with humility, and the great Pope listened to the advice of his cardinals and stopped giving away these treasures which had been so carefully collected by his predecessors. The Pope's modesty and humility are the reasons why there are so few coats of arms of himself in the

91

The arms of St. Pius V sculpted on the outer wall of S. Stefano degli Abissini (above) and on the Holy Office (below).

Lo stemma di S. Pio V compare scolpito, oltre che sul Palazzo del Santo Uffizio (in basso), anche sulla parete esterna della chiesa di S. Stefano degli Abissini (in alto).

Das Wappen des Hl. Pius V gemeisselt am Palast der Kongregation der Glaubenslehre (unten), und an der Aussenseite der Kirche S. Stefano degli Abissini (oben).

pontifical apartments, although they had been partly rebuilt by him.

The blazon of Pope St. Pius V was: *"d'oro a tre bande di rosso"*; bendy gold and *gules*.

There are six examples of his arms in the Vatican: one in the Cortile della Sentinella, one in the Cortile del Belvedere, on the tower which bears his name, the Torre Pia, and one at the end of the Bernini Colonades; his arms are in the chapel of the Swiss Guard, which he had built in honour of St. Martin and St. Sebastian, and also a sculpted coat of arms on the corner of the Palazzo del S.Uffizio, the Holy Office on the left side of St. Peter's Square; Pius V commissioned that Palace to be built.

Having reached the first floor where the Sala Ducale and Sala Regia are located, I remind my guests that in the Sala Regia the Pope always received kings, and in the Sala Ducale the sovereign dukes of Italy, Parma and Modena, for example, or the accredited ambassadors to the Holy See.

This is reflected in the frescos which recalled for the benefit of these illustrious visitors some of the great events in the history of the papacy and its relationship to temporal power.

Giorgio Vasari who painted the two enormous frescos of the Battle of Lepanto during the pontificate of Pius V, certainly did not under-estimate the worth of his own work. "It is one of the most beautiful paintings I have ever executed!", he wrote modestly to the Grand Duke of Tuscany, Cosimo I de'Medici; he went on to say that he had worked himself into such a state of enthusiasm that he felt he was fighting the Turks with his own hands and was directly involved in the conflict with the Turks.

Vasari must be counted among the ten great artists who had been working in the Apostolic

St. Pius V (1566–1572)
S. Pio V (1566–1572)
St. Pius V (1566–1572)
ANTONIO MICHELE GHISLIERI.

Palace since the pontificate of Paul III.

On the other walls in the Sala Regia one can see frescos depicting 'The Reconciliation of Frederic Barbarossa with Alexander III', 'The Victory of Pipin over Astolfo','The Investiture of Peter II of Aragon by Innocent III','The donation of Liutprando', The donation of Charlemagne', 'Henry IV at Canossa pleading to be pardoned by Gregory VII', 'Gregory IX excommunicating Frederic II', 'St. Bartholomew's night and the slaughter of the Huguenots', 'Charles IX justifying himself before parliament', and 'Gregory XI bringing back the papacy from Avignon to Rome'. The last fresco is by Giorgio Vasari, who signed it in Greek letters.

Pius V died in 1572. The *'fasce rosse'*, the bends *gules*, were succeeded by *'il drago d'oro'*, the golden dragon of Ugo Boncompagni from Bologna, who as Gregory XIII gave to the world the Gregorian calendar and the Gregorian University.

93

IV

GREGORY XIII (1572–1585)

Credit for the completion of the magnificent decorations in the Sala Regia belongs to Gregory XIII, Ugo Boncompagni (1572–1585). Here on the floor is the inscription: «AULAM REGIAM VARIO MARMORE STRAVIT», and on the four walls is further evidence: the dragon from his armorial bearings, designed in a different style, and the rather enigmatic motto «VIGILAT – FOELIX PRAESAGIUM – A QUO ET AD QUEM – NON COMMOVEBITUR». These are the *imprese* of Pope Boncompagni. High up, near the large window facing North, is the full blazon: *"al drago alato di oro nascente su fondo rosso"*; *gules* a demi-dragon gold – and the name of the Pope in large letters.

Gregory XIII wanted to commemorate the famous night of St. Bartholomew on the wall which receives the light from the large window and complete with it the decoration of the Sala Regia. Many writers have written about the fresco and the poet Stendhal wrote: "in Europe is a place where massacres are actually publicly exalted!".

Gregory XIII (1572–1585)
Gregorio XIII (1572–1585)
Gregorius XIII (1572–1585)
UGO BONCOMPAGNI.

Opposite top. The winged dragon of Pope Boncompagni,Gregory XIII, in the third Loggia of the Apostolic Palace. Below: Gregory XIII presiding over the commission he had nominated for the reformation of the Julian Calendar. The arms under the painting are those of the cardinals who were members of the commission.

Lato opposto in alto: il drago alato di Papa Boncompagni, Gregorio XIII, nella terza loggia del Palazzo Apostolico Vaticano. In basso: Gregorio XIII presiede la commissione da lui nominata per la riforma del calendario giuliano. Gli stemmi sotto l'illustrazione appartengono ai Cardinali membri della Commissione.

Ggenüber oben: Der beflügelte Drache von Papst Boncompagni, Gregorius XIII, in der Loggia auf der dritten Etage des Apostolischen Palastes im Vatikan. Unten: Gregorius XIII leitet den Vorsitz der von ihm ernannten Kommission zur Verbesserung des Julianischen Kalenders. Die Wappen unter dem Germälde gehören den Kardinälen, die Mitglieder der Kommission waren.

COLOUR PLATES

IX

Left to right, top: Arms of Sixtus IV; external wall of the Sistine Chapel. Arms of Innocent VIII; Apostolic Palace. Bottom: Arms of Alexander VI; Cortile della Guardia Svizzera. Arms of Leo X; third Loggia, Apostolic Palace.

Da sinistra a destra in alto: Stemma di Sisto IV; muro esterno della cappella Sistina. Stemma di Innocenzo VIII; Palazzo Apostolico. In basso: Stemma di Alessandro VI; Cortile della Guardia Svizzera. Stemma di Leone X; terzia loggia del Palazzo Apostolico.

Links nach rechts, oben: Wappen des Sixtus IV; Aussenmauer der Sixtinischen Kapelle. Wappen des Innozenz VIII; Apostolischer Palast. Unten: Wappen des Alexander VI; Hof der Schweizer Garde. Wappen des Leo X; dritte Loggia im Apostolischen Palast.

X

Left to right, top: Arms of Paul III; Sala Regia. Arms of Julius III; Prefecture of the Papal Household. Bottom: Arms of Marcellus II; 'Grotte', Basilica Vaticana. Arms of Paul IV; Sala Ducale.

Da sinistra a destra in alto: Stemma di Paolo III; Sala Regia. Stemma di Giulio III; Prefettura della Casa Pontificia. In basso: Stemma di Marcello II; 'Grotte', Basilica Vaticana. Stemma di Paolo IV; Sala Ducale.

Links nach rechts, oben: Wappen des Paulus III; Sala Regia. Wappen des Julius III; Präfektur des päpstlichen Haushalts. Unten: Wappen des Marcellus II; 'Grotte', Basilica Vaticana. Wappen des Paul IV; Sala Ducale.

XI

Arms of Julius III; ceiling in the Prefecture of the Papal Household.

Stemma di Giulio III; soffitto della Prefettura della Casa Pontificia.

Wappen des Julius III; Decke der Präfektur des Päpstlichen Haushalts.

XII

Top: Arms of Gregory XIV; bottom: of Innocent IX; Apostolic Palace.

In alto: Stemma di Gregorio XIV; in basso: di Innocenzo IX; Palazzo Apostolico.

Oben: Wappen des Gregorius XIV; unten: des Innozenz IX; Apostolischer Palast.

ALEXANDER·VI·PONT·MAX·
CALIST·III·PONT·MAX·NEPOS·
NATIONE·HISPANVS·PATRIA·

Psal. 24.

VIAS TVAS DOMINE DEMONSTRA MIHI.

Praelucet ad victoriam.

Non tibi, duassan.

Aeternum viuo CLEMENTIS nomine, signant
CLEMENTEM coeli, sydera, serta, manus.

P. Ludoicus Medardus.

COLOUR PLATES

XIII

Biblioteca Vaticana. *"Theatro del Mondo"* (Ortelius); J. B. Vrients, Antwerp, 1608. Frontispiece: Clement VIII and his arms; frontespizio: Clemente VIII e suo stemma; Titelbild: Klemens VIII und sein Wappen.

XIV

Left to right, top: Arms of S. Pius V; Palazzo del Sant'Uffizio. Arms of Clement VIII; Sala Clementina. Bottom: Arms of Gregory XV; Cappella del Coro. Arms of Innocent X; Cortile di San Damaso.

Da sinistra a destra, in alto: Stemma di S. Pio V; Palazzo del Sant'Uffizio. Stemma di Clemente VIII; Sala Clementina. In basso: Stemma di Gregorio XV; Cappella del Coro. Stemma di Innocenzo X; Cortile di San Damaso.

Links nach rechts, oben: Wappen des St. Pius V; Palazzo del Sant'Uffizio. Wappen des Klemens VIII; Sala Clementina. Unten: Wappen des Gregorius XV; Cappella del Coro. Wappen des Innozenz X; Cortile di San Damaso.

XV

Left to right, top: Arms of Gregory XIII; second Loggia. Arms of Paul V; Basilica Vaticana. Below: Arms of Urban VIII; Vatican Basilica. Arms of Alexander VII; Piazza di San Pietro.

Da sinistra a destra, in alto: Stemma di Gregorio XIII, seconda loggia. Stemma di Paolo V; Basilica Vaticana. In basso: Stemma di Urbano VIII; Basilica Vaticana. Stemma di Alessandro VII; Piazza San Pietro.

Links nach rechts, oben: Wappen des Gregorius XIII; zweite Loggia. Wappen des Paulus V; Basilica Vaticana. Unten: Wappen des Urbanus VIII; Basilica Vaticana. Wappen des Alexander VII; Piazza San Pietro.

XVI

Arms of Leo X; ceiling of the Sala dei Chiaroscuri.

Stemma di Leone X; soffitto della Sala dei Chiaroscuri.

Wappen des Leo X; Decke des Sala dei Chiaroscuri.

The arms of Pope Boncompagni, the winged dragon, appear very often in the Vatican Palaces.

Lo stemma di Papa Boncompagni, il drago alato, compare frequentemente nei Palazzi Vaticani.

Das Wappen des Papstes Boncompagni, der beflügelte Drachen, ist sehr oft in den Vatikanischen Palästen zu sehen.

Pope Gregory's election to the papacy took place in the year of that infamous massacre, which Caterina de Medici justified before the Pope and the whole of Europe as 'an act of self-defence'. She described it as the reaction to a plot against the King and the royal family, which was miraculously discovered at the last moment. The massacre had been the answer to an attempt to establish the Protestant religion with violence in France.

After such explanations, the Visible Head of the Holy Roman Church had no option but to congratulate that Most Christian King on his ''holy and most remarkable success '', in which could be seen the intervention of Providence, – the same Providence which had given victory to the Christian Fleet in the waters of Lepanto in the previous year. This event is also recalled in a fresco on the walls of the Sala Regia. Vasari was called for that purpose in great haste from Florence. He was given magnificent quarters in the Belvedere where he lived *a guisa di un sovrano* – in the style of a king.

On 1 May 1573, the frescos in the Sala Regia were all complete and covered the entire walls. The Pope spent an hour alone with the artist, admiring the paintings. On May 21, the feast of Corpus Domini, the Pope solemnly inaugurated the Sala Regia in the presence of many illustrious guests. This was the first contribution by Pope Boncompagni to the artistic enrichment of the Vatican Palace.

Under the pontificate of Gregory XIII the building in the city was restarted with new vigour. He commissioned the Chiesa del Gesù to be built and also S.Maria in Vallicella. He ordered the building of the Roman College and was responsible for the first work on the Palazzo del Quirinale. In the Vatican Basilica he built a beautiful chapel, located near his own tomb on which there is a very impressive bas-relief. On each floor of the Apostolic Palace is a representation of his coat of arms, testifying to the work carried out during his pontificate.

Going from the Sala Regia to the Sala Ducale, which was partly decorated by Lorenzo Sabbatini during the pontificate of Gregory XIII and whose coat of arms can be seen on the embrasures of the windows, we enter the Sale dei Paramenti, which are very beautiful but not open to visitors. Here the Pope dresses in his liturgical vestments before presiding over solemn ceremonies in the Sistine Chapel.

The decorations in the Sala dei Palafrenieri and the Sala della Falda, are rather mediocre.

The sucessors to Raphael, Sabbatini, Mascherino, Laureti etc., were mere decrators rather than artists. In the Loggias on the second and third floor one can see more of their decorative style; it can hardly be described as skilled artistic painting.

Starting in the third Sala, one can see an abundance of winged dragons from the Pope's coat of arms: in each of the squares of the coffered ceiling is one dragon in relief and in colour, and a Latin inscription recalls all the deeds of the Pope's pontificate.

The fresco by Antonio Tempesta is of great historical importance because it shows the city of Rome in detail. The fresco depicts the long procession on 11 June 1580, when the relics of St. Gregory Nazianzeno were taken from the Benedictine Convent at Campo Marzio to the Gregorian Chapel in the Vatican Basilica, which had just been completed. The procession wound along the Via della Scrofa, the Piazza S.

The arms of Gregory XIII in Castel Sant'Angelo.
Lo stemma di Gregorio XIII nel Castel Sant'Angelo.
Das Wappen von Gregorius XIII im Castel Sant'Angelo.

99

The Tower of the Winds, overlooking the Court of the Library, was built (1579) by Gregory XIII as an astronomical observatory, to the North of the Gallery of Maps.

La Torre dei Venti, che sovrasta il Cortile della Biblioteca, è l'osservatorio astronomico che Papa Gregorio XIII fece sorgere (1579) a nord della Galleria delle Carte Geografiche.

Der Torre dei Venti, der über dem Cortile della Biblioteca emporragt, ist Sitz des astronomischen Observatoriums, das Papst Gregorius XIII in 1579 nördlich der Gallerie der Landkarten gebaut hat.

Apollinare, along the ancient Via Papale, and crossed the bridge of S.Angelo and along to St. Peter's Basilica, as yet without its dome.

From the Loggia we enter the Sala Bolognese where we can see on the floor the inscription «GREGORIUS XIII, ANNO IUBILAEI MDLXXV» and one wall is covered entirely with a map of Bologna, the town were the Pope was born. We are now in the private apartments of Pope Boncompagni. It is for this reason that we find on the floor below the Pope's name on all doors and windows, and there is no shortage of dragons.

One of the rooms of Gregory XIII is also the Chapel of Matilda. Cardinals and members of the Curia can attend a Spiritual Retreat which is preached here every year during the first week of Lent in the presence of the Pope. During the last war the Supreme Pontiff also used to celebrate Midnight Mass at Christmas in this Chapel for the members of the Diplomatic Corps accredited to the Holy See.

From here we go through a Sala which was much admired by the contemporaries of Gregory XIII and arrive in the large gallery which has the Vatican Gardens on one side and the Cortile del Belvedere on the other.

We now arrive at the entrance to the museums, where we find another representation of a winged dragon.

This is the famous Galleria delle Carte Geografiche where we can see the beautifully painted maps of all the regions of Italy and the Papal States, including Avignon. The maps were painted on cardboard by the Dominican Friar Ignazio Danti between 1580 and 1583. In recognition for his work Frà Ignazio Danti was consecrated a bishop.

100

Here Gregory XIII also built the Torre dei Venti from where he could study the stars. If one leans out of a window of the tower, one can again see the sculpted winged dragon of the Pope. There is also a very large dragon on the wall behind the old clock of the Cortile di S.Damaso.

The Sala Superiore, with its frescos by Circignani and by Brill, was used by the Pope during his preparation of the Gregorian calendar, and one can see the meridian of Rome traced on the floor.

To the scholar of heraldry there is little of interest here among the data of the epact, the excess of the solar over the lunar year, and the equinoxes, but nevertheless one cannot ignore the major contribution the Pope made to our civilisation: the Gregorian calendar. This was a milestone in history.

The Pontifical Gregorian University.
La Pontificia Università Gregoriana.
Die Päpstliche Universität Gregoriana.

On the uppermost floor, in the third Loggia we see once again under the wings of the Pope's dragon the inscription which recalls this great historical event: «GREGORIUS XIII PONT. MAX. UT SANCTUM PASCHA SUO IN PERPETUUM TEMPORE CELEBRETUR, RATIONEM ANNI DIU PERTURBATAM RESTITUIT». Because of a mistake made by Julius Caesar, the time lapse which occurred was eleven minutes and fourteen seconds every solar year; this added up to a twenty-four hour day every 128 years. After fifteen centuries, the calendar needed a major adjustment.

V

SIXTUS V (1585–1590)

We have now reached the pontificate of Sixtus V, Felice Peretti (1585–1590), the Pope best remembered for the Acqua Felice, the Via Sistina and the Obelisks.

Judging by the enormous amount of work that was carried out during his five-year pontificate, it could be said that he was like a force of nature. It was obviously no coincidence that he chose the Lion as the main charge in his armorial bearings. Alluding to his native town Montalto, he added a triple mount as a second charge, and in the right paw of the lion he placed the fruits of a pear tree, alluding to the family name Peretti; on the bend on which he had placed the triple mount, he added an eight-pointed star. The complete blazon reads: *"d'azzurro al leone d'oro impugnante un ramo di pero fruttato di tre pezzi del secondo, attraversato da una banda di rosso caricata di un monte di tre pezzi alla italiana posto nel senso della banda sormontato da una stella di otto punte, il tutto d'oro"*; – *azure* a lion holding a branch of a pear tree gold, and a bend *gules* over all, charged with an eight-pointed star *or* in chief and a triple mount *or* in base.

The arms of Sixtus V.
Lo stemma di Sisto V.
Das Wappen von Sixtus V.

The bronze door of the Vatican Library, built by Sixtus V whose coat of arms rises above the cornice. On the door are two coats of arms and the name of Urban VIII; the bees and letters are gilded.

La porta di bronzo della Biblioteca Vaticana costruita da Sisto V, il cui stemma raggiunge la cornice. Sulla porta, due stemmi ed il nome di Urbano VIII: api e lettere dorate.

Die bronze Tür der Vatikan Bibliothek, die von Sixtus V gebaut wurde, dessen Wappen über dem Sims der Tür zu sehen ist. Auf der Doppeltür sind zwei Wappen und der Name des Urbanus VIII: die Bienen und Buchstaben sind vergoldet.

Sixtus V (1585–1590)
Sisto V (1585–1590)
Sixtus V (1585–1590)
FELICE PERETTI.

Bronze bust in the Vatican Library.
Busto bronzeo nella Biblioteca Vaticana.
Bronzebüste in der Vatikanischen Bibliothek.

Both his complete armorial bearings and individual charges from his coat of arms can be seen in the magnificent Salone Sistino, which today forms part of the Vatican Museums but which architecturally is part of the Biblioteca Vaticana, which he also had built.

Here we are directly above the Sala di Consultazione, well known to scholars and students. The bookcases contain manuscripts and early printed works which were transferred here from the rather humid and dark place where they had been kept since the pontificate of Sixtus IV (1471–1484).

Pope Peretti, the architect of original and grandiose buildings, had no qualms about cutting right across the magnificent architectural perspective of the Cortile del Belvedere; it is possible that he did so deliberately to stop once and for all the rather worldly entertainments and theatre plays which were performed there at the time of the Renaissance.

The splendid Salone Sistino gives us an idea what Rome looked like at the end of the sixteenth century and it also helps us to recall the main events during the pontificate of Sixtus V.

On one of the frescos is a lion on a green mountain: what exactly does this representation tell us? It symbolises one of the main achievements of Pope Sixtus V, and heraldry gives us the explanation as unexpectedly as it is helpful. The Pope liberated the Papal States from the plague of the *brigantaggio*, roaming bandits and robbers. To be effective in his endeavour to purge the country from this plague, he ordered the best known brigands to be hanged from the Ponte Sant'Angelo; this had the desired effect on their followers.

Fresco in the Salone Sistino recalling the suppression of the brigands in the Papal States, and below, the Pope provides sustenance for his subjects.

L'affresco nel Salone Sistino che ricorda l'opera di Sisto V per la repressione del brigantaggio nei suoi Stati, e in basso: il Papa procura il benessere ai suoi sudditi.

Fresko im Salone Sistino, das die Unterdrückung der Räuber durch Sixtus V in seinen Staaten zeigt, und unten: der Papst versorgt die Bürger mit Nahrung.

The junction where the Via della Conciliazione meets the Piazza Pio XII, and where the buildings housing the Congregations of the Roman Curia are situated.

Termine di Via della Conciliazione su Piazza Pio XII, dove sono situati i Palazzi delle Congregazioni della Curia Romana.

Einmündung der Via della Conciliazione in die Piazza Pio XII, wo die Gebäude der Kongregationen der Römischen Kurie liegen.

But how was it possible to recall such events in a painting without causing offence ? The answer lies in the fresco where two of the Pope's charges from his coat of arms have been enlarged and transformed: on a mountain stands a magnificent lion, holding his dexter paw in a threatening gesture; he represents Sixtus V as Grand Executioner, who from high above restores and maintains order in his territory, the Papal States. Below, the sheep graze peacefully at the foot of the mountain, while guard dogs search in all directions for brigands.

In the other fresco we see Sixtus V providing bread and sustenance for all his subjects. The lion, king of beasts, is shown shaking the trunk of a pear tree with his front paws, making the fruit fall to the ground to be gathered for food.

Lions and mountains make up the main motifs for the decorations in the Salone Sistino. They continue along the adjacent gallery as a decorative motif with additional, most apropriate mottoes, like that under the lion "*Si rugiet, quis non timebit?*"

Such examples demonstrate the subtle and practical aspects of heraldry and its usefulness in interpreting and understanding the hidden meaning in works of art. I often wonder how many visitors pass by these frescos day after day without understanding what is represented here or, most likely, without even knowing anything about Pope Sixtus V.

We now go to the upper floor to the Sala di Costantino. Besides the papal coat of arms above the inscription ≪*Aulam constantinianam . . . . . pro loci dignitate . . . . . absolvit*≫, and the frieze where lions and mountains alternate, we find here the *imprese* of Pope Peretti. The first one is the mountain with the motto *mons in quo beneplacitum est Deo*; next we see the lion with the motto *Justus ut leo confidens*; this is followed by the representation of the Apostle Peter's little boat with the motto *Duc in altum*; finally a representation of St. Francis of Assisi with the motto *Domum meam quae labitur repara*, which recalls that the Pope was a member of the Franciscan Order. On the walls in the recesses of the upper windows is yet another lion with the motto *vigilat pro custodia*.

The columns and obelisks painted on the ceiling have no heraldic significance; they merely recall two different achievements of Sixtus V : the erection of the obelisks in front of the main basilicas, and the placing of statues of the Princes of the Apostles on the Traiana and Antonina columns. The inscriptions *Sic de Traiano Petrus victore triumphat* and *Sic Antonium sub pede Paulus habet* refer to the statues.

The golden age of the Renaissance had passed. The Church now placed her Saints on columns and relics on obelisks.

It may be helpful to walk down to St. Peter's Square and end this excursion in front of the obelisk. On our way there, I remind my visitors that those popes who had been great builders, had also, of necessity, been great destroyers of buildings. Sixtus V, who reminds us of Julius II because of his patronage of the arts and architecture, not only demolished the famous Settizonio di Settimio Severo, which Bramante regarded, next to the Colosseum, as the most important and beautiful architectural treasures of ancient Rome and ancient times, but he also demolished the venerable Palazzo Laterano where so many Councils had met. Pope Peretti had erected the building we can see there today.

And yet he did exactly what so many of his predecessors had done: he took a pick-axe to

On the right of the Basilica is the Apostolic Palace. On the last floor of the Palace on the extreme right are the Pope's private apartments.

A destra della basilica il Palazzo Apostolico. All'ultimo piano del corpo di destra del palazzo, l'appartamento privato del Papa.

Rechts von der Basilika ist der Papstpalast in dessen obersten Etage im rechten Flügel des Palastes sich die Privatgemächer des Papstes befinden.

The Hall of Sixtus V is the reading room of the Library which Domenico Fontana built for Sixtus V, (1587), cutting across Bramante's Belvedere Courtyard.

Il Salone Sistino è la sala di lettura della Biblioteca di Sisto V che Domenico Fontana eresse (1587) tagliando il bramantesco Cortile del Belvedere.

Der Salone Sistino ist der Lesesaal der Bibliothek Sixtus V. Domenico Fontana baute ihn in 1587. Er durchteilte mit diesem Gebäude den von Bramante geschaffenen Cortile del Belvedere.

the ancient Vatican Basilica and built a new one.

Sixtus V is responsible for three major achievements which can best be seen from the centre of St. Peter's Square; they testify to his endeavour to add beauty to the city of Rome and to the Vatican: he erected the obelisk in the centre of St. Peter's Square, he built the Apostolic Palace which was destined to become the residence of future popes, and by having the dome built he was responsible for the completion of the Vatican Basilica, which had been built over the tomb of St. Peter.

I draw my visitors' attention to the four small lions on which the obelisk rests and to the triple mount and the star with which the obelisk is crowned. The are the heraldic charges of Pope Sixtus V.

The inscription *Vicit leo de tribu Juda* also makes an heraldic allusion, but one which can only be fully understood by scholars who are familiar with the ancient custom of using an *imprese* to convey a message and who were considered *iniziati* or initiated in the subtelties of this practice.

I have already mentioned that Sixtus V built the official residence of the popes, the Apostolic Palace, which has become a familiar sight to millions of pilgrims, and where that famous window is brightly lit often into the late hours of the night.

The buildings of Gregory XIII which faced northwards, proved both unhealthy and inadequate. Sixtus V did not hesitate to cut right through the gigantic block of buildings. It was only because his pontificate was so short that he did not complete this particular project. The eye trained in heraldry will immediately

108

notice the lion of Sixtus V above the windows on the first floor.

To bring this excursion to a close, let us take one more look at the dome of St. Peter's Basilica, one of the greatest, and perhaps even the greatest of all architectural masterpieces in history. Michelangelo had died over twenty years before when the cardinals went into the conclave to elect the successor to Gregory XIII (1585), and in unison entreated the future pope to complete the work on St. Peter's Basilica which had been dragging on for over a century. Sixtus V was not the kind of man to be daunted by such a task, and before he died, he had the great pleasure of seeing from his room in the Palazzo Quirinale the dome, which Michelangelo had designed, and which now dominated the skyline of Rome.

Today, the pilgrim who comes to pray at the *Confessione* of the Apostle Peter can lift up his eyes to the dome above and see the name of Pope Peretti next to that of St. Peter. The year of the Pope's death was also the year when the dome had been completed: «SANCTI PETRI GLORIAE SIXTUS PP.V. ANNO MDXC PONTIF. V».

''To the glory of St. Peter – Pope Sixtus V – in the year 1590 – the fifth year of his pontificate''. The inscription which commemorates the energetic Pope who had Michelangelo's dome built directly above the *Confessione* of the Basilica.

''Alla gloria di San Pietro – Sisto Quinto Papa – anno 1590 – quinto del suo pontificato''. L'iscrizione commemorativa del'energico Pontefice che portò a compimento la cupola michelangiolesca sopra la *Confessione* della basilica.

''Zu Ehren des Heiligen Petrus – Papst Sixtus V – im Jahre 1590 – im fünften Jahre seines Pontifikats''. Diese Beschriftung erinnert an den tatkräftigen Papst, der den Dom von Michelangelo direkt über dem Bekenntnisaltar der Basilika hat bauen lassen.

TU ES PETRUS ET SUPER HANC PETRAM AEDIFICABO
ECCLESIAM MEAM ET TIBI DABO CLAVES REGNI COELORUM

VI

FROM URBAN VII (1590)
TO
LEO XI (1605)

URBAN VII (1590)   GREGORY XIV (1590–1591)
INNOCENT IX (1591)   CLEMENT VIII (1592–1605)
LEO XI (1605–)

Alluding to heraldic charges from papal coats of arms, a typical Roman *bon mot* soon greeted the election of Urban VII, Giovanni Battista Castagna (1590) as successor to Sixtus V with satire: *Ai Romani Stufi di pere il Sacro Collegio regala adesso le castagne;* – the Romans who had become tired of pears (Pope Peretti), were given chestnuts (Pope Castagna) by the Cardinals instead!

But the witty citizens of Rome did not have much time in which to enjoy their joke because Urban VII died only twelve days after he was elected. He was buried in the Basilica della Minerva, and the only coat of arms belonging to him is carved on his funeral monument. His blazon was : *"troncato da una fascia d'argento: nel primo di rosso alla castagna fruttata di un pezzo e fogliata di quattro pezzi il tutto d'oro; nel secondo d'oro a tre bande di rosso"*; bendy silver and *gules*, a chief *gules* upheld by a fillet or gold and *gules*, a chief *gules* upheld by a fillet and leaved gold.

Just before his death he made a gesture which is of some interest to heraldic scholars and certainly testifies to the nobility and humility of Urban's spirit: The Palazzo del Vaticano and the Palazzo del Quirinale were almost

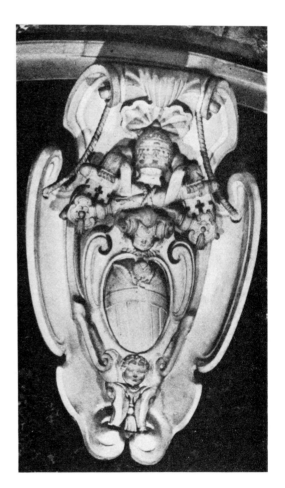

The arms of Urban VII.
Lo stemma di Urbano VII.
Das Wappen von Urbanus VII.

111

Urban VII (1590)
Urbano VII (1590)
Urbanus VII (1590)
GIOVANNI BATTISTA CASTAGNA.

completed, and Domenico Fontana intended to place Urban's coat of arms outside the palaces; however, the Pope gave strict instructions that the armorial bearings of his predecessor were to be placed there.

From an heraldic point of view, the next Pope, Gregory XIV, Niccolò Sfondrati (December 1590 – October 1591), was not much luckier than Urban VII because his pontificate only lasted ten months; but he lived long enough to see the lanterna in the cupola petriana, in the dome of the Basilica, completed. He also had some work done on the Torre Pia (so named after Pope St. Pius V). This

The arms of Gregory XIV surmount an empty niche in the right aisle of the Vatican Basilica because the Pope's statue was never sculpted; he reigned only for ten months.

Lo stemma di Gregorio XIV sormonta una nicchia vuota nella navata destra della Basilica Vaticana poichè la statua del Pontefice nun fu mai eseguita. Gregorio XIV regnò per dieci mesi.

Das Wappen von Gregorius XIV ist über einer leeren Nische im rechten Seitenschiff der vatikanischen Basilika weil sein Denkmal nie geschaffen wurde. Er regierte nur für zehn Monate.

is the reason why his name was carved above one of the windows, and his coat of arms adorns the ceilings of two of the new Halls of Tapestries in the Vatican Museum. His armorial bearings can also be seen on his tomb, on the right side of the aisle in the Vatican Basilica: *"inquartato: nel primo e nel quarto d'oro alla banda doppio-merlata d'azzurro accostata da due stelle dello stesso e caricata di un filetto d'oro; nel secondo e nel terzo d'argento al cipresso terrazzato, il tutto al naturale"*; quarterly, first and fourth, gold a bend battled on both sides *azure*, charged with a bendlet silver, between two stars of eight points azure, second and third, silver, a cypress tree on a terrace, all proper.

Innocent IX, Giovanni Antonio Facchinetti (October-December 1591), was the third pope who had a very short reign; his pontificate lasted just two months. Unlike his predecessors, he left no coat of arms behind in the Vatican Basilica, but we know that his blazon was: *"d'argento al noce sradicato al naturale"*; *argent*, a wallnut tree uprooted proper.

We now reach the pontificate of Clement VIII, Ippolito Aldobrandini (1592–1605). In contrast to his predecessors, charges from his coat of arms are in great abundance in the entire Apostolic Palace: the embattled and counter-embattled bend and his eight-pointed stars can be seen almost everywhere. He was the first pontiff who continued work on the Apostolic Palace after the interruption of four conclaves in eighteen months.

Clement VIII lost no time in countinuing the work that had been started in the pontificate of Sixtus V. On November 18, 1593, the Feast of the Dedication of the Vatican Basilica, he blessed the dome of St. Peter's. He had a gigantic bronze ball placed on the dome with a cross that stood five meters above the ball. He then ordered the remnants of the old basilica to

Gregory XIV (1590–1591)
Gregorio XIV (1590–1591)
Gregorius XIV (1590–1591)
NICCOLÒ SFONDRATI

Arms of Innocent IX (1591)
Lo stemma di Innocenzo IX (1591)
Das Wappen von Innozenz IX (1591)
GIOVANNI ANTONIO FACCHINETTI.

113

The arms of Clement VIII. Ceiling in the Sala del Concistoro.

Lo stemma di Clemente VIII. Soffitto della Sala del Concistoro.

Das Wappen von Klemens VIII. Decke des Sala del Concistoro.

be demolished, and the walls which had been built by Bramante around the old presbytery removed. He had the dome covered with layers of lead, and after having the inside of the dome decorated by Giuseppe Cesari, the Knight from Arpino, Clement VIII had placed in large letters inside the dome what we can regard as the Charter of the Church of Jesus Christ: «TU ES PETRUS ET SUPER HANC PETRAM AEDIFICABO ECCLESIAM MEAM ET TIBI DABO CLAVES REGNI COELORUM» – You are Peter and upon this rock I shall build my Church and to you I will give the keys of the Kingdom of Heaven.

114

The inscription in the dome which links the name of St. Peter with that of Sixtus V, is not the only tribute to the memory of Pope Peretti. If one looks carefully at the mosaics by the Cavaliere di Arpino, one notices that the vertical bars which divide the various sections end at the bottom with lion heads.

Clement VIII also had the great papal altar installed. The High Altar which on Maundy Thursday becomes the *lavata*, is made of marble which was cut at Foro di Nerva. The altar was built directly above the one erected by Callistus II in 1123; the latter would not have been large enough for this new basilica; besides, the little that was left of it had almost been buried. It is possible that the ground level of the old Constantinian Basilica was lower; it was probably at the level of the new Grottos.

Under the altar he had a chapel built near the tomb of the Apostle Peter; the chapel was named after him: Clementina. Pope Clement also had a secret passage built which enabled him to go more easily from the Apostolic Palace to pray at the tomb of St. Peter. Here we find the armorial bearings of the Pope, but a more beautiful coat of arms in multi-coloured marble is on the floor of the other Cappella Clementina, near the Sacristy on the left side of the aisle.

The blazon of Clement VIII was: *"d'azzurro alla banda doppio-merlata d'oro accostata da sei stelle di otto punte, tre al capo e tre in punta poste nel senso della banda, il tutto d'oro"*; azure, a bend battled on both sides gold, between six eight-pointed stars gold, three stars above and three below the battled bend.

An inscription which is repeated once more high up in the dome of the chapel reads: «CLEMENS VIII PONT.MAX. ANN.SAL. MDCI PONT.X».

Clement VIII (1591–1605)
Clemente VIII (1591–1605)
Klemens VIII (1591–1605)
IPPOLITO ALDOBRANDINI.

Mobile of Clement VIII.
Mobile di Clemente VIII.
Mobile von Klemens VIII.

115

Mobile of Clement VIII.
Mobile di Clemente VIII.
Mobile von Klemens VIII.

One must admire the skill of the artists who sculpted the arms of Pope Aldobrandini on the marble ballustrades of the altar in the Cappella Clementina. The Pope's arms have also been cut into the small granite pillars round the Arco delle Campane; they have been carved on the columns leading to the famous Portone di bronzo, the Bronze Door, and again on the crowning cornices of the Apostolic Palace. Here one must remember that the walls were built by Pope Sixtus V and the roof was put on the building by Clement VIII.

It is interesting that there is no heraldic memento to be found of that memorable event when Henry IV of France was reconciled with the Church. This celebration took place right here in the Porch of the Basilica in the pontificate of Clement VIII.

On September 17, 1595, Cardinals du Perron and d'Ossat representing their Sovereign at the ceremony, were beaten on their shoulders with a rod at the start of each verse of the sung *Miserere*, as a punishment for their Sovereign.

Imprese of Pope Aldobrandini in the Sala Clementina.
Impreses di Papa Aldobrandini nella Sala Clementina.
Imprese vom Papst Aldobrandini im Sala Clementina.

Clement VIII built the magnificent Aula in the Vatican where the Dutchman Paul Brill painted the martyrdom of Pope St. Clement, and where Giovanni Alberti painted that magnificent perspective on the ceiling. This pre-dates, and, indeed, anticipates the bold concept employed by the celebrated painter Andrea Pozzo, a Jesuit Father, who painted a false dome in the Church of S.Ignazio. The coat of arms of Pope Aldobrandini also decorates the ceiling of the Sala del Concistoro which is nearby.

Let us now go once more into St. Peter's Basilica and look at the tomb of the successor to Clement VIII, Pope Leo XI, Alessandro de'Medici, whose pontificate only lasted from 1 to 27 April 1605. The sculpted roses on the side of his tomb are the only personal symbols and they allude to his short pontificate in the Vatican, *"Sic florui"*, and the inscription underlines that: *"ad summam Ecclesiae Dei felicitatem ostensus magis quam datus"*.

The bas-relief recalls the event when Henry IV formally ratified his abjuration of the Protestant Faith and the restoration of full diplomatic relations between the Holy See and France. The documents were signed by Pope Clement VIII and given to Cardinal Alessandro de'Medici, the future Pope Leo XI, who was to present the documents to the King.

The Cardinal Legate de'Medici was solemnly received in France, and the King himself accompanied him as far as Montlhéry. Legend has it that when the document was to be signed, no table could be found, and that King Henry placed the scroll on his knee with the words "one can sign anywhere, as long as one signs with a happy heart". This scene is also recalled on the bas-relief, though the document is signed on a table, and the bearded

The arms of Clement VIII are sculpted in the arched balusters of the altars of St, Gregory the Great and of the Transfiguration.

Lo stemma di Clemente VIII è scolpito sui pilastri delle balaustre degli altare di San Gregorio Magno e della Transfigurazione.

Das Wappen von Klemens VIII ist in den gewölbten Geländersäulen der Altäre des Hl. Gregorius dem Grossen und der Verklärung gemeisselt.

117

Detail of the bas-relief on the front of the Monument to Leo XI. It shows the Pope when he was still a cardinal, receiving the document of abjuration from Henry IV.

Particolare del Monumento a Leone XI. Il bassorilievo sulla fronte del sarcofago rappresenta il Papa, ancora cardinale, che riceve l'abiura di Enrico IV.

Das Detail des Flachreliefs an der Vorderseite des Monuments von Leo XI zeigt den Papst als er noch Kardinal war und das Dokument der Abschwörung von Heinrich IV in Empfang nahm.

King is shown with his hand resting on the Gospels, taking the oath to remain faithful to the Church.

Leo XI was a loyal friend to the French. He lived in France for two years as Papal Legate. It is an amazing coincidence that young French artists who once received the coveted *Prix de Rome* from the French Government, did so in the famous Villa Medici sul Pincio. This Palace belonged to the Medici Pope Leo XI.

It goes without saying that the monument erected in honour of Leo XI is crowned once again by the roundels of the Medici, that illustrious family which had already given three Popes to the Church, Leo X (1513–1521), Clement VII (1523–1534), Pius IV (1560–1565), and now, in the person of Cardinal Alessandro de'Medici, its fourth Supreme Pontiff, Leo XI.

VII

PAUL V (1605)
TO
GREGORY XV (1623)

PAUL V (1605–1621)   GREGORY XV (1621–1623)

With Clement VIII (1592–1605) and his immediate successor, Leo XI (1605), *"ostensus magis quam datus"*, we have crossed the threshold of the seventeenth century into the Baroque age, which draws attention to itself even in some of the Vatican buildings.

The first Pope of that era is he whose name can be seen in huge letters on the façade of St. Peter's Basilica; one must be blind or distracted not to notice this monumental inscription which has immortalised his name as well as that of his family and his native city for centuries: «PAULUS V BURGHESIUS ROMANUS».

Paul V, Camillo Borghese (1605–1621), was elected to the papacy during a very impassioned conclave. First it appeared that the votes were being cast for Cardinal Bellarmino, then it seemed certain that Cardinal Baronio would be elected, but in the end it was Cardinal Borghese, then fifty-two years old, who succeeded to the papacy and who reigned for over fifteen years. He resided either in the Vatican Palace or in one of the villas he had built in Rome. A contemporary observed that "he was more enthusiastic with his building programme than any of his predecessors, and he was the right man to renew papal patronage of the arts and architecture in a grandiose and splendid style".

Paul V (1605–1621)
Paolo V (1605–1621)
Paulus V (1605–1621)
CAMILLO BORGHESE.

119

In the city of Rome he is mainly remembered by the Palazzo del Quirinale, the Palazzo Borghese and the Capella della Basilica Liberiana, where his mortal remains were interred in 1621. The Villa Borghese is perhaps the outstanding testimony of the *mecenatismo*, the patronage of the Pope's nephew, Cardinal Scipione Caffarelli Borghese, who built this magnificent villa in the pontificate of his uncle, Paul V, betwen 1613 and 1616.

In the Vatican itself, Pope Borghese was absolutely single-minded; his sole aim was to complete, St. Peter's Basilica once and for all time.

Above the central door of the Basilica and above the Loggia della Benedizione is the Pope's coat of arms: *"d'azzurro al drago alato coronato d'oro con le ali aperte e seminate di occhi; al Capo, dell'Impero cioè all'aquila spiegata di nero coronata imbeccata e rostrata del campo"*; *azure* a dragon with raised wings gold, the chief of the Empire *or* an eagle with his wings spread *sable*, beaked and crowned *or*.

The uppermost of the two heraldic beasts is the eagle of the Holy Roman Empire. It was Austino Borghese, one of the Pope's ancestors, an ambassador accredited to the Court of the Emperor Sigismund (1410–1437), who had been granted the privilege of augmenting his armorial bearings with the imperial eagle.

The arms of Paul V on the ceiling in the entrance hall to St. Peter's Basilica.

Lo stemma di Paolo V sul soffitto dell'atrio della Basilica di San Pietro.

Das Wappen von Paulus V in der Vorhalle der St. Peter Basilika.

On the impressive façade of St. Peter's Basilica, Paul V left a perpetual memento of his pontificate behind: his name and place of birth and his coat of arms: *PAUL V – CITIZEN OF ROME*. He reigned for fifteen years and left many grandiose buildings behind.

Sulla imponente facciata di San Pietro restano, a perenne ricordo, il nome di Paolo V, ''Burghesius Romanus'' e il suo stemma. Regnò per quindici anni lasciando grandi opere edilizie.

Auf der imposanten Fassade der St. Peter Basilika hat Papst Paulus V ein Denkmal an sein Pontifikat gesetzt. Man sieht dort seinen Namen, Paulus V, seine Herkunft, Bürger von Rom, und sein Wappen. Er war Papst für fünfzehn Jahre und hat viele grosse Bauwerke hinterlassen.

The Eagle of the Holy Roman Empire recalls a privilege granted to an ancestor of Paul V.

L'aquila del Sacro Romano Impero ricorda un privilegio accordato ad un antenato di Paolo V.

Der Adler des Heiligen Römischen Kaiserreiches war einem der Ahnen von Paulus V gewährt worden.

Although the many buildings which were erected during the pontificate of Paul V delight and even overwhelm us today with their magnificence, we must always remember that the greatest builders were also the greatest destroyers of older buildings, often, however, brought about by necessity.

Clement VIII had limited his demolition work to the apse of the ancient Constantinian Basilica. The rest was left to Paul V to demolish, disregarding protests by Baronio and many others who refused to resign themselves to watching helplessly while those magnificent witnesses of ancient times crumbled under the pick-axe wielded with such enthusiasm and fervour by the workers of Pope Borghese.

One only has to think of that brilliant façade, shining in gold and glorious colours, with in the centre Christ giving his Blessing. For thirteen centuries millions of pilgrims had passed by this spectacular building. To pacify the traditionalists (as they were called), it was officially announced that the ancient basilica was about to collapse, and that sooner or later the basilica would have to be demolished anyhow. In fairness to Paul V it must be said that he showed greater respect for antiquity than any of his predecessors of the Renaissance era had. He saved and conserved many of the tombs and venerated relics from the ancient Constantinian Basilica and, in addition, he had an accurate inventory of the old basilica drawn up, and all its parts or monuments which had to be demolished he had drawn or painted for posterity.

The major question under discussion was the area the new basilica should occupy. Two ideas were put forward: should the new basilica occupy the entire area of the old basilica or only the area around the tomb of the Apostle Peter?

122

The discussion became quite heated between two powerful pressure groups: those who supported the architectural blueprint of a Greek-Cross-structure, which had been suggested by Bramante and Michelangelo, and the party which favoured a blueprint based on a Latin-Cross-structure. Because of the powerful influence of Carlo Maderno, those supporting the Latin Cross plan won the day, and it it was decided to begin without delay with the building of the central nave.

In true baroque style, Paul V asked Carlo Maderno to start with the façade. Because the demensions envisaged for the new basilica were so enormous, it once again became necessary to use the pick-axe before building. First, the Pope ordered the demolition of the Court of Innocent VIII, which had housed the offices of the Sacred Rota, and then the Loggia of Paul II, together with the bell tower; finally the small palace of the Cardinal Archpriest fell victim to progress. The famous mosaics of Navicella by Giotto were rescued just in time, and after having them restored and resited several times, Paul V finally had them moved to the Porch above the central door.

Before entering the Basilica, let us pause for a moment in front of this imposing façade which has been criticised so often. It most certainly gives the impression that it was built without interruption during a single pontificate. And yet, thanks to heraldry, we can see quite clearly that this was not the case. For example, let us look at the clocks which seem to be held up there by angels. Directly under the dials one can see the *fleurs-de-lis* from the coat of arms of Pius VI (1775–1799), who reigned as Pope during the years of the French Revolution. These and other ''augmentations'' fit so well into the over-all structure and harmony of the building that the casual

On the Via della Conciliazione two small fountains have survived. The eagle and dragon of Paul V are carved in niches.

Lungo Via della Conciliazione restano due fontanelle. Nella nicchia sono scolpiti l'aquila e il drago di Paolo V.

Auf der Via della Conciliazione findet man noch zwei kleine Brunnen, und in den Nischen sind der Adler und Drachen von Paulus V gemeisselt.

Facing the Basilica, the fountain on the right which was erected in the pontificate of Paul V, and a detail of the armorial decorations which shows the corrosion caused by the water over nearly four centuries.

Guardano la facciata della Basilica: la fontana destra costruita durante il Pontificato di Paolo V, e dettagli delle decorazioni araldiche dimostranti la corrosione causata dall'aqua nel corso di circa quattro secoli.

Der Brunnen auf der rechten Seite vor der Fassade der Basilica: ein Detail der heraldischen Skulpturen, die zeigen wie sehr das Wasser des Brunnens während der letzten vierhundert Jahre die Skulpturen korrodiert hat.

observer could easily be deceived. Not so the scholar of heraldry, who can place each part and attribute it to the correct papal patron.

Of course, the question immediately arises as to what had been where the clocks are today.

There were, or better, there should have been, small bell towers, decorated with the arms of Pope Paul V, displaying the dragon and the imperial eagle. Indeed, we know that work on one of these bell towers had been well under way, but the tower had to be demolished with the utmost speed because the architects discovered – fortunately just in time before disaster struck – that the bell tower was making the entire building unsafe and was upsetting the static equilibrium of the basilica. A few of the parts of the missing bell tower can now be seen above the porch of S.Maria in Travestere.

Just before entering the Basilica it is worth glancing at the adjacent building to our right. It dates from the pontificate of Leo X, but Paul V had a new façade put on it. At one time this building housed the Apostolic Secretariat; today we find there the offices of the papal Master of Ceremonies and some offices belonging the the Secretariat of State. The coat of arms of Paul V can be seen on the central *cancello* of the Basilica which dates from the same time as the façade, and again, high up on the stucco ceiling of the porch, gilded on a white background.

The eagle and the dragon from the Pope's armorial bearings, sculpted individually, can also be seen on the small pillars in front of the door which links the porch with the Apostolic Palace. Both heraldic beasts are also on the door knocker of the famous Bronze Door, *il Portone di Bronzo*, through which enter all those who go to a special audience with the Pope.

Let us now briefly go into the Basilica. On Palm Sunday 1615 the Romans looked at the magnificent spectacle we see today for the first time. The central nave have been completed and the partition wall which had been placed by Paul III between the old and the new Basilica had been completely taken down. The Romans were particularly proud that this magnificent building had finally been completed by one of their own citizens.

Those looking for the eagle and the dragon on the ceiling will be disappointed; they used to be there in the colourful mosaics by Marcello Provenzale who, incidentally had also restored the Navicella by Giotto. We know that the eagle and dragon looked beautiful in the mosaic ceiling. Sadly, they were later taken out, and their place was taken by a small angel blowing on a *fleur-de-lis*. Both are heraldic charges from the arms of Pope Braschi, Pius VI, who had the ceiling restored almost two hundred years later.

To see the eagle and the dragon again, we have to go down the entire nave and descend to the *Confessione*. The statue of the kneeling pope which was there until the recent restoration work, was that of Pius VI, who seems to follow us everywhere, but the coat of arms on the walls, in multi-coloured marble, is that of Paul V. It was he who continued and carried out the work begun by Clement VIII in the Grottos and in the *Confessione*. The inscription in the Nicchia dei Pallii explains this: «SACRA B. PETRI CONFESSIO A PAULO PAPA V EIUS SERVO EXOSNATA ANN. DOM. MDCXV. PONT. XI».

One cannot end an heraldic excursion looking at the arms of Paul V without looking at the fountains with which the Pope enriched the Vatican, beginning with the most famous of them, designed by Maderno, which stands in

125

St. Peter's Square. Unfortunately, the water which has been overflowing from the upper basin for almost four centuries has left heavy mineral deposits on the eagle and the dragon which were sculpted below. But to compensate for the disappointment, those sculpted on the small pillars surrounding the fountain are clearly visible.

Next I take my visitors to see the fountain in the Cortile del Belvedere, and from there we go through the covered passage, known as the Grottone, to the Vatican Gardens. We come out at the Piazza della Zecca where we can see the most beautifully executed coat of arms of Paul V, who had a small villa built here. Paul V used the staircase we can see to go down to the Vatican Gardens. Today, the building from which the staircase leads is an annexe to the museums, and is best known for its fresco by Nozze Aldobrandini. There is a typically baroque fountain here; two towers are crowned by dragons which frame, in quite an original way, several water-jets, which come from an altar that has a monstrance in the middle and three candles on either side.

More formal but less stylish is the fountain dell'Aquilone; its huge basin is decorated with dragons, and the fountain is crowned with a colossal eagle. The Pauline aquaduct which brought water from Lake Bracciano to supply the district of Trastevere was the first made use

Over one of the doors in the Secret Archives hangs the portrait of their founder, Paul V; the next door is surmounted by the founder's coat of arms.

Al di sopra di una delle porte dell'Archivio Segreto è appeso il ritratto suo fondatore, Paolo V, il cui stemma sovrasta la porta successiva.

Über einer Tür des Geheimarchivs hängt das Gemälde des Gründers, Paulus V, dessen Wappen über der nächsten Tür hängt.

of by the Vatican Gardens; the aquaduct also supplied the *fontanoni* near S.Pietro in Montorio and the Ponte Sisto.

The fountain in S.Andrea della Valle is also decorated with the arms of Paul V, who put the fountain into the Piazza Scossacavalli, which disappeared when the Via della Conciliazione was built. Two smaller versions of this fountain can be seen in Borgo, in the old Palazzo dei Penitenzieri, and they too show the Borghese arms.

Paul V was succeeded by Gregory XV, Alessandro Ludovisi (1621–1623). His pontificate only lasted two years, and he is best rememberedd for founding the Sacred Congregation *De Propaganda Fide*. His tomb, sculpted by Legros, is in the Church of S.Ignazio, but his coat of arms :*"di rosso a tre bande d'oro ritirate al capo"* – *gules* three bends gold retraits in chief –, can only be seen in the corners of the central medallion which decorates the ceiling in the Cappella del Coro in St.Peter's Basilica.

On the other hand, the *api* – the bees of Pope Barberini, Urban VIII (1623–1644), had the opportunity of finding their way into many places in the Vatican during that Pope's long pontificate of over twenty years. They offer a rich field of exploration to the scholar of heraldry, and they justify an entire heraldic excursion in themselves.

Gregory XV (1621–1623), ALESSANDRO LUDOVISI. During his pontificate which lasted only two years, he founded the Congregation *De Propaganda Fide*. His coat of arms also adorns the dome in the Choir Chapel (below).

Gregorio XV (1621–1623), ALESSANDRO LUDOVISI. Nel suo pontificato di appena due anni istituì la Congregazione *De Propaganda Fide*. Il suo stemma orna anche la cupola della cappella del coro (in basso).

Gregorius XV (1621–1623), ALESSANDRO LUDOVISI. Während seines zweijährigen Pontifikats hat er die Kongregation *De Propaganda Fide* gegründet. Sein Wappen ist auch in der Kuppel der Chorkapelle zu sehen (unten).

VIII

URBAN VIII (1623–1644)

During the pontificates or Urban VIII, Innocent X and Alexander VII, the Vatican Basilica, the Apostolic Palace and St. Peter's Square took on the appearance we know today. This took all place at the peak of the age of Baroque.

One name dominated the entire era: Bernini, the 'Michelangelo' of the seventeenth century.

When Urban VIII, Maffeo Barberini (1623–1644) was elected to the papacy, Bernini was not as yet twenty-five years old but he was already very famous. Pope Urban's predecessor, Gregory XV, had conferred upon the young Bernini the highest Order of Knighthood: the Supreme Order of Christ. When Bernini's old friend Cardinal Maffeo Barberini was elected to the papacy, the new Pope immediately sent for him and said: "Sir Knight, it is most fortunate for you that Maffeo Barberini is now the Pope, but it is even more fortunate for Us that Cavaliere Bernini lives in Our pontificate". Although the Pontiff was aware that his action might cause jealousy and envy, he handed over to Bernini the whole Vatican project to complete it as he pleased.

We have now reached the period where all Roman creativity is focused on St. Peter's Basilica. The actual building had been completed under Paul V, but now the time had come to furnish the enormous nave and decorate the bare walls inside. Bernini set about this task with his uniquely fertile imagination; this is also one of the reasons why the heraldic *api*, the bees of Pope Barberini, seem to swarm all over St. Peter's Basilica.

The bronze baldachin by Bernini rises over the altar called *Confessione*, because it stands above the tomb of St. Peter, who 'confessed' his faith by the sacrifice of his martyrdom.

Il baldacchino in bronzo del Bernini si erge sull'altare detto della *Confessione* perchè sorge sul luogo della tomba di San Pietro che 'confessò', cioè attestò col martirio la sua fede.

Der Bronzebaldachin von Bernini wölbt sich über dem Bekenntnisaltar, so genannt weil er über dem Grabgewölbe des Apostels Petrus steht, der mit dem Martyrium seinen Glauben 'bekannte'.

129

Urban VIII (1623–1644)
Urbano VIII (1623–1644)
Urbanus VIII (1623–1644)
MAFFEO BARBERINI.

Beginning with the High Altar above St. Peter's tomb, and called the *Confessione* because the Apostle Peter confessed his Faith by the sacrifice of his martyrdom, we can see eight very large coats of arms on the base of the pillars of the famous bronze *Baldacchino*. The grace and softness and the delicate touch of the artist who executed these monumental heraldic shields are truly remarkable.

Naturally, heraldic scholars, but also many pilgrims who admire that magnificent *Baldacchino*, are curious to learn the reason for the bees in those coats of arms. It is not always easy to trace the origins of armorial bearings and especially the reasons for the heraldic charges of the armiger, but in the case of Pope Barberini the explanation is not difficult to find.

Originally, the Barberini bees were quite ordinary wasps, or worse still, some historians maintain that they had been rather vulgar and unpleasant horseflies. Urban VIII was descended from the Tafani family, – *tafani* meaning horseflies or blood-suckers. The Tafani family were small merchants in Ancona, and they retained the name Tafani until, having become quite wealthy, they were able to buy the Castello Barberini near Siena. From then on the family name was changed to Barberini and the three heraldic horseflies in the family's coat of arms were enobled and changed into three golden bees: *"alle tre api d'oro in campo azzurro"*; azure three bees *or*. The Barberini bees can be seen, in no particular arrangement, all over the twisted columns of the famous *Baldacchino*, among the decorative angels and laurel leaves.

The *Baldacchino* of the papal altar is as high as the Palazzo Farnese and weighs over one hundred tons. It is hard to imagine how many difficulties had to be overcome when it was

130

erected. Each of the four twisted columns was meticulously weighed on gigantic scales which had been invented by Bernini's brother Luigi, who had also invented the movable scaffolding which was used by the *sampietrini*, the workmen permanently employed on the fabric of St. Peter's to regularly clean the ceiling of the basilica. Seven years after work on the *Baldacchino* had begun, this sumptuous work of art was finally unveiled on the Feast of SS. Peter and Paul, 29 June 1633 *"universali omnium admiratione et plausu"*.

It is well known that Bernini used bronze taken from the Pantheon for the *Baldacchino*, but one cannot agree with contemporary comment which was far too cynical and, indeed, gratuitous in its implication: *"Quod non fecerunt Barbari fecerunt Barberini"*. Furthermore, it is important to bear in mind that the old bronze girders of the Temple of Agrippa, which had been used by Bernini, had not even been visible, and the commemorative inscription which refers to the spoiling of the temple does not exaggerate when it says that Urban VIII used these *"decora inutilia"*, useless adornments, for the greater glory of the Apostle Peter.

The *Baldacchino* was described by Milizia as "a real frenzy, and truly an absurdity"; Bruzi, on the other hand, described it as *"opus pulchritudine et magnificentia non infra Phidiae et Praxitelis praestantiam"*, "a real work of art of exceptional beauty and magnificence, in no way inferior to the superb work of the Athenian sculptors Phidias and Praxiteles". Putting aside these two extreme views, one must agree with Gaetano Bossi, who said that the *Baldacchino* blends in perfectly with the vastness and majesty of the basilica, and although quite different in style, it is in total harmony with its surroundings.

A base of one of the spiral columns of the bronze baldachin (page 128) of the papal altar in St. Peter's Basilica, decorated with the 'Api' – the Bees of Pope Barberini.

Uno dei basamenti delle colonne tortili del baldacchino (pagina 128) dell'altare papale in S. Pietro, ornato dalle api di Papa Barberini.

Der Sockel einer der spiralen Säulen des Bronzebaldachins (Seite 128) des päpstlichen Altars in St. Peter, geschmückt mit den 'Api' – den Bienen des Papstes Barberini.

The pier with the reliquary which holds the lance of St. Longinus.

Il pilone con il reliquiario contenente la lancia di S. Longino.

Der Stützpfeiler mit dem Reliqienschrein der Lanze des Hl. Longinus.

Emile Male gave a justification for the *Baldacchino*, using, metaphorically speaking, the language of the artist. He maintained that it was necessary to remind the whole world that the Apostle Peter lay buried under these triumphal columns (though nobody had ever denied that Rome had the glory of owning the relics of St. Peter). It had therefore to be stated clearly, and for the whole world to see, that the first Pope of the Holy Roman Church was the cornerstone upon which the Church was built. The statement of truth from the Gospels, which the Protestants were trying to misinterpret and distort, was therefore displayed in huge letters in the centre of the dome of St. Peter's Basilica: «TU ES PETRUS ET SUPER HANC PETRAM AEDIFICABO ECCLESIAM MEAM».

Even before the four pillars for the *Baldachino* were completed, Bernini started on the sumptuous decoration of the four massive pentagonal piers upon which the *cupola*, the dome, rests, and which were designed by Michelangelo. He raised the spiral columns of the ancient Constantinian Basilica, and under each of the loggias he placed the coat of arms of Pope Barberini. He carved four large reliquaries into the piers where the four most important relics belonging to the Basilica were to be placed: a fragment of wood from the Holy Cross; the so-called linen cloth of St.Veronica; the lance of St. Longinus, which had been given as a present to Innocent VIII by the Sultan Baiazet; and the head of St. Andrew. The four large niches can be seen in the piers with the statues of St. Helena with the True Cross, St. Veronica holding the linen cloth, St.Longinus with his lance and St. Andrew with his saltire cross.

The statue of St. Longinus was sculpted by Bernini himself, the other three by Andrea Bolgi, Francesco Mochi and the Flemish sculptor Francesco Du Quesnoy.

132

An unexpected and dramatic event occurred towards the end of 1636 which stopped the work that was being carried out at a feverish pace on the foundations of the piers. An enormous crack appeared in the dome. Was it possible that this had been caused by this activity ? That was certainly the accusation made by Bernini's enemies. An avalanche of written and verbal abuse fell upon the architect who was being held personally responsible for the collapse of the Basilica, expected daily.

It is said that when Bernini asked the artist Mochi about the breeze which so delicately seemed to move the beautifully sculped dress of St.Veronica, the sculptor promptly answered: "the wind blows from the crack in the dome which is there because of your genius".

The news of the damage to the dome naturally caused much apprehension in the Vatican. But as soon as some calm had been restored and reason prevailed the work was continued, and two years later, in 1638, the four major relics were placed in the reliquaries in the massive piers. To make public veneration of the relics easier, three were originally placed into the reliquary of St. Veronica and the head of St. Andrew into the reliquary of St. Helena.

There is a memorable postscript about the relic of St. Andrew: in 1964, during the Second Vatican Council, over three hundred years after the Saint's head was placed into this magnificent reliquary in St. Peter's Basilica, Pope Paul VI, in a gracious gesture of reconciliation, returned the head of St. Andrew to the Orthodox Bishop of Patrasso, the town where the Apostle had met his martyrdom. The author had the honour of being appointed a member of the commission which returned this sacred relic.

The pier with the reliquary which held until 1964 the head of St. Andrew.

Il pilone con il reliquiario che fino al 1964 conteneva la testa di S. Andrea.

Der Stützpfeiler mit dem Reliquienschrein in dem bis 1964 das Haupt des Hl. Andreas aufbewahrt wurde.

133

The arms of the Countess Matilde of Canossa on her monument erected in the right aisle of St. Peter's Basilica.

Lo stemma della contessa Matilde di Canossa, sul monumento erettole nella navata destra della Basilica di San Pietro.

Das Wappen der Gräfin Matilde von Canossa auf ihrem Grabmal, das in dem rechten Seitenschiff der St. Peter Basilika errichtet wurde.

In 1639 Bernini married, but a year later he was working on new projects, especially on the grandiose statue of Urban VIII in Campidoglio.

Let us now go to the Cappella del Coro dei Canonici Vaticani, the Choir Chapel of the Canons of the Vatican Basilica. Heraldically it is a 'beehive' of prayers because it is full of Barberini bees; one can see them carved in wood on the stalls of the canons. They seem not only to be carrying the bidding prayers up to heaven, but also the mutterings of the venerable prelates, who owe a great debt to Pope Barberini for this magnificent chapel. There are Barberini bees on the iron railings and on the monumental door as well as on the sides of the altar in the Chapel of the Most Holy Sacrament.

We have now reached the monument erected in honour of the Countess Matilda of Tuscany whose ashes were brought here by Urban VIII. The statue was sculpted by Bernini, and on the bas-relief he recalls the historical event of Canossa. There are no Barberini bees on this monument because the Pope had expressly wished that only the coat of arms of the Countess and the motto *"Tuetur et unit"* should be on it.

However, the golden winged insects accompanied Pope Barberini to his own tomb; Bernini himself sculpted the monument to his friend and great benefactor. Looking at the tomb, we see immediately that the bees, the heraldic charges, have left the coat of arms and settled all over the tomb. We have now reached the zenith of the age of Baroque.

But what is this bat-like creature which seems to be writing the name of the deceased? It is the skeleton of death, but one has to look at the monument more closely to see and appreciate yet another aspect of Bernini's genius. Few people even notice it unless it is pointed out to them: a book, sculpted in black marble, shows clearly the name of the dead Pontiff written on it, but one page has not been quite turned over by the scrivener, and a small portion of the previous page is visible, and on that small area we can discern just a single letter, the initial of Urban's predecessor, Gregory XV. The Barberini bees seem to remain with the Pope in the hereafter and accompany him beyond his death.

The Romans, tired of paying heavy taxes, only to see members of the Barberini family enrich themselves, soon composed their own sarcastic epitaph for the Pope: ≪*Pauca haec Urbani sint verba incisa sepulcro – Quam bene pavit apes, tam male pavit oves*≫; ''There are few words written on the tomb of Urban – but how well he looks after the bees and how badly after his flock''.

This judgement on Urban VIII was quite unjust; it came about because of favouritism he had shown to his nephews and because of the expenses of his military ventures. Contrary to the peaceful appearance of his coat of arms, the Pope was very much '*rebus bellicis maxime intentus*' – set on belligerent ventures with great fervour.

He changed the Castel S.Angelo into a fortress and installed eighty canons which were cast from bronze taken from the Pantheon and again the cause of much of the peoples' anger. He also fortified the Janiculean walls, and his coat of arms can be seen on them about twenty times!

As to the Pope's nephews, we must not forget that we owe to them the magnificent Palazzo Barberini, several famous churches and other

An ingenious idea of Bernini: on the tomb of Urban VIII, Death turns the last page of the large marble book and one can see just the initial of Urban's predecessor, Gregory XV.

Una geniale trovata del Bernini: sul grande libro marmoreo del Monumento sepolcrale di Urbano VIII, la Morte volta l'ultima pagina lasciando vedere solo la prima lettera del nome del predecessore Gregorio XV.

Eine geniale Idee von Bernini: auf dem Grabmal von Urban VIII, der Tot schlägt die letzte Seite eines grossen, in Marmor gemeisselten Buches um, und man kann den Anfangsbuchstaben des Namens seines Vorgängers, Gregorius XV, sehen.

The Bronze Door, placed by Bernini at the beginning of the north colonnade of St. Peter's Square.

Il Portone di Bronzo collocato dal Bernini all'incollatura del porticato nord di Piazza San Pietro.

Das Bronzeportal von Bernini and der Biegung der nördlichen Kolonnaden des St. Petersplatzes.

buildings. In fact, the Barberini building projects caused Fraschetti to say, though with some exaggeration, ". . . the bees of Pope Barberini sit on all the most beautiful buildings of the seventeenth century that can be seen in Rome".

In the Apostolic Palace itself, apart from several inscriptions to the effect that during his pontificate certain restorations had been carried out, his coat of arms appears only twice: on the second floor in the Sala della Contessa Matilda, which was later changed to the sacristy of the chapel dedicated to her Patron Saint, and where spiritual retreats are held even today, and in the private chapel of the Pope. During a conclave I could, theoretically of course, take my visitors from the Cortile dei Pappagalli up a mysterious staircase which leads to a kitchen, and higher up still, to the dining room of the cardinals assembled here to elect the new pope. Going up this secret staircase even further, they would see some rather mediocre frescos commemorating the most important events during the pontificate of Urban VIII.

Of course, being unable to see these frescos, one might compensate for this by looking at some very similar paintings which can be found in the *anticamera* of the Cardinal Secretary of State. They are depicted along the cornices, alternating with the inevitable Barberini bees.

Heraldically speaking, we shall stay with 'winged creatures'. Our next excursion begins in front of a dove which surmounts the gracious fountain in the Cortile di S.Damaso, and which is the main heraldic charge from the armorial bearings of Pope Barberini's successor, Innocent X, Giovanni Battista Pamphili.

136

IX

INNOCENT X (1644–1655)

There are few visitors or, indeed, members of the Curia who, when crossing the Cortile di S.Damaso give a thought to Pope Innocent X, Giovanni Battista Pamphili (1644–1655). His famous painting by Velasquez hangs in the Galleria Doria Pamphili, and his bronze statue by Alessandro Algardi can be found in the Palazzo dei Conservatori which was designed by Michelangelo.

And yet it was Innocent X who had that delightful fountain built under the clock in the Cortile. The fountain seems to welcome those who walk towards the lifts which take members of the Curia and others to the various floors of the Apostolic Palace.

Rome is famous all over the world for its many fountains; of course, fountains differ in beauty and age. How different is this lovely little fountain in the Cortile di S.Damaso from the famous Fontana dei Fiumi, the Fountain of the Four Rivers, which Innocent X had built by Bernini in front of his magnificent palace in the Piazza Navona ! There the four rivers, the Nile, the Ganges, the Danube and the River Plate roar into an enormous basin, and here in the Cortile, a small jet of water falls softly with a gentle splatter into the basin; during the long hours of the afternoon, the gentle splashing of water is often the only sound of life in this silent courtyard.

But this little fountain not only has its delightful charm: more significantly, it is important to students of heraldry because it introduces them to the coat of arms of Innocent X.

Innocent X (1644–1655)
Innocenzo X (1644–1655)
Innozenz X (1644–1655)
GIOVANNI BATTISTA PAMPHILI.

137

The Cortile di San Damaso is the heart of the Vatican Palaces. Under Pope Pamphili's coat of arms, between the first Loggia and the porch is an inscription which recalls the second 'discoverer' of the water which Pope Damaso had channeled into the Vatican and with which he administered baptism.

Cuore dei Palazzi Vaticani è il cortile di San Damaso. Sotto lo stemma di Papa Pamphili, tra il balcone della prima loggia e il portico, è murata una lapide che ricorda il secondo scopritore dell'acqua incanalata da Papa Damaso per amministrare il battesimo.

Der Cortile di San Damaso ist das Herz der vatikanischen Paläste. Unter dem Wappen des Papstes Pamphili, zwischen dem Balkon der ersten Loggia und dem Portal, ist eine Steinplatte zum Andenken an den zweiten Entdecker des Wassers, das Papst Damaso in den Vatikan kanneliert hatte, um das Sakrament der Taufe zu geben.

These are the same *fleurs-de-lis* and the same dove that one can see in the Piazza Navona and on the corners of the Palazzo Doria Pamphili which faces the Piazza del Collegio Romano. During the years of the pontificate of Innocent X, the two families of Doria and of Pamphili founded a new branch. To the herald, their coat of arms with its unusual chief presents a problem in its precise blazoning. The official Italian blazon is: *"di rosso alla colomba posante d'argento imbeccante un ramo di ulivo in sbarra al naturale: capo di tre pezzi d'azzurro caricato di tre gigli d'oro"*; Galbreath gives a blazon with further details about the chief, and it is his eye for meticulous detail which makes the Pamphili chief most unusual: *"gules,* a dove silver holding an olivebranch *vert,* and a chief *azure* charged with three *fleurs-de-lis* gold divided by two pallets *retraits* in base *gules".* Originally this was the chief of Anjou, *capo d'Angiò.* A tombstone dating from 1600 in San Pietro in Montorio shows an alternative and certainly older version of the Pamphili chief: *"azure* sustained by an inverted label of four points and charged with three *fleurs-de-lis* gold.

Coming back to the Cortile di S. Damaso, a rather sophisticated Latin inscription explains why the courtyard was named after Pope S. Damaso, because in this very place on the Vatican Hill, Pope Damaso discovered a natural spring with its waters flowing down-hill: «*aquam vaticani collis incerto olim a capite deerantem a Beato Damaso inventa scaturigine*» [*scaturigo,* f. = a bubbling spring] put behind . . . spring.] After having the water channelled, he had a fountain built, and he used the water to administer the Holy Sacrament of Baptism. This legend is shown on the bas-relief. Sadly, with the passing of time, all traces of this precious spring were lost. However, in the inscription it is also recalled that the founder of the second fountain was

Innocent X: ≪*Rursum amissam Innocentius X Pont. Max. conquisitam repertamque ac mire probatam fonti recens extructo restituit*≫. This is the reason the Pope's coat of arms is sculpted on it. The inscription does not mention that the bas-relief was the work of Alessandro Algardi.

Had the fame of Bernini already fallen into decline? Sadly, when Urban VIII, his great patron had died, the unfortunate Cavaliere Bernini found himself as much in disgrace as did the entire Barberini family.

We don't know how much Pope Innocent X, who preferred Borromini to Bernini, listened and yielded to the advice of Bernini's enemies, but we know that the Pope authorised the domolition of a bell tower which Bernini had begun building on the left side of the Basilica. The unfortunate artist was even forced to assist in the demolition of his own work and help his rival on his way to fame and fortune. The pontificate of Innocent X had begun badly for Bernini.

Fortunately, it was only a passing phase, because in 1647 Innocent X enthusiastically approved Bernini's plans for the Fontana dei Fiumi on the Piazza Navona. The star of the great Master rose again, but this did not stop Alessandro Algardi from making his own mark on the world of the arts and architecture, as he was one of the few artists who had no need to engratiate himself with Bernini.

In St. Peter's Basilica are two important works of art which Alessandro Algardi executed during the pontificate of Innocent X: the famous bas-relief showing the abjuration of Henry IV, and which he sculpted on the tomb of Leo XI, and at the end of the left side of the nave, the gigantic altar piece, truly a painting

A small fountain under the coat of arms of Innocent X in the Cortile di San Damaso.

Una piccola fontana sotto lo stemma di Innocenzo X nel cortile di San Damaso.

Ein kleiner Brunnen unter dem Wappen von Innozenz X im Cortile di San Damaso.

in stone. The work on this *pittura pietrificata* took Algardi four years to complete, from 1646 until 1650. It shows S. Leo I halting Attila and his hordes near Mantua in 452. Algardi idealised the scene as much as Raphael did in the Stanze. But it is the prerogative of the artist to embellish history.

Let us now turn to the centre of the nave and look at some of the work commissioned by Innocent X. The nave had been made longer under Paul V (1605–1621), but the pillars had remained bare stone. In 1647 Pope Pamphili asked Bernini to line the pillars with marble and decorate them with medallions in time for the Holy Year of 1650.

Once again it is heraldry which serves as the best guide. On the floor we see a very large coat

Cortile di San Damaso

140

Cortile del Belvedere.

of arms of Innocent X made of multi-coloured marble. The inscription «ANNO IUBILAEI MDCL» shows that the work had been completed in time for the Holy Year. Where the nave begins, the Pope had the famous *disco di porfido*, the porphyry disk, inlaid in the flooring; (porphyry is a hard rock composed of crystals of red and white feldspar, that was anciently quarried in Egypt). It is one of the very few surviving relics from the ancient Constantinian Basilica.

Heraldry helps us to date the decoration of the pillars. To the ordinary tourist or pilgrim, those doves with an olivebranch in their beaks may appear just decorative, or, at best, remind

141

The nave had been made longer under Paul V, but the pillars had remained bare stone. In 1647, Innocent X asked Bernini to line the pillars with marble and decorate them with medallions in time for the Holy Year of 1650.

La navata era stata prolungata da Paolo V, ma i pilastri erano rimasti spogli. Fu appunto Innocenzo X che, nel 1647, ordinò al Bernini e ai suoi aiuti di rivestirli di marmi e di medaglioni, facendo in modo che tutto fosse pronto per l'anno santo 1650.

Das Mittelschiff wurde unter Paul V verlängert, aber die Säulen verblieben kahl. In 1647 hat Innozenz X Bernini beauftragt, die Säulen mit Marmor zu bemänteln und mit Medaillons zu verzieren, und diese Arbeit für das Heilige Jahr 1650 zu vollenden.

him of similar representations he may have seen sculpted or painted in the catacombs. On the other hand, the heraldic scholar knows that the dove with the olivebranch is the main heraldic charge from the coat of arms of Innocent X, and they testify quite independently of any narrative that this work was carried out in his pontificate between 1644 to 1655. Even very few heraldic scholars know that these armorial doves were designed by Nicolas Sale, a French artist, who is described as being 'di cristianissimi costumi', 'of the highest Christian virtues'. Sale had been employed by Bernini as major-domo, and being so near the great Master all the time, he finally discovered his own vocation as a sculptor.

Apart from the heraldic doves of Pamphili, the pillars are decorated with huge medallions, depicting forty early popes who had been canonised, dancing cherubs, tiaras and the crossed keys of St. Peter. One of the best known biographers of Bernini, Fraschetti, agrees that the medallions and decorations lend a certain richness and magnificent splendour to the Basilica, but he considers the portraits of the early popes "pontefici agonizzanti", "pontiffs in real agony", the cherubs "mostruosi i putti", "monstrous children", and the doves "galline le colombe", "old chickens".

Certainly, these decorations cannot be regarded among the most beautiful in the Basilica, but we must remember that only the concept of the medallions and the manner in which the pillars should be decorated were Bernini's. Unfortunately, the execution of his brilliant concept was left to rather second-rate artists, such as Bolgi, Fancelli, Bonarelli and Raggi, and sometime to even less than mediocre decorators !

142

Innocent X had those snow-white angels put along the cornices high up on the ceiling; they seem to defy the law of gravity floating up there. More angels were placed in the Chapels of the Most Holy Sacrament and of the Choir of the Canons of the Vatican Basilica; they were sculpted by Bernini's brother Luigi.

Looking back once more towards the end of the nave, directly above the central door, we must admire the impressive armorial bearings of Innocent X, just below those of Paul V. There is no need to read the monumental inscription there, but it is well worth the effort taking a closer look at the bussola where *fleurs-de-lis* alternate with doves.

We shall now hasten our steps towards the next pontificate, that of Alexander VII (1655–1677). We no longer find works of art by Algardi because he had died in 1654, but still awaiting us are the final masterpieces by Bernini: in the Basilica the *Cattedra of St. Peter*, the bronze throne which shows the same baroque sense of movement as does the *Baldacchino*, the Scala Regia, the royal staircase which leads to the first floor, and the famous *Colonnato*, the colonnade, where the mountains and stars, heraldic charges from the arms of Alexander VII, can be found in abundance.

The dove, a heraldic emblem of Innocent X.
La colomba, un emblema di Innocenzo X.
Die Taube, ein heraldisches Emblem von Innozenz X.

143

X

ALEXANDER VII (1655–1667)

With the pontificate of Alexander VII, Fabio Chigi (1655–1667), we have reached the peak of the Baroque era. It is a point of arrival but also one of conclusion because Alexander VII was to give to the Vatican its final appearance what we see today. In the next three centuries his successors made only some very minor modifications. As in the pontificates of the predecessors of Alexander VII, Bernini was once again the architect of the most significant buildings.

When Monsignore Fabio Chigi was created a cardinal in 1652, he commisioned some work to be done in the Basilica of S. Maria Maggiore, and following the example of his predecessor Urban VIII, on the day Alexander VII was elected Pope, he sent for Bernini and gave him the opportunity to create some more masterpieces.

I have already mentioned the outstanding creations of Bernini at the conclusion of our last excursion: in the Vatican Basilica the monumental *Cattedra Trionfante* in gilded bronze with the famous *Gloria*; the magnificent Scala Regia in the Apostolic Palace, and the world-famous Colonnato in the Piazza S.Pietro.

Let us start our excursion from the end of the colonnnade in St. Peter's Square and walk towards its centre. From here we have the best opportunity of studying the armorial bearings of Alexander VII. We notice right away that the arms at the start of the colonnade are smaller

Alexander VII (1655–1667)
Alessandro VII (1655–1667)
Alexander VII (1655–1667)
FABIO CHIGI

Opposite: The Scala Regia by Bernini leads up to the first floor of the medieval part of the Papal Palace. Above the arch are the quatered arms, Chigi-Rovere, of Alexander VII.

Lato opposto: per la Scala Regia del Bernini si sale al primo piano del corpo medioevale del Palazzo Pontificio. Sopra l'arco lo stemma 'inquartato', Chigi-Rovere, del committente Papa Alessandro VII.

Gegenüber: Die von Bernini erbaute Scala Regia führt in das erste Stockwerk des mittelalterlichen Gebäudeteils des Papstpalastes. Oberhalb des Bogens sieht man das quartierte Chigi-Rovere Wappen des Auftraggebers Alexander VII.

145

The quartered arms of Alexander VII.
Lo stemma 'inquartato' di Alessandro VII.
Das quartierte Wappen von Alexander VII.

and appear incomplete compared to those in the centre arches. If anybody is to be held responsible for this, I suppose it has to be Pope Julius II who, although he died more than one and a half centuries before the coats of arms of Alexander VII were placed there, granted armorial bearings to the famous banker Agostino Chigi, as can be seen in the documents which are still available for the student of heraldry to examine:

'' *Ut arma et insignia arbore quercus cum glandibus aureis . . . perpetuo uti possetis . . . donavimus et concessimus''*.

From the sixteenth century onwards, the Rovere family and the Chigi family had become related, That is the reason why in some coats of arms the mountains of the Chigi family appear by themselves, in others with the uprooted oaktree of the Della Rovere family.

However, the correct and complete blazon of the armorial bearings of Pope Alexander VII is: ''*inquartato: nel primo e nel quarto di Della Rovere d'azzurro alla pianta di Rovere sradicata d'oro, i rami passati in doppio decusse; secondo e terzo di Chigi di rosso al monte di sei pezzi all'italiana accostato in capo da una stella di otto punte il tutto d'oro''*; ''quarterly, first and fourth the arms of the Della Rovere family, *azure*, an oaktree uprooted gold; second and third the arms of Chigi, *gules*, a star of eight points gold above a sextuple mount (*all'italiana* = in Italian fashion) gold''.

From the arms on the colonnade we learn that the work was carried out under Alexander VII, who blessed the foundation stone on 28 August 1657, in the third year of his pontificate.

We have grown accustomed to the perfect proportions of the monumental Piazza S.Pietro,

146

and we give little thought to Bernini's first concept of it for which he had made provision in all his other designs. Bernini had planned St. Peter's Square to be rectangular and not oval. Also, we are not always aware of the audacity of that great architect who dared challenge the views and opinions of the 'conservative' and 'traditionalist' establishment who looked upon Bernini's project as an unashamedly scandalous luxury; they claimed that it was a threat and danger to public health because the plan inevitably invisaged the demolition of some buildings but especially because of the enormous foundations that would be needed. Lastly they protested because the plan contained a provision for a large amphitheatre which, in their opinion, would dwarf the majesty of the Basilica itself.

Once again common sense prevailed, and this massive lobby of protesters created the opposite effect to what they wanted. After all, thousands of Romans would find work on these building sites while Bernini spent most of his time solving technical problems.

Looking at that magnificent panorama of the colonnade, the first question that comes to mind is : " what are all those statues doing on those crowning cornices, where they appear to be dancing and floating in a breeze "? They are a typical answer to the requirements of the Baroque Age; according to the taste of the times, the colonnade would have been considered bare and dull without them. Having drawn attention to the statues, the way they seem to move and dance to a certain rhythm, and how their garments seem to sway in a breeze, it is only fair to say that such innovations angered those who preferred the strict and silent simplicity of the Middle Ages.

Emile Mâle was quite correct when he said of these figures: ". . . such an expression did not

The Baroque Throne of St. Peter in gilt bronze, constructed by Bernini between 1656–1666, during the papacy of Alexander VII.

La barocca Cattedra di San Pietro in bronzo dorato, costruita dal Bernini negli anni 1656–1666 nel Pontificato di Alessandro VII.

Den vergoldeten baroque Bronzethron des Apostels Petrus schuf Bernini zwischen 1656–1666 während des Pontifikats von Alexander VII.

147

Above and opposite: The colonnade which surrounds St. Peter's Square was completed during the pontificate of Alexander VII, who had blessed the foundation stone on 28 August 1657.

In alto e lato opposto: il colonnato che abbraccia la piazza S. Pietro venne compiuto sotto il pontificato di Alessandro VII, il quale ne aveva benedetto la prima pietra il 28 agosto 1657.

Oben und gegenüber: die Kolonnade, die den St. Peters Platz einschliesst, wurde im Pontifikat von Alexander VII vollendet. Er hatte den Grundstein am 28. August 1657 gesegnet.

displease anybody then, and it should not prevent us today from admiring those masters, most of whom interpreted the spirit of Christianity of that time and made statements which the Middle Ages had not made".

Bernini was the greatest of these masters, and it would be presumptuous to say that the colonnade with those figures has no statement to make.

Let us quicken our step because we have only just started our heraldic exploration. Once we have passed through the Portone di Bronzo, we follow the long corridor which leads to the Scala Regia. The arch leading up the majestic staircase is adorned with the full armorial bearings of the Chigi – Della Rovere family; the pontifical coat of arms is held by two supporters, angels blowing trumpets as if to hail the glory of the Pope who commissioned the artist.

On our right we see famous monument of the Emperor Constantine on his horse, seeing in the sky the cross and the words "In hoc signo vinces". Bernini carved the entire monument with its many figures out of a single block of marble, and it overpowers the visitor with its elegance and unparalleled craftsmanship. In its design and superb execution it balances the sculpture of Charlemagne by Cornacchini perfectly. That monument was moved during the next century and placed at the far end of the porch leading to the Basilica.

We may well question the reason why two great historical figures, Constantine and Charlemagne, both better known for their secular rather than their spiritual or ecclesiastical fame, were given such prominent places in the greatest of all the Basilicas in the world. The reason is the same that persuaded

Urban VIII to erect a monument to the Countess Matilda in St. Peter's Basilica. The Holy See wanted to show its appreciation of those to whom it felt endebted with regard to the Church States. As far as Constantine and Charlemagne are concerned, it is moving to behold that the great founders of the Occidental and Oriental Empires watch over the tomb of that humble Fisherman of Galilee, the Apostle Peter.

The beauty of the Scala Regia forces the vistitor into silent admiration. Its harmony and magnificent perspective are due to the skillful positioning of the columns and pillars. It is a matter of opinion whether we have reached the era of architectural perspective with the Scala Regia. The Baroque Age has often been blamed for merely seeking grandeur, and finding it in pomp and outward appearance. But this certainly does not apply to the Scala Regia. Bernini himself considered it his most important architectural achievement. He used to say that the talent of a great artist should not be judged by works which he could create without obstacles and restrictions and which, in turn, would allow him total freedom to express his imagination. An artist should be judged by works he had undertaken where his freedom of space and movement had been restricted, and where he had to work within an inadequate and often extremely difficult framework.

Bernini encountered enormous practical and technical difficulties, but he succeeded in transforming the dark, narrow and asymmetric corridor leading to the Sala Regia and the Sistine Chapel into the most beautiful and harmonious staircase, full of light.

In the same pontificate, Bernini began another, probably even more famous, master-

149

The 140 statues of Apostles, Popes and Bishops which Bernini placed on the colonnades of St. Peter's Square.

Le 140 statue di Apostoli, Papi e Vescovi, che il Bernini pose sulle colonne della Piazza di San Pietro.

Die 140 Figuren der Apostel, Päpste und Bischöfe, mit denen Bernini die Kolonnaden des St. Petersplatz gekrönt hat.

piece in St. Peter's Basilica: the *Cattedra trionfante* But before approaching the gilt bronze 'triumphant throne of St.Peter', let us halt for a moment at the threshold of the Basilica and try to imagine what the scene must have looked like when a gigantic machine-like construction occupied the space now taken up by the *Baldacchino* over the *Confessione*. It was an enormous task to decorate the apse and to solve so many technical problems.

Alexander VII had rejected the idea of building a tomb for a pope in this most prominent position of the Basilica. He decided to place here the most important symbol of the *Magisterium* of the Apostle Peter: the *Cattedra*, which for centuries had been venerated with celebrations taking place on a special feast day. The gilt bronze chair is supported by statues of two doctors of the Latin Church, St. Ambrose and St. Augustine, and two doctors of the Greek Church, St. Athanasius and St. Chrysostom.

Above the throne is a radiant sunburst in gilded stucco which, with angels and clouds, encircles a stained glass window portraying the dove, the symbol of the Holy Spirit.

This gigantic work was solemnly inaugurated one year before the death of Alexander VII, on 18 January 1666, the feast day of the *Cattedra* of St. Peter in Rome.

The base of the *Cattedra* is adorned with four coats of arms of the Chigi family: each coat of arms is 1.75 metres high and the four figures of the doctors of the Church reach a height of 5 metres. For the casting of this enormous shrine, Bernini used 191,283 pounds of bronze; – 14,891 pounds more than he had used for the *Baldacchino* over the *Confessione*. And yet the

150

weight appears to defy gravity and lift itself up into the air.

When it was completed, rather contradictory judgements were passed on this magnificent monument. According to Burckhard, it was "the most ordinary work the artist had done; just a decorative element thought up at the spur of the moment and some improvisation". Muñoz calls it "the most beautiful decoration of any apse in a Christian Temple and a masterpiece to be proud of". Mâle underlines and interprets the religious meaning of Bernini's *Cattedra*, although its meaning may well escape many visitors who admire it: "The *Cattedra* is glorified as the symbol of Catholic truth against the Protestant Reformation. The Fathers of the Church bow before the *Magisterium* of the *Cattedra* of Rome". The dove, representing the Holy Spirit, enlightens the entire scene, and Mâle concludes that "without the Reformation, we would probably not have had the monument of the *Cattedra* of St. Peter because it would have been unnecessary to assert what was not disputed".

At the far end of the Basilica, on the left side of the aisle, in the passage behind the pier with the relic of St.Veronica, we find the tomb of the Pope to whom we owe a great debt for these masterpieces, Alexander VII. This tomb was also built by Bernini, who once again used his architectural genius when he utilised an existing arch which would have posed an unsurmountable obstacle to a lesser artist. He placed the actual tomb above the arch. Death, represented on the left, seems with one hand to lift the pall, which is sculpted out of Sicilian stone, and in the other hand he holds an hour glass which he shows to the Pope, telling him that the hour of his death has come.

The figure on the right represents *la Verità*, Truth. If one knocks very lightly with one

The tomb of Alexander VII is one of Bernini's masterpieces in the Vatican Basilica. From the pall made of Sicilian jasper, the figure of Death holds in the right hand an hour glass which warns the Pope that his last hour has come.

La tomba di Alessandro VII, uno dei capolavori del Bernini, nella Basilica Vaticana. Dalla coltre di diaspro siciliano la Morte protende la destra che impugna una clessidra, per avvertire il Pontefice che sta per scoccare la sua ultima ora.

Das Grabmal des Papstes Alexander VII ist eines der Meisterwerke von Bernini in der vatikanischen Basilika. Vom Bahrtuch streckt der Tod die rechte Hand aus, in der er ein Stundenglass hält, das den Papst warnt, dass seine letzte Stunde gekommen ist.

151

finger against the figure of Truth, one hears a metallic sound. It was neither Bernini's intention nor his wish that the figure should be cast in metal, but a higher power, presumably Alexander VII himself, imposed his will on the artist.

Three pontificates and seven years later, Innocent XI observed: "normally truth pleases very little, but here *la Verità*, Truth seems to please a little too much!" – In 1776, the year of his accession to the papacy, he asked Bernini to cover the statue with a lamination which would give the impression that it was sculpted in stone.

Bernini, this faithful and loyal servant to the Pope, who was to follow him in death soon afterwards, obeyed immediately.

Two views of Bernini's colonnade. Since the beginning of the sixteenth century the families of Chigi and Della Rovere had become related. This is the reason why the heraldic mountains of the former are sometimes represented on their own and sometimes with the oak tree of the Della Rovere.

Due vedute del colonnato berniniano. Dagli inizi del secolo XVI le famiglie dei Chigi e dei Della Rovere erano imparentate. Ecco perchè i 'monti' dei primi vengono raffigurati talvolta da soli, talvolta con la quercia dei Della Rovere.

Zwei Blicke auf die Kolonnade von Bernini. Seit dem sechszehnten Jahrhundert waren die Familien Chigi und Della Rovere miteinander verwandt. Das ist der Grund, warum manchmal die heraldischen Berge der Chigi allein erscheinen und auf anderen Wappen zusammen mit dem Eichenbaum der Della Rovere.

XI

CLEMENT IX (1667)
TO
INNOCENT XII (1700)

CLEMENT IX (1667–1669)   CLEMENT X (1670–1676)
INNOCENT XI (1676–1689)   ALEXANDER VIII (1689–1691)
INNOCENT XII (1691–1700)

The death of Alexander VII must be considered the end of an era. From now on, the armorial bearings of the Supreme Pontiffs no longer adorn the building in such profusion because the Vatican, that small City-State where St. Peter's successor resides, had only very few new buildings added to it.

For this reason we must rely more than before on pontifical arms as they were carved on popes' tombs or perhaps appeared on monuments they had erected or restored, or inside the Apostolic Palace on frescos, on tapestries, ceilings or inlaid in marble floors. We shall find 'mobili' of popes on doors, along cornices and friezess, on railings along staircases and on all manner of objets d'art.

It is sad to have to admit that many of these later coats of arms, particularly those from the eighteenth century onwards, with very few exceptions show a distinct artistic deterioration. Heraldically speaking, the coats of arms become overloaded, complicated, and sometimes the blazoning is a nightmare for the heraldic scholar.

Nothing could be farther removed from the simplicity we find in the armorial bearings of

Clement IX (1667–1669)
Clemente IX (1667–1669)
Klemens IX (1667–1669)
GIULIO ROSPIGLIOSI.

153

The coat of arms of Clement IX is on the base of the first two statues of angels on the Sant'Angelo Bridge.

Lo stemma di Clemente IX si trova sulla base delle due prime statue di Angeli a ponte Sant'Angelo.

Das Wappen von Klemens IX kann man auf den Sockeln der ersten beiden Statuen der Engel auf der Sant'Angelo Brücke sehen.

Eugene IV, Pius II and III, the Medici Popes, from the elegance of the coats of arms of Julius III or Marcellus II, when we look at the coats of arms of, for example, Benedict XIII (1724–1730), Clement XIII (1758–1769), Clement XIV (1769–1774), Pius VI (1775–1799), Pius VII (1800–1823) and others.

In brief, from now on we can speak of a quantitative and qualitative decline in pontifical armorial representations. Of course, there are always exceptions to the rule, and, indeed, continuing with the immediate successors of Alexander VII, we find armorial bearings which are heraldically and artistically very pleasing. The are some very beautiful and simple coats of arms of later Popes; Benedict XIV (1740–1758) and Paul VI (1963–1978) whose armorial bearings are in true medieval tradition, the latter having his 'mobili' displayed in a most elegant design on the marble surround of a door.

I draw special attention to colour plate I: « Full Circle », which shows the evolution of pontifical heraldry over five hundred years far more clearly than words can.

But let us return to the successor of Alexander VII. We only have to look at the base of the two angelic statues on the Ponte S. Angelo; there we see the elegant and simple lozenges of Clement IX, Giulio Rospigliosi (1667–1669). There are sadly only very few example of that Pope's coat of arms in Rome. The name of Clement IX is mainly associated with the Jansenite controversy and the 'Clementine Peace'. It was his destiny to spend his short pontificate trying to resolve tensions he had inherited from his predecessors, and he found no time to commission magnificent buildings. Nevertheless, he patronised several artists, among them Bernini, whom he commissioned to decorate the Ponte S.Angelo

154

The Bridge of Sant'Angelo and the two statues of the angels. Clement IX reigned only for one and a half year. He died on 9 December 1669 shortly after hearing the news of the conquest of the island of Candia by the Turks.

Ponte Sant'Angelo e le due statue degli Angeli. Clemente IX regnò un anno e mezzo. Morì il 9 dicembre 1669 poco dopo aver appreso la notizia della conquista dell'isola di Candia da parte dei turchi.

Die Sant'Angelo Brücke und die beiden Statuen der Engel. Klemens regierte nur für anderthalb Jahre und starb am 9. Dezember 1669, kurz nachdem er die Nachricht erhalten hatte, dass die Insel Candia den Türken zum Opfer gefallen war.

with carvings and statues. It is for this reason that we can admire his coat of arms at the beginning of the bridge and study his blazon: "*inquartato d'oro e d'azzurro a quattro losanghe dell'uno nell'altro*"; "quarterly gold and *azure*, four lozenges counter-changed".

Although everybody admires the statues, few notice the coat of arms with its classical blazon and elegant lines, let alone the Pontiff's name which Bernini had carved at the base as well. Bernini had designed all the statues for the Ponte S. Angelo but he personally sculpted only two of them. These are known as 'The Angel of the Cross' and 'The Angel of the Crown of Thorns'. The original statues by Bernini can now be seen in the choir of S.Andrea delle Fratte.

The arms of Clement X. The defence of Europe against the Turks and the famine which was raging in the Papal States prevented him from undertaking great building works.

Lo stemma di Clemente X. La difesa dell'Europa contro i turchi e la carestia che infierì negli Stati della Chiesa, non gli permisero di intraprendere grandi opere edilizie.

Das Wappen von Klemens X. Die Verteidigung Europas gegen die Türken und die Hungersnot im Kirchenstaat verhinderten ihn grosse Bauarbeiten zu unternehmen.

It appears that Clement IX, as Sixtus V (1585–1590) had done before him, used the concept of decorating this famous ancient monument to add Christian symbols for the veneration by pilgrims who would cross the bridge on their way to St. Peter's Basilica and the tomb of the Prince of the Apostles. He asked Bernini to incorporate in his sculptures a 'Way of the Cross'.

The name of Clement IX was carved only once, in a Latin inscription on the base of the first angel on the bridge. Sadly, like the coat of arms which Bernini carved there, it was completely walled in by his successor in 1672.

From the Ponte S.Angelo we go back to the Vatican and pause for a moment in St. Peter's Square in front of the fountain on the left as we face the Basilica. The fountain looks absolutely identical and contemporary to the one on the right which was built by Paul V (1605–1621) and which bears that Pontiff's coat of arms. Even to the observant student, both fountains look alike. One needs the eyes of an eagle and extraordinary determination to find any heraldic representation on this one. But there is: right at the bottom of the basin of the fountain is the coat of arms of Clement X, Emilio Altieri (1670–1676) : *"d'azzurro a sei stelle d'argento, 3:2:1:, alla bordura del primo indentata del secondo"*; *"azure* six stars silver, arranged 3:2:1:, and a border indented silver and *azure"*.

Although the fountains could be twins, they are not only separated by almost the width of St. Peter's Square but by the span of more than half a century and seven pontificates.

Another example of the armorial bearings of Clement X, but far more visible, is in the porch of the Basilica; on the floor that was

156

extensively restored during the preparations for the Second Vatican Council, where it can be found near the coats of arms of Leo XIII (1878–1903) and of John XXIII (1958–1963). In their own way, the three heraldic representations testify to the continuity of the pontifical ministry.

To see an even better example of the coat of arms of Clement X, we must walk right down the aisle, just before we reach the *Cattedra* of St.Peter, on the right of the nave, where we find the tomb of the Pope. However, I always take my visitors back once more to the Chapel of the Most Holy Sacrament. Most pilgrims and visitors are attracted by Bernini's splendid tabernacle, which was inspired by the famous little temple by Bramante in S.Pietro in Montorio, and the sculpted angel kneeling on the right. Few seem to pay attention to the papal coat of arms which adorns the altar or to the date which is carved there, giving the years when the chapel was decorated: 1674–1676, the last two years of the pontificate of Clement X.

Clement X descended from the noble family Altieri.
Clemente X discende dalla nobile famiglia degli Altieri.
Klemens X stammte von der Adelsfamilie Altieri ab.

Clement X (1670–1676)
Clemente X (1670–1676)
Klemens X (1670–1676)
EMILIO ALTIERI

157

The tomb of Clement X was designed by Mattia de' Rossi. The statue of the Pope by Ercole Ferrata is flanked by the figures of Kindness and Mercy.

Il Monumento sepolcrale di Clemente X disegnato da Mattia de' Rossi. La statua del pontefice, di Ercole Ferrata, è fiancheggiata da quelle della Benignità e della Clemenza.

Das Grabmal von Klemens X wurde von Mattia de' Rossi entworfen. Neben der Statue des Papstes von Ercole Ferrata stehen die Figuren der Güte und der Barmherzigkeit.

There is an amusing anecdote about the armorial bearings of Clement X. During the four months of the conclave (1669–1670) from which Cardinal Altieri finally emerged as the elected Pope, the cardinals had many spare hours during which little could be done. Cardinal Decio Azzolini even found time to compose a little poem about Cardinal Altieri's coat of arms and he made him listen to it:

≪Altier, le stelle tue son fisse o erranti?
S'erranti son, non ti diranno il vero:
E se son fisse, no andranno avanti≫,

which roughly translated means :

≪Altieri, are your stars fixed stars or do they wander in the sky ?
If they are wandering stars, they will not tell the truth,
But if they are fixed they will not go forward≫.

Cardinal Altieri, without losing his composure replied quickly:

≪Decio, le stelle mie non sono erranti,
Ma fisse son, e col motto del cielo
Per favore divino andranno avanti≫.

≪Decio, mine are not travelling stars but fixed,
And because the very sky above us moves,
By the Grace of God, they still go forward≫.

Altieri's stars indeed moved forward, but when he learned that he had been elected Pope, the venerable old gentleman, now eighty years old, burst into tears, and it took the cardinals a whole hour to persuade him to accept their choice. His pontificate lasted six years.

The successor to Clement X was Innocent XI, Benedetto Odescalchi (1676–1689), whose

158

mortal remains rest in a crystal casket near the statue of Pius XII who beatified him. His only known coat of arms can be seen on his tomb in the left aisle.

The defence of Europe against the invading Turks and the dreadful famine which raged throughout the Papal States, made it impossible for him to devote any financial resources to the building of great monuments or palaces.

The armorial bearings of Innocent XI are depicted on the bas-relief and they appear quite different from the armorial representations we have seen so far. The French sculptor Etienne Monnot represented the liberation of Vienna, the most important event during the Pope's pontificate, the battle in which the Polish King John Sobieski distinguished himself.

Above the relief is a coat of arms which appears very complicated: *"d'argento a sei incensieri di rosso, 3:2:1:, posti fra tre burelle del secondo; al capo d'argento, caricato di un leone passante di rosso, il capo abbassato, sotto un altro capo dell' Impero: d'oro all'aquila spiegata di nero, imbeccata, rostrata e coronata d'oro"*;. Galbreath rendered the following blazon in English: «Silver, three bars *gules* accompanied by a lion passant in chief and six (3,2,1) cups all *gules*, with a chief of the Empire». I must explain that the *tre burelle* are heraldic horizontal ornamental bars, and not even the learned Galbreath recognised the 'cups' as incense burners. Heraldry always leaves freedom of interpretation.

Innocent XI was succeeded by Cardinal Pietro Ottoboni of Venice, who took the name Alexander VIII (1689–1691). Once again, the pontificate was too short for the Pope to commission any monuments or large build-

Innocent XI (1676–1689)
Innocenzo XI (1676–1689)
Innozenz XI (1676–1689)
BENEDETTO ODESCALCHI

159

Above: the arms of Pius IV; Porta del Popolo. Opposite: the "eagle checky" of Innocent XIII.

In alto: lo stemma di Pio IV; Porta del Popolo. Lato opposto: "l'aquila scaccata" di Innocento XIII.

Oben: das Wappen von Pius IV; Porta del Popolo. Gegenüber: der "karierte Adler" von Innozenz XIII.

Alexander VIII (1689–1691)
Alessandro VIII (1689–1691)
Alexander VIII (1689–1691)
PIETRO OTTOBONI.

ings. To see his coat of arms, we must go to the first floor of the Apostolic Palace into the Cappella Paolina. To reach the chapel, we either go up the sumptuous Scala Regia or walk up the much more modest Scala dei Morti, the Staircase of the Dead. Before the parish church of S.Anna dei Palafrenieri was built, dead cardinals and prelates were taken down the Staircase of the Dead to the Basilica of St. Peter for the Requiem Masses.

Both the Sistine Chapel and the Pauline Chapel can be reached from the Sala Regia. Though less famous than the Sistine Chapel, the Pauline Chapel also has frescos by Michelangelo. Alexander VIII had the chapel restored, and he is remembered with his coat of arms on the ceiling. One again, we see the Eagle of the Empire, this time double-headed, and the blazon reads: *"troncato; nel primo dell'Impero: d'oro alla aquila spiegata bicipite di nero, coronata del campo sulle due teste; nel secondo, trinciato d'azzurro e di verde pieni, alla banda d'argento attraversante"*; "party bendwise *azure* and *vert*, a bend gold and a chief gold with a double-headed eagle *sable"*.

If we want to see the double-headed eagle again, a very unusual charge in pontifical heraldry, we must go down to St. Peter's Basilica again, right down to the Choir nave, where on the left side, opposite the monument of Clement X, the nephew of Alexander VIII had a sumptuous tomb erected for his uncle. The bronze statue was sculpted by Giuseppe Bartosi, who also sculpted the bas-relief. The statues, depicting Religion and Prudence, are the work of Angelo Rossi.

We end this heraldic excursion in front of the tomb of Innocent XII, Antonio Pignatelli (1691–1700), the Pope whose pontificate lasted

The arms of Alexander VIII.
Lo stemma di Alessandro VIII.
Das Wappen von Alexander VIII.

into the eighteenth century. The coat of arms of Innocent XII can be seen in the Cappella del Battistero, immediately on the left as one enters the Basilica. His blazon reads: *"d'oro a tre pignatte di nero 2:1:, le due al capo affrontate"*; again, Galbreath gives a very short and liberal interpretation of the Pope's arms: "Gold, three jugs *sable"*; (*pignatta*, f., is a cooking-pot, secondly, the arrangement 2:1: gives the positioning of the pots, and thirdly, *affrontate* means that the two cooking-pots face eachother).

The origin of the Pope's family arms is shrouded in legends: we are told that the three pots recall the pots, filled with gold and jewels, which one of his ancestors found in Constantinople during his stay there at the time of the fourth Crusade; another legend says that the three pots recall the occasion when a member of the Pignatelli family used three incendiary vessels with which he put an enemy fleet to flight. Both legends are fascinating, and heraldry interprets them with artistic licence.

This is a very apt way of closing the seventeenth century and, incidentally, this particular heraldic excursion.

Innocence XII, ANTONIO PIGNATELLI, and his arms.
Innocenzo XII, ANTONIO PIGNATELLI, e suo stemma.
Innozenz XII, ANTONIO PIGNATELLI, und sein Wappen.

163

XII

CLEMENT XI (1700)
TO
CLEMENT XII (1740)

CLEMENT XI (1700–1721) INNOCENT XIII (1721–1724)
BENEDICT XIII (1724–1730) CLEMENT XII (1730–1740)

Clement XI, Giovanni Francesco Albani (1700–1721), the pope whose pontificate starts with the eighteenth century is the author of the famous bull *Unigenitus Dei Filius*, condemning 101 Jansenist propositions. He stood firm against powerful pressure groups who tried to reverse the Pope's decision by appealing to a general council; Clement XI, however, excommunicated the appellants and finally the French government forced the *parlement* to register the bull. He is also the Pope who wrote that beautiful prayer: "My God, I believe in you, increase my faith . . . .". Pope Albani was elected at a most turbulent time in history, and he accepted the great responsibility of ruling the Church only after the four theologians whom he consulted told him that after having been unanimously elected, he could not refuse the tiara with a clear conscience.

During the twenty-one years of his pontificate he did not enrich the Vatican with many buildings or works of art; therefore one can only find a few examples of his coat of arms. I shall, however, show it to you where you would least expect it: in the chapel of the Governor of the Vatican City State. It is true, the Palazzo del Governatorato is one of the many buildings erected in in the pontificate of Pope Pius XI (1922–1939), but how often –

Clement XI, GIOVANNI FRANCESCO ALBANI, and (opposite) his coat of arms on the obelisk above the fountain in the Piazza del Pantheon.

Clement XI, GIOVANNI FRANCESCO ALBANI, e (lato opposto) suo stemma sul basamento dell'obelisco sulla fontana nella piazza del Pantheon.

Klemens XI, GIOVANNI FRANCESCO ALBANI, und (gegenüber) sein Wappen das den Sockel des Oelisks über einem Brunnen im Piazza del Pantheon verziert.

165

The arms of Clement XI: doorlock and keyhole on the outer door of the Church of Sant'Anna dei Palafrenieri.

Lo stemma di Clemente XI: serratura della porta e buco della serratura sulla porta esterna della chiesa di Sant'Anna dei Palafrenieri.

Das Wappen von Klemens XI: Schloss und Schlüsselloch an der Aussentür der Kirche von Sant'Anna dei Palafrenieri.

especially in Rome – do we find remnants of antiquity incorporated in new buildings! The balustrade of the altar in the Governor's Chapel, for example, comes from a chapel which was demolished centuries ago.

And here is the coat of arms of the Albani family in multicoloured marble: "*d'azzurro, alla fascia d'oro accompagnata in capo da una stella di otto punte e in punta da un monte uscente di tre pezzi all'italiana, il tutto d'oro*"; "*azure,* a fess between a star of eight points in chief, and a triple mount Italian fashion in base, all gold". All the other coats of arms with the eagle in chief and the three roundels remind us of Pius XI.

Let us walk back to the Cortile del Belvedere, almost a heraldic museum on its exterior, and go towards the wing where the fire-brigade is quartered. The coat of arms above the three arches is that of Clement XI who strengthened this part of Bramante's beautiful building.

Just a few steps from here, on the door of the parish church of S.Anna dei Palafrenieri, I can show you a heraldic curiosity: the stylized coat of arms of Pope Albani on the outside plate of the lock. The keyhole is cut into the top mount and the star above.

Clement was the first Pope who had the idea of housing the pontifical museums in one group of buildings, an Idea only realised by his successors.

His coat of arms also adorns the so-called large niche in the Cortile della Pigna, and the ceiling above the statue of Charlmagne which he had commissioned from Agostino Cornacchini, the same artist who some years later, in 1775, carved the monumental Holy Water stoups.

166

We would look in vain for the armorial bearings of Clement XI inside the Basilica. Although the monument to Queen Christina of Sweden and the mosaics in the domes of the Chapels of the Most Holy Sacrament and of the Presentation of the Virgin were completed in his pontificate, his pontifical arms cannot be seen anywhere, Stranger still, even in the Choir of the Chapel of the Canons of the Vatican, where the Pope's mortal remains rest, a simple slab of marble indicates his resting place; carved onto it are the words which he himself dictated: «CLEMENS XI P.M. – HUIUS BASILICAE – OLIM VICARIUS – POSTEA CANONICUS – SIBI VIVENS PONI IUSSIT – ORATE PRO EO»; «CLEMENT XI SUPREME PONTIFF – FIRST VICAR – LATER A CANON OF THIS BASILICA – ORDERED THIS STONE TO BE LAID DOWN WHILE HE WAS STILL ALIVE – PRAY FOR HIM».

Clement XI supported James Stuart, pretender to the throne of England against the Elector of Hannover. The painting shows him being received in Rome by a cardinal on his arrival in exile in 1715. He is buried in the tomb erected by Canova in St. Peter's.

Clemente XI sostenne Giacomo Stuart, pretendente al trono d'Inghilterra contro l'Elettore di Hannover. Il dipinto lo raffigura mentre è ricevuto da un cardinale a Roma dove si stabilì dal 1715. Il suoi resti riposano in San Pietro nel sepolcro eretto dal Canova.

Klemens XI unterstützte Jakob Stuart, Prätendent des englischen Thrones gegen den Kurfürsten von Hannover. Das Gemälde zeigt seinen Empfang von einem Kardinal, als er in Rom eintrifft, um sich dort niederzulassen in 1715. Er ist in Canovas Grabmahl in St. Peter begraben.

167

Innocent XIII (1721–1724)
Innocenzo XIII (1721–1724)
Innozenz XIII (1721–1724)
MICHELANGELO DEI CONTI

Clement's successor, Innocent XIII, Michelangelo dei Conti (1721–1724), was descended from the same family who had given already three Popes to the Church: Innocent III (1198–1216), Gregorius IX (1227–1241) and Alexander IV (1254–1261). The pontificate of Innocent XIII only lasted two and a half years, and most of that time he was ill. His coat of arms with the eagle *scaccata* is carved on the small columns along the first landing of the Scalinata di Trinità dei Monti, the famous Spanish Steps.

In the Vatican, or better, on St. Peter's Square, Pope Conti thought of placing a surround at the base of the obelisk and adorning it with '*duplice ornato*', a double heraldic ornamentation: four metal eagles, the main heraldic charge in his own armorial bearings, were placed on the four *Leoni Sistini*, the lion from the coat of arms of Sixtus V, who had commissioned Fontana to move the obelisk from the circus of Nero to St. Peter's Square. He also replaced the old railings, which can be seen on old prints, with a circle of sixteen granite boulders, which came from columns of the old basilica near the churchyard of St. Marta. The treasurer of the Fabric of St. Peter's Basilica, Mons.Ludovico Sergardi, praised this work highly in his book "*Discorso sopra il nuovo ornato della guglia di S.Pietro*" which was published in 1723.

It is worth taking a closer look at the coats of arms of Innocent XIII at the base of the obelisk; they were crafted with the same delicate touch as those on the columns of the Spanish Steps. Sadly, it is impossible to discern the colouring of the blazon from them : "*di rosso all'aquila dal volo abbassato scaccata di nero e d'oro, coronata, imbeccata e rostrata d'oro*"; "*gules* an eagle checky gold and *sable*, crowned, beaked and armed gold". Another coat of arms can be seen on the Pope's tomb in the Grottoes.

168

The coat of arms of the next Pontiff, the Dominican Benedict XIII, Pietro Francesco Orsini (1724–1730), from an ancient noble Roman family, is both complicated and introduces an element of ugliness into pontifical heraldry. Thankfully, the Pope's arms can only be seen once in the Vatican: on a wall in the Cortile del Belvedere. It can neither be found in St. Peter's Square, on which he spent 80,000 scudos to have it paved for the first time, nor in St. Peter's Basilica, where he consecrated twenty-one new altars and which he enriched with a new bell.

Benedict XIII was deeply attached to his Religious Order, the Dominicans, and he decided to add the armorial bearings of his Order to the extremely complicated family arms. Such an idea had never occurred to his predecessors Paul IV, who belonged the Teatine Order, the Dominican St. Pius V, nor to the Franciscan Sixtus V. However, encouraged by the example of Benedict XIII, the conventual monk Clement XIV, the Benedictine Pius VII and the Camaldolesian Benedictine Gregory XVI augmented their arms with those of their Order, thereby ruining the simplicity of their papal arms.

As if it had not been enough to combine the complicated Orsini arms with those of the Dominican Order, Benedict XIII also added the arms of Gravina (Puglia), because in 1660 at the time he entered the Order, Pietro Francesco Orsini had succeeded in 1660 to the title of Duke of Gravina, though it passed to his younger brother in 1669 on his making his religious vows and taking the name Vincenzo-Maria.

The coat of arms may be deeply religious but it is a heraldic monstrosity. There are very few examples of his armorial bearings in Rome, and only one – the one I already mentioned – in

The Dominican Benedict XIII, PIETRO FRANCESCO ORSINI, (1724–1730), introduced some controversial augmentations to pontifical heraldry. He added the armorial bearings of his Religious Order to the arms of his family; (Cortile del Belvedere).

Il domenicano Benedetto XIII, PIETRO FRANCESCO ORSINI, (1724–1730), introduce nell'araldica pontificia elementi alquanto discutibili con l'aggiungere lo stemma di un ordine religioso a quello del proprio casato; (cortile del Belvedere).

Der Dominikaner Benedikt XIII, PIETRO FRANCESCO ORSINI, (1724–1730), führte eine diskutabele Neuigkeit in päpstliche Heraldik ein. Er fügte seinem Familienwappen das des Dominikaner Ordens bei; (Cortile del Belvedere)

A stone tablet above a holy-water basin in memory of the many altars Benedict XIII had consecrated in the Vatican Basilica.

Una lapide sopra un'acqua-santiera a ricordo dei numerosi altari consecrati nella Basilica Vaticana da Benedetto XIII.

Eine in Stein gemeisselte Gedenktafel über einem Weihwasserbecken erinnert an die vielen Altare, die Benedikt XIII in der vatikanischen Basilika geweiht hat.

the Vatican, which is not surprising as it is one of the most complicated blazons in the history of the papacy:

"*partito: il primo di Orsini (di rosso a due bande d'argento) al capo di Anguillara: d'argento caricato di un'anguilla di verde ondeggiante in fascia; il capo abbassato sotto un altro capo: d'argento caricato di una rosa di rosso bottonata d'oro; nel secondo d'azzurro alla torre di tre ordini al naturale, aperta e finestrata di nero terrazzata di verde. Al capo, della Religione Domenicana: d'argento, mantellato di nero caricato del cane giacente d'argento, ingollante una torcia accesa posta in sbarra, timbrato di una corona antica attraversata da un decusse formato da un gambo di giglio in banda fiorito e fogliato al naturale e da una palma di martirio in sbarra al naturale; il tutto sormontato da una stella di otto punte d'oro*".

Galbreath gives the following blazon:

"Party, dexter, silver three bends *gules*, a chief silver charged with an eel (azure) (Orsini); sinister, *azure* a tower silver (Gravina); a chief of the Dominican Order, *chapé sable* and silver, in a base a dog spotted silver and *sable* couched holding a lighted torch in his mouth and his paws lying on a book, surmounted by a palm branch and a branch of lilies crossed in saltire all proper and passed through a crown gold, in chief a star of eight rays silver".

At the other end of spectrum of good taste, simplicity and beauty were the armorial bearings of Benedict's successor, Clement XII, Lorenzo Corsini (1730–1740), and no greater contrast could be imagined:

"*d'argento, a tre bande de rosso, attraversate da una fascia d'azzurro*"; "bendy silver and *gules*, a fess azure".

170

Descended from an ancient Florentine family, he became a cardinal in 1706 and entertained the outstanding artists of the day as well as the leading members of the Roman Curia and society in his palace in the Piazza Navona. Once he had become Pope, he was troubled by blindness which eventually became total, but he nevertheless left his name and coat of arms on the famous Fontana di Trevi, on the façade of the Lateran Archbasilica, and in S.Giovanni dei Fiorentini, to name but three of him most famous works.

In 1732 he enlarged the *Biblioteca Apostolica* in the Vatican, adding to it a wing adjacent to the one where the beautiful frescos had been painted in the pontificate of Paul V, whose coat of arms therefore adorns the entrance hall to the Sala di Consultazione. Clement XII opened the first public museum of antiquities in Europe. The collections of beautiful *objets d'art*

Although afflicted by blindness which in time became total, Clement XII, LORENZO CORSINI, (1730–1740), left his coat of arms on many monumental buildings such as the façade of San Giovanni in Laterano and the Fontana di Trevi, one of the masterpieces of the baroque age.

Nonostante fosse afflitto da una cecità, che con il tempo divenne completa, Clemente XII, LORENZO CORSINI, (1730–1740), lasciò il suo stemma in opere monumentali come la facciata di San Giovanni in Laterano e la Fontana di Trevi, uno dei capolavori del barocco.

Obwohl er von Blindheit leidete, die am Ende total war, hat Klemens XII, LORENZO CORSINI, (1730–1740), sein Wappen auf vielen monumentalen Bauwerken hinterlassen, zum Beispiel auf der Fassade von San Giovanni in Laterano und auf dem welt-berühmten Trevi Brunnen.

Clement XII (1730–1740)
Clemente XII (1730–1740)
Klemens XII (1730–1740)
LORENZO CORSINI

with which Sixtus IV and Julius II had enriched the Campidoglio and the Belvedere were hitherto regarded as private possessions. Clement XII, however, made them part of the Vatican Museum for all to admire.

His public-spirited generosity was the reason for the humorous epitaph the Romans gave him: *"Sono stato un ricco abate – Un comodo prelato – Un povero cardinale – Un papa spiantato"*; "I was a rich abbot, quite wealthy as a prelate, a poor cardinal and a penniless pope".

As far as our heraldic excursion is concerned, the only example of the armorial bearings in colour of the penniless pope is in the Vatican Basilica on the ceiling of the Cappella di S.Petronilla.

If by chance any of my visitors join the pilgrims on 31 May and attend the Holy Mass which is celebrated for France, (a service attended by the French Ambassador to the Holy See and concluded with the recitation of the *De Profundis* for the soul of King Louis XI), I suggest that they should look up at the arms on the left arch over the altar of St. Petronilla, hoping that the Saint will intercede with Our Lord for our temporary heraldic distractions. . . .

172

XIII

BENEDICT XIV (1740)
TO
PIUS VI (1799)

BENEDICT XIV (1740–1758) CLEMENT XIII (1758–1769)
CLEMENT XIV (1769–1774) PIUS VI (1775–1799)

Benedict XIV, Prospero Lambertini (1740–1758), a man of letters, a connoisseur of the arts, and a brilliant canon lawyer, enjoyed a popularity which was not only rare but unique for a pontiff: one can say without exaggeration that from the day he became pope, to the day of his death, he had the unstinting respect of all.

In the Biblioteca Apostolica he founded the Museo Sacro and in the left aisle at the entrance to the dome in the Basilica he had the Maria Clementina Sobieska Monument errected for the pious wife of the son of King James II, James Stuart, who as pretender to the British throne styled himself James III. The Stuart Monument is facing that of his wife on the other side of the left aisle.

In the right aisle, behind the pier with the relic of St. Longinus, is the Pope's own monument, and his tomb is decorated with his armorial bearings.

It is a most beautiful coat of arms: unfortunately, heralds are in total disagreement as to its correct blazoning. Mons. Barbier de Montault stated that the correct blazon was "*a pali alternati d'oro e di rosso*"; others disagree and give the blazon: "*d'oro a tre pali di rosso*", and others "*d'oro a quattro pali di rosso*".

On the tomb of Benedict XIV in St. Peter's Basilica one can see an alternative version of his coat of arms with only three gold pales. According to some heraldic scholars there should be four pales.

Sul Monumento sepolcrale di Benedetto XIV in San Pietro si vede il suo stemma a pali alternati che, secondo alcuni araldisti, dovrebbero essere quattro. Qui ne risultano solo tre.

Auf dem Grabmal von Benedikt XIV in St. Peters Basilika sieht man sein Wappen mit lediglich drei golden Pfählen. Gemäss gewisser Heraldiker, soll der Papst vier Pfähle im Wappen geführt haben.

173

The monument to Maria Clementina Sobieska, wife of James Stuart, pretender to the throne of England. The portrait in mosaic is held by the figure of Charity.

Monumento a Maria Clementina Sobieska, moglie di Giacomo Stuart, pretendente al trono d'Inghilterra. Il ritratto, in mosaico, è sorretto dalla Carità.

Das Monument der Maria Clementina Sobieska, Gattin von Jakob Stuart, Prätendent des englischen Thrones. Die Figur der Caritas hält das Mosaikbild.

The interpretations range from an unspecified number of red and gold pales, to a gold field with three red pales and a gold field and four red pales.

Count Pasini-Frassoni states that he speaks with authority when giving the blazon on the tomb. However, he repeats all the same mistakes which appeared on private and 'official' prints of that era with the exception of one which he himself adds to the already existing confusion. He placed the four pales in a blue field instead of a gold one!

Prospero Lambertini was the son of a highly respected Senator of Bologna. The noble, though impoverished, Lambertini family had always claimed descent from the Royal House of Aragon, and they have always borne four pales *gules* on a field of gold in their armorial bearings.

I feel sorry for the authority-claiming Count, but I must say that the correct coat of arms of Benedict XIV can be found at the bottom of the semi-circle, and twice on the north-facing façade of the Cortile del Belvedere. All these are identical with the one on his tomb in the right aisle facing the pier of St. Longinus in the Vatican Basilica.

I find it singularly unfortunate that even the *Annuario Pontificio*, when it still contained a section showing the armorial bearings of all popes, a practice which was discontinued in the pontificate of Paul VI, published the wrong coat of arms of Benedict XIV, showing only three pales. The proper blazon should read: *"d'oro a quattro pali di rosso"*; *"Gold, four pales gules"*. When compiling his Papal Heraldry in 1930, immediately after the signing of the Lateran Treaty which created the Vatican City State, Galbreath was well aware of possible

174

shortcomings. However, he maintained that there existed coins with Pope Lambertini's arms impaled with the arms of Benedict XIII, thus making them the most elaborate coat of arms ever to have been borne by a pope. Galbreath was wrong; when Prospero Lambertini was a cardinal, several portraits of him appeared with coats of arms as adornments. Some of these bear his arms impaled with those of Benedict XIII, to whom he owed his elevation to the cardinalate in 1728. In 1724, when he had already been Promotor of the Faith for some years, Benedict XIII created him titular Archbishop of Theodosia, in 1727 Archbishop of Ancona. Until the Pope's death, he remained his closest adviser. In accordance with the practice of the time, it is most likely that Cardinal Prospero Lambertini was granted the special privilege of impaling his personal arms with those of the reigning pontiff. Benedict XIV's arms were not the most elaborate arms in the history of the papacy: that record belongs to Benedict XIII.

Also in the Cortile del Belvedere we find the coat of arms of Clement XIII, the Venetian Carlo Rezzonico (1758–1769), and we notice the two-headed eagle of Pope Ottoboni, Alexander VIII (1689–1691). Through a branch of the Rezzonico family which had settled in Como, the Rezzonicos were Barons of the Empire.

Clement XIII had the old Bramante buildings strengthened and his armorial bearings were placed there:'' *Inquartato; nel primo di rosso alla croce d'argento; nel secondo e nel terzo d'azzurro alla torre in due ordini al naturale, merlata alla guelfa, aperta e finestrata di nero; nel quarto di rosso a tre sbarre d'argento. Sul tutto uno scudo d'oro timbrato di una corona all'antica e caricato di un'aquila spiegata bicipite di nero coronata del campo sulle due*

Benedict XIV (1740–1758)
Benedetto XIV (1740–1758)
Benedikt XIV (1740–1758)
PROSPERO LAMBERTINI.

175

*teste''; "Quarterly, first, *gules*, a cross silver, second and third, *azure* a tower silver, fourth, *gules* three bends sinister silver; over all a scutcheon gold with an ancient coronet also gold, with a two headed eagle *sable* crowned gold".

The arms of Clement XIII can also be seen on the second floor of the Apostolic Palace, woven in the tapestries in the Sala del Consistoro, which he had restored. Further examples of the Pope's arms are in St. Peter's Basilica on the iron railings which enclose the Choir Chapel and on his tomb at the far end of the right aisle, facing the pier containing the relic of St. Helena. His tomb is a masterpiece by Antonio Canova, who portrays the Pope in an attitude of profound piety between two beautiful lions, crouching on a plinth, one sleeping, one awake, at the feet of the figures of Death and of Religion.

Tomb of Clement XIII.
Tomba di Clemente XIII.
Grabmal von Klemens XIII.

176

On a wall in the Cortile del Belvedere (opposite) one can see the coat of arms of Clement XIII. It was placed there in memory of the work he had carried out strengthening the old building by Bramante. The arms of Clement XIII feature the double-headed eagle of the Holy Roman Empire.

Nel cortile del Belvedere (lato opposto) è murato uno stemma di Clemente XIII a ricordo dei lavori compiuti per consolidare la vecchia costruzione del Bramante. Nello stemma di Clemente XIII compare l'aquila a due teste del Sacro Romano Impero.

Im Cortile del Belvedere (gegenüber) kann man das Wappen von Klemens XIII sehen, das an die Bauarbeiten erinnert, die der Papst angeordnet hatte, die alten Gebäude von Bramante zu verstärken. Im Wappen führt Klemens XIII den zwei-köpfigen Adler des Heiligen Römischen Kaiserreiches.

The arms of Clement XIII (1758–1769), CARLO REZZONICO; Wallhanging in the Sala del Concistoro.

Lo stemma di Clemente XIII (1758–1769), CARLO REZZONICO; arazzo nella Sala del Concistoro.

Das Wappen von Klemens XIII (1758–1769), CARLO REZZONICO: Wandteppich im Sala del Concistoro.

178

The next two popes were once again great builders: Clement XIV, Giovanni Vincenzo Ganganelli (1769–1774), who is mainly remembered for suppressing the Society of Jesus (the Jesuits), and Pius VI, Giovanni Angelo Braschi (1775–1799), the most famous of the victims of the French Revolution, and whose pontificate brings the eighteenth century to a close. Both Popes gave their name to the Pio-Clementine Museum.

Clement XIV had the idea of housing all the antique statues and sculptures in a new building; in spite of the Holy See's terrible financial state, Clement carried on acquiring statues and sculptures in great numbers, and the Capitoline Museum, which had been founded in 1471 by Sixtus IV for classical sculptures, could no longer accommodate the new acquisitions. Between 1771 and 1773, in the garden of Innocent VIII, where the Cortile del Belvedere now gently slopes, the Gallery of Statues was erected. There the coat of arms of Clement XIV greets the visitors to the museums; it can once more been seen above the door leading to the Room of Busts.

I have earlier commented on the poor heraldic quality of the armorial bearings of Clement XIV. He followed the example of Benedict XIII and insisted on augmenting his coat of arms with a chief of his monastic order, the Conventual Franciscans, whom he always regarded as his religious family.

To his personal coat of arms which was simple and heraldically excellent "*azure, a fess gules* between three stars of six points gold in chief, and a triple mount gold in base", the Pope added charges until it resulted in a quite different blazon: "*d'azzurro alla fascia cucita di rosso, accompagnata in capo dell'impresa della Religione Fracescana (due braccia decussate, un*

Monument to Clement XIV (1769–1774), GIOVANNI VINCENZO GANGANELLI, in the Basilica of the Holy Apostles is the first Roman work by Antonio Canova.

Monumento a Clemente XIV (1769–1774), GIOVANNI VINCENZO GANGANELLI, nella Basilica dei Ss. Apostoli, prima opera romana di Antonio Canova.

Das Grabmal von Klemens XIV (1769–1774), GIOVANNI VINCENZO GANGANELLI, in der Basilika der Heiligen Apostel, ist das erste römische Werk von Antonio Canova.

179

The *'Nicchione'*, built by Pirro Ligorio about 1561, is the centre of the south façade of the building housing the Pio-Clementine Museum.

Il *'Nicchione'*, realizzato da Pirro Ligorio intorno al 1561, è il centro dei prospetto sud degli edifici che ospitano il museo Pio-Clementino.

Der von Pirro Ligorio um 1561 erbaute *'Nicchione'* bildet das südliche Zentrum des Gebäudekomplexes, der das Pio-Clementino Museum beherbergt.

braccio posto in bànda al naturale di carnagione e con mano ferita di rosso; un braccio posto in sbarra, vestito di nero; il tutto sormontato da una crocetta di nero), posta su tre stelle di otto punte d'oro; in punta da un monte uscente di tre pezzi all'italiana d'oro".

Above the three gold stars he placed a chief with two arms crossed in saltire, one arm in natural complexion and a hand bearing a red wound (stigmata), the other arm clad in a black sleeve (of a Franciscan) and the hand also with stigmata, all surmounted by a black cross. The three mountains in Italian fashion remain at the base of the arms. Galbreath gives the field of the chief as silver.

Clement XIV was not buried in St. Peter's Basilica but in the Church of the Twelve Apostles which is still entrusted to the Conventual Franciscans. There we can admire the monument built for him by Canova, who, as we have seen, had also built the tomb of his predecessor Clement XIII which was, however, only completed five years later in 1792.

With Canova begins a new chapter in the arts: neo-classicism. In fourteen years Pius VI (1775–1799) managed to add to the Pio-Clementine Museum the Greek Cross Room, the Rotonda, the Room of the Muses and the Room of the Animals. He was very enthusiastic about the projects planned by Clement XIV and firmly set on carrying them out as soon as he had been elected to the papacy in 1775. He did not listen to the criticism and rebukes that he was wasting hundreds of thousands of scudi on buildings and especially "those unnecessary and ugly galleries"; he continued to amass antique masterpieces so that they could be exhibited properly. When one considers that Julius II and his immediate successors had acquired only about twenty sculptures between

Above: on the floor of the Sacristy in St. Peter's Basilica one can see the arms of Pius VI in multi-coloured marble. Left: one of the very rare examples of the former and extremely complicated coat of arms of Pius VI.

In alto: sul pavimento della Sacrestia di S.Pietro appare lo stemma Pio VI in marmi policromi. A sinistra: uno dei rarissimi esemplari del primitivo e complicato stemma di Pio VI.

Oben: auf dem Boden der Sakristei in der St. Peter Basilika kann man das Wappen von Pius VI in vielfarbigen Marmor eingelegt sehen. Links: eines der sehr seltenen Exemplare des ehemaligen und höchst komplizierten Wappens von Pius VI.

181

Pius VI (1775–1799)
Pio VI (1775–1799)
Pius VI (1775–1799)
GIOVANNI ANGELO BRASCHI ·

them, Clement XIV bought about fifty, while Pius VI alone had purchased some six hundred sculptures, it is no surprise that it is called the Pio-Clementine Museum.

The coat of arms of Pope Braschi, Pius VI, decorates several halls and can also be seen on the cornices of the pillars in the niches of the Rotonda.

Its blazon reads: *"di rosso, alla pianta di giglio di tre gambi posti in sbarra, fioriti e fogliati al naturale, terrazzata di verde, accantonata a destra da una testa di Eolo soffiante sulla pianta con soffio d'argento posto in banda; al capo: d'argento, caricato di tre stelle di otto punte d'oro, per inchiesta"*.

Galbreath reads the blazon as follows: *"gules*, a head of Boreas in the dexter chief blowing on a natural lily proper on a terrace *vert*, a chief silver with three stars of eight points gold".

Galbreath adds that Pius VI had set several heraldic precedents: first he replaced the double-headed imperial eagles of his paternal coat of arms with three silver roses *"di rosso a tre rose d'argento"*.

Pope Braschi then exchanged the three roses for a real heraldic novelty: the head of Boreas blowing on a lily.

His first venture into setting a heraldic record was when he abandoned his family arms completely, having borne them during the first few months of his pontificate: "quarterly, first and fourth, gold a two-headed eagle *sable* surmounted by an imperial crown, second and third, *azure* a fess silver, charged with three stars of six points gold and accompanied by two *fleurs-de-lis* silver, one in chief and one in base; over all a scutcheon *gules*, three roses silver

182

with three stars of eight points gold". Examples of the Pope's early armorial bearings are very rare.

One angel, two eagles with two heads each, five *fleurs-de-lis*, six stars of six rays, three stars of eight rays . . . . . surely that is too much even for the grace of God to allow in a single coat of arms. No wonder that he was asked by *Pasquino* to put them back to where they belonged, as if Pius VI had actually stolen them. [*Pasquino*, a legendary entity, purportedly resided in a niche in some monument. It was a most democratic invention, and Romans who had a complaint were able to write it down, and in due course it would find its way to those to whom it was directed]. Pius VI received a rather amusing request in verse; it is not very good poetry but the message comes across clearly: *"Rende all'Impero l'aquila – De' francesi il giglio al re – Al ciel rendi le stelle – Il resto, o Braschi a te"*; "Give the eagle back to the emperor – to the King of the French give back their *fleurs-de-lis* – give the stars back to the heavens – and the rest, o Braschi, you can keep".

History does not tell us if it was because of the admonishment by *Pasquino* that the eagle, the *fleurs-de-lis*, and six of the nine stars disappeared from the arms of Pius VI. However, he kept the angel blowing on a *fleur-de-lis* below the chief of three stars.

It is this coat of arms that we see in the sacristy of St. Peter's Basilica and that adorns all the other works of art he is responsible for.

Like Clement XI and Benedict XIV, Pius VI had been a Canon of the Vatican Basilica, and he knew from personal experience the discomfort and inconvenience caused by the old sacristy, which was quite inadequate for this vast basilica.

The statue of Pius VI in prayer, a work by Canova.
La statua di Pio VI in preghiera, opera del Canova.
Die Statue von Pius VI im Gebet, ein Werk von Canova.

183

The entrance to the Palace Pius VI had built for his former colleagues, the Canons of St. Peter.

L'ingresso del Palazzo costruito da Papa Braschi per i suoi vecchi colleghi, i canonici di S.Pietro.

Der Eingang zum Palast den Pius VI für seine ehemaligen Kollegen, die Domkapitulare von St. Peter, hat bauen lassen.

In the early years of the seventeenth century, in 1607 there had been a plan to build a new sacristy where the entrance to the Chapel of the Most Holy Sacrament is today; later the plan was changed to where we now have the Choir of the Canons. Bernini under Alexander VII, Filippo Juvara under Clement XI, and Alessandro Galilei under Clement XII had all proposed similar projects. Pius VI ordered new plans to be drawn up and the he finally chose the blueprint of the architect Carlo Marchionni. First the Pope acquired certain slum property adjacent to St. Peter's Basilica and had it demolished; he then errected a magnificent though somewhat cold building, and not one but three separate sacristies: one general sacristy, one for the canons, and one for the incumbents with rooms and corridors which linked sacristy with the Basilica.

Those who showed some tolerance described it as "if not beautiful, it is magnificent"; the famous Abbot Cancellieri said: "the only defect of the building is that it was erected next to those gigantic masterpieces of Bramante and Michelangleo".

The coat of arms of Pius VI can be found almost everywhere; it is on Holy Water stoups, on cornices and it stands out particularly in the general sacristy where it has been inlaid in multi-coloured marble. At the top of the staircase which bears his name is a statue of the Pope, sculpted by Agostino Stemma, and his coat of arms is held by two lions which were sculpted by Francesco Franzoni.

In the Basilica the Pope's arms can be seen carved on the ceiling in the central nave and on inlaid altar frontals of side altars. Then his arms are on the metal gates which close the *Confessione*. Finally, they can be seen on those eccentric railings and on the two clocks of St.Peter's Basilica by Valadier.

184

It is rather fascinating to learn that one of the clocks showed the time "*all'italiana*", and the other probably Greenwich Mean Time. This practice was maintained until 31 December 1846, the year of the accession to the papacy of Pius IX. A brief Latin inscription explains that the clocks were placed there in 1789, in the fourteenth year of the pontificate of Pius VI. It is rather ironic that the clock of St. Peter's Basilica started to work as the French Revolution began.

Having completed the sacristies, Pius VI had a five-storey palace built for his colleagues, to which Pius XI had another storey added , the Palazzo della Canonica or Palazzo del Capitolo di San Pietro. On the front of the palace, a majestic coat of arms, supported by two eagles, dwarfs a small Latin inscription.

Heraldry has left nothing behind to remind us of that tragic day in February 1798 when the seventy-one year old Pope was dragged away from Rome, forced to cross the Alps in terrible conditions and literally imprisoned in Valence, where he died on 29 August 1799.

The mortal remains of Pius VI were transferred by order of Pius VII and laid to rest in the Vatican Grottoes. A simple inscription marks his resting place. The statue of that great Pope by Canova, which shows the Pontiff kneeling in prayer, is now also in the lower part of the Grottoes.

The representative of the revolutionary government said "*Le ci-devant Pape est mort* – the former Pope is dead – he will be the last one, and with him the superstition will end".

With the death of Pius VI the papacy did not end, not even the history of pontifical heraldry. His death merely closed the eighteenth century.

The clocks of St. Peter's Basilica started to work as the French Revolution began.

Gli orologi di S. Pietro hanno cominciato a funzionare con la Rivoluzione Francese.

Die Uhren der St. Peter Basilika zeigten die Zeit zum ersten Mal, als die französische Revolution begann.

PIVS·VII·PONT·MAX·AN·XXII·

PIVS VII

XIV

PIUS VII (1800)
TO
PIUS IX (1878)

PIUS VII (1800–1823)   LEO XII (1823–1829)
PIUS VIII (1829–1830)   GREGORY XVI (1831–1846)
PIUS IX (1846–1878)

Following the heraldically misguided examples of the Dominican Pope Benedict XIII and the Franciscan Pope Clement XIV, the first of the pontiffs in the nineteenth century, Pius VII, Luigi Barnabà Gregorio Chiaramonti (1800–1823), added to his family coat of arms the armorial bearings of the Benedictine Order, which he had joined at the age of fourteen and where he had taken the name Gregorio. Unlike the other two pontiffs I mentioned, he did not place the religious arms in chief but impaled his coat of arms, placing the Benedictine arms on the sinister side:

"*partito; nel primo, della religione benedettina (d'azzurro al Calvario con croce di due braccia attraversata dalla parola* PAX *in caratteri stampatelli romani, il tutto d'oro); nel secondo, trinciato d'oro e d'azzurro pieni, alla banda d'argento caricata di tre teste di moro bendate d'argento, poste nel senso della banda e questa attraversante sul trinciato. Al capo, d'azzurro caricato di tre stelle, di sei punte d'oro, male ordinate (Chiaramonti)*".

The coat of arms of Pius VII bears also the arms of the Benedictine Order to which he belonged.

Lo stemma di Pio VII reca l'emblema dei Benedettini, l'Ordine cui apparteneva.

In seinem Wappen führt Pius VII auch die Embleme des Benediktinerordens, dem er angehörte.

Pius VII (1800–1823)
Pio VII (1800–1823)
Pius VII (1800–1823)
BARNABA GREGORIO CHIARAMONTI

"Impaled, on the sinister side the arms of the Benedictine Order (*azure* on the mountain of Calvary [represented as a mount in three parts in Italian fashion] a double traversed cross and across centrally in Roman capital letters the motto PAX, all in gold); on the dexter side party bendwise, gold and *azure*, a bend silver with three Moors' heads *sable*, their eyes bandaged silver; a chief *azure* three stars gold with six rays, arranged 1 : 2 ".

Galbreath differs substantially in his blazon of the Dominican Order which he gives as "Silver, a triplemount *vert* bearing a cross of Calvary *sable* with the word PAX *sable* in fess all over"; he also gives eight-pointed stars in the chief of the Chiaramonti arms".

Until the pontificate of Benedict XV (1914–1922), the arms of Pius VII decorated that magnificent drapery designed by Bernini to camouflage the asymmetric appearance of the sumptuous Sala Ducale. In fact, Galbreath remarked on these armorial bearings which were placed above the beautiful and delicately sculpted drapery held up by four cherubs or putti, by Pius VII to commemorate some renovation which had taken place in that part of the Apostolic Palace during his pontificate. Forturnately, some later restorations removed all traces of this armorial addition which had certainly not contributed to the beauty of Bernini's concept.

To compensate for this, Pope Chiaramonti's coat of arms can be seen at the entrances of Galleria Lapidaria and to the Vatican Museums.

In spite of the turbulent political events which dominated his entire pontificate, he continued with the building work that had been started by his predecessor Pius VI and he

188

PIO·VII·CLARAMONTIO·CAESENATI·PONTIFICI·MAXIM
HERCVLES·CARD·CONSALVI   ROMANVS·AB·EO·CREATV

even built an additional museum for sculptures which bears his name, Museo Chiaramonti. In 1822 he had the Braccio Nuovo constructed, a wing which ran parallel to the one Sixtus V had built to divide the Cortile del Belvedere and house the *Biblioteca Vaticana*.

In 1816 he moved the *Pinacoteca* to the Borgia Apartments and ordered the renovation of the staircase which leads from the Cortile di S.Damaso to the museums; but none of these building works were commemorated with his coat of arms. Only an inscription in Latin tells us that in the twenty-second and penultimate year of his pontificate Pius VII contributed financially to the restoration of this staircase which was in need of repair: *"scales antea climacotas et vetustate squallentes in hanc commodiorem spectabilioremque formam redegit"*.

Lastly, his coat of arms can be seen on his tomb which is rather cold and was sculpted by the famous Protestant artist Thorwaldsen; it is situated halfway along the left aisle near the Cappella Clementina.

The arms of Pius VII
Lo stemma di Pio VII
Das Wappen von Pius VII

189

Above: the coat of arms of Leo XII (1823–1829), ANNIBALE DELLA GENGA; St. Peter's Basilica. Below: the arms of Pius VIII (1829–1830), FRANCESCO SAVERIO CASTIGLIONE, at the entrance of the Sacristy.

In alto: lo stemma di Leone XII (1823–1829), ANNIBALE DELLA GENGA; Basilica di S. Pietro. In basso: lo stemma di Pio VIII (1829–1830), FRANCESCO SAVERIO CASTIGLIONE, sull'ingresso della Sacrestia.

Oben: das Wappen von Leo XII (1823–1829), ANNIBALE DELLA GENGA; St. Peter Basilika. Unten: das Wappen von Pius VIII (1829–1830), FRANCESCO SAVERIO CASTIGLIONE, über dem Eingang zur Sakristei.

Neither Pius VII nor the three Popes who followed him left many heraldic records in the Vatican. For example, the armorial bearings of Leo XII, Annibale della Genga (1823–1829), *"l'aquila dal volo abbassato e coronata d'oro in campo azzurro"*; *"azure* an eagle with its wings lowered and crowned gold", can only be seen on his tomb, which is in the right aisle as one enters St. Peter's Basilica.

The same is true of Pius VIII, Francesco Saverio Castiglione, whose pontificate only lasted from 31 March 1829 to 30 November 1830, exactly twenty months. His tomb is at the entrance to the corridor leading to the sacristy in the left aisle opposite the shrine of St. Andrew. His armorial bearings are those of the Castiglione family and the same as those borne by Pope Celestine IV in 1241, whose pontificate lasted only fifteen days: *"di rosso al leone sorreggente una torre, aperta del campo, merlata alla guelfa, il tutto d'oro"*; *"gules* a lion rampant holding in his paw a tower embattled in the Guelphic fashion, all gold".

Gregory XVI, Bartolomeo Alberto Cappellari (1831–1846), had entered the strict Camaldolese Order at the age of eighteen, and when he was elected to the papacy, he chose to impale his personal arms with those of his religious Order. His complete blazon reads:
"partito; nel primo della religione camaldolese (d'azzuro, al calice d'oro, sormontato da una stella cometa ondeggiante in palo, del medesimo, e affiacanto da due colombe d'argento affrontate e in atto di bere nel calice); nel secondo (Cappellari): troncato, da una fascia di rosso caricata da tre stelle d'oro: il primo d'azzurro caricato da un cappello ecclesiastico con due fiocchi di nero; il secondo d'argento pieno"; "impaled; in the sinister part the armorial bearings of the Camaldolese Order, *azure,* a chalice gold between two silver

190

Gregory XVI also belonged to a Religious Order, the *Camaldolesi*. The two doves drinking from a chalice are part of the Order's arms. The hat on the impaled side of the arms recalls the Pope's family, the Cappellari.

Anche Gregorio XVI apparteneva ad un Ordine religioso, quello dei Camaldolesi, il cui grazioso emblema reca due colombe che bevono in un calice. La presenza del cappello nell'altra parte del blasone ricorda il casato del Pontefice: Cappellari.

Gregorius XVI gehörte auch einem religiösen Orden an, den *Camaldolesi*. Die beiden Tauben, die aus dem Kelch trinken, sind Teil des Wappens das der Orden führt. Der Hut auf der anderen Hälfte des Wappens erinnert an die Familie des Papstes, die Cappellari.

doves, facing each other and drinking from the chalice, surmounted in chief by a comet gold set pale-wise; in the dexter part the arms of Cappellari, party fess-wise *azure* and silver, a fess *gules* charged with three stars gold, in the field *azure* an ecclesiastical hat with one tassel pending either side *sable*, the other field silver".

The ecclesiastical hat used by Gregory XVI as the heraldic charge for his personal arms

191

Gregory XVI (1831–1846)
Gregorio XVI (1831–1846)
Gregorius XVI (1831–1846)
BARTOLOMEO ALBERTO CAPPELLARI.

This ventilation grill was placed into the floor of the basilica in the pontificate of Pius IX in 1857.

Questa griglia per ventilazione fu posta nel pavimento della basilica durante il pontificato di Pio IX nel 1857.

Dieses Entlüftungsgrille ist in den Boden der Basilika eingelassen worden während des Pontifikats von Pius IX in 1857.

derives from the Italian ''cappello'', which refers to the Pope's surname Cappellari. His personal armorial bearings are therefore 'canting arms' or 'arma parlante'.

Gregory XVI did not commission any new buildings but ordered substantial extensions to be added to existing ones. This made it possible to house two more important art collections in the Vatican Museum: the Etruscan Museum in 1837 and the Egyptian Museum in 1839. He also restored the Vatican Gardens, a Latin inscription stating that: ''with great care did he restore them to their former splendour''. He planted many more trees, had more pathways laid and elegant fountains constructed. On the fountain he had built in the garden of the Pinacoteca, near the Latin inscription, his coat of arms has been carved twice.

The armorial bearings of Gregory XVI can be seen twice in colour at the entrance to the third loggia which he had restored. Today this loggia leads to the offices of the Papal Secretariat of State.

The long pontificate of Pius IX, Giovanni Maria Mastai-Ferretti (1846–1878), gave him the opportunity of having his coat of arms represented in many places in the Vatican: ''inquartato: nel primo e nel quarto di Mastai (d'azzurro al leone coronato poggiante su una palla, il tutto d'oro); nel secondo e nel terzo di Ferretti (d'argento a due bande di rosso''; ''quarterly, 1 & 4 the arms of Mastai (azure a lion rampant, crowned, standing on a roundel, all gold); 3 & 4 the arms of Ferretti (silver two bends gules)''.

On entering the Apostolic Palace through the Bronze Door, we see for the first time, immediately on our right, the staircase which leads to the Cortile di S.Damaso; Pius IX had

192

the old, sloping staircase taken out and this new one built. Under his coat of arms a stone plaque states that Pius IX had this new staircase built in 1860 in the hope that the buildings of the Vatican could be reached more conveniently.

The major renovations undertaken in the pontificate of Pius IX were on the ceiling in the Audience Halls on the second floor of the Apostolic Palace, among them the Hall known today as Sala del Trono, where until the pontificate of Paul VI the Popes received the Credentials of newly accredited ambassadors to the Holy See. Large coats of arms of Pius IX remind the visitor of the enormous renovations carried out here.

The armorial bearings of Pope Mastai-Ferretti cannot be seen on a tomb in St. Peter's Basilica. The Pope was buried in the Basilica di S. Lorenzo fuori le Mura.*

However, his coat of arms can be seen in many other places in the Apostolic Palace: it is painted in the frescoes by Alessandro Mantovani in the East wing of the Loggia di S.Damaso; the arms can be seen in the Sala dell'Immacolata which was decorated with murals by Francesco Podesti in 1858, depicting the extraordinary privileges of the Blessed Virgin Mary; on 8 December 1854, Pius IX had defined the Immaculate Conception of the Blessed Virgin Mary and her freedom from original sin.

Other armorial representations are in the Sala Braschi, on a glass door next to the sacristy of the Vatican Basilica, in St. Peter's Square on

* When his mortal remains were transferred from their temporary resting place in St. Peter's to the Basilica of St. Lawrence, during the night of the 13 July 1881, an anticlerical Roman mob, howling and shouting, attempted to halt the procession and throw the Pope's body into the Tiber.

Pius IX (1846–1878)
Pio IX (1846–1878)
Pius IX (1846–1878)
GIOVANNI M.MASTAI-FERRETTI.

Pius IX takes leave of Ferdinand II of Naples on
6 April 1850.

Congedo di Pio IX da Ferdinando II di Napoli il
6 aprile 1850.

Pius IX nimmt Abschied von Ferdinand II von
Neapel am 6.April 1850.

the pedestals of the Princes of the Apostles, and
at the bottom of the wide shallow steps leading
from the Basilica. His arms are also on the base
of the old cast-iron gas lamps along the Via
delle Fondamenta; today the same lamps use
electricity. Going farther afield, the arms are on
the Northern side of the Ospizio di S. Marta,
a charitable institution which still offers
hospitality to pilgrims.

With Pius IX another era of the history of the
Church comes to an end. The Franco-Prussian
War interrupted the First Vatican Council
which the Pope had inaugurated in December
1869. While the decline and total loss of the
temporal power of the papacy caused it new
and serious problems, fortunately pontifical
heraldry remained uneffected by these drastic
events and continued to flourish.

194

AQVA PIA MDCCCLXXIII

The quartered coat of arms of Pius IX. The lion belongs to the family of Mastai, the heraldic bends to the Ferretti family.

Lo stemma inquartato di Pio IX. Il leone è dei Mastai, le bande dei Ferretti.

Das quartierte Wappen von Pius IX. Der Löwe gehört der Mastai Familie, die heraldischen Schrägbalken der Ferretti Familie.

195

XV

LEO XIII (1878–1903)

The new conditions experienced by the papacy after the loss of its temporal power, undoubtedly brought about many changes in the administration and government of the Church. It did not prevent the 'august Prisoner of the Vatican' from exercising his patronage of the arts and architecture and the results were glorious and memorable. We need only look at the work carried out in some of the churches in Rome during the pontificate of Leo XIII, Gioacchino Pecci (1878–1903), the apse in St. John Lateran, the episcopal church of the popes, the tomb of his predecessor Pius IX, in San Lorenzo fuori le Mura or the Cappella dei SS. Cirillo e Metodio in the Church of St. Clement, to realise that although the conditions of his pontificate differed greatly from that of Pius IX, Leo XIII continued with extensions in Rome and in the Vatican itself.

The principal heraldic charges of the Pope's coat of arms were a pine tree, two *fleurs-de-lis* and a comet. Pope Pecci descended from an ancient family from Siena, and his branch of the family had moved to the Papal States during the sixteenth century.

As soon as he had been elected to the papacy, everybody saw a confirmation of the cardinal's choice in Malachy's prophecy: *"Lumen in coelo"*, a light in the sky, to many an obvious allusion to the comet in his coat of arms.

Leo XIII (1878–1903)
Leone XIII (1878–1903)
Leo XIII (1878–1903)
GIOACCHINO PECCI.

The arms of Leo XIII. A stained glass window; Scala del Palazzo Apostolico.

Lo stemma di Leone XIII. Una finestra a vetri istoriati; scala del Palazzo Apostolico.

Das Wappen von Leo XIII. Ein bemaltes Fenster; Treppe im Apostolischen Palast.

The arms of Leo XIII have as heraldic charges a pine tree, two *fleurs-de-lis* and a comet; his contemporaries saw in his arms a confirmation of the prophecies of Malachy: "*Lumen in coelo*".

Lo stemma di Leo XIII è formato da un pino, da due fiordalisi e una cometa, nella quale i contemporanei amarono vedere confermata la profezia di Malachia: "*Lumen in coelo*".

Im Wappen von Leo XIII sind eine Kiefer, zwei *fleurs-de-lis* und ein Komet. Seine Zeitgenossen sahen darin eine Bestätigung der Prophezeiung des Malachias: "*Lumen in coelo*".

His full blazon was: "*d'azzurro al cipresso terrazzato sulla pianura erbosa, il tutto al naturale; attraversato da una fascia ristretta d'argento, addestrata al capo da una stella cometa d'oro posta in banda e accompagnata in punta da due gigli di Francia d'argento*".

The blazoning of Pope Pecci's coat of arms and the interpretation of the '*mobili*' varies both in the Vatican and in the churches of Rome. Count Pasini-Frassoni insisted that the comet and the two *fleurs-de-lis* were silver and not gold. The *Annuario Pontificio* which, as I mentioned before, used to publish the pontifical coats of arms until the pontificate of Paul VI, depicts the tail of the comet like a 'bar sinister', whereas Pasini-Frassoni and Galbreath place the tail of the comet '*posta in banda*' – to the dexter. Rietstap, probably the most reliable herald of his time, exercises great diplomatic prudence by giving the blazon of the charge as "a golden comet with its tail downwards", which of course, allows it to be depicted according to personal preference, to the dexter or to the sinister. Different representations can be seen in the Vatican as well; for example, in the Borgia apartments the tail of the comet is on the dexter side '*in sbarra*', like a bar sinister; in the porch of St. Peter's Basilica, we can see the comet '*in banda*' on the sinister side.

The arms of Leo XIII adorn three places which this Pope opened for the first time to the outside world, especially to scholars and those involved in cultural pursuits. Among his greatest achievements, one which guarantees him a place of glory among scholars, was that for the first time in 1881 he allowed outsiders access to the Vatican Archives. This is the reason why the green pine of his coat of arms stands out several times from the ceiling of a hall that was recently redecorated and which can now be entered directly from the Cortile del Belvedere. An exhibition of the Oecumenical Councils was held in this hall in 1964.

We move from the Vatican Archive to the second sanctuary of culture, the *Biblioteca Vaticana* which we enter through the Sala di Consultazione. From the inscription we learn of his great merits, how he enriched this famous place of learning by a new constitution and new rules, as well as by the addition of finely bound books which he took from the Borgia apartments where they seemed to have been kept in the past purely to keep Pinturicchio's frescos company. Finally we come to the third place, the Vatican Museum, which that great friend of literature and art so generously enriched.

In the first two rooms of the Borgia apartments, the one showing the Prophets and Sybils, and the room depicting the Creed with the Prophets and Apostles, the armorial bearings of Pope Leo XIII and Alexander VI alternate. In the last room of the apartments we find a bust of Leo XIII and his death mask, and on the wall yet another Latin inscription stating that in the twentieth year of his pontificate, this building with its pictures and decorations had been renovated, the floor had been completely relaid, and the entire apartment restored to pristine condition, and that the Pope had rededicated the building.

Not satisfied with what he had achieved so far, he also opened to the public the Museum of Sculptures and the Gallery of the Candelabra. There we can admire the most beautiful coat of arms of Leo XIII and perhaps the most famous armorial bearings in the Vatican: it is made entirely from lapis lazuli, and a ballustrade has been placed around it to prevent visitors from accidentally stepping on it.

The Galleria dei Candelabri. On the first floor one can see the coat of arms of Leo XIII.

La Galleria dei Candelabri. In primo piano lo stemma di Leone XIII.

Die Galleria dei Candelabri. Auf dem ersten Geschoss sieht man das Wappen von Leo XIII.

The Palazzina of Leo XIII in the Vatican Gardens, which houses the headquarters of Vatican Radio, a number of studios and transmitters.

Palazzina di Leone XIII, nei Giardini Vaticani, dove risiede la Direzione Generale della Radio Vaticana e dove sono situati alcuni studi e impianti dell'emittente.

Die Villa Leos XIII, in den Vatikanischen Gärten, in der sich die Generaldirektion von Radio Vatikan und einige Studios und Sendeanlagen befinden.

The patronage of the arts given by Leo XIII has a theological justification, should that be necessary. That has been glorified in the frescos by Ludovico Seitz and by Torti, which represent among others *la Verità*, historical Truth, recalled by the register of the chronological succession of the popes, and the painter Mateiko presenting Pope Leo XIII with a painting depicting the liberation of Vienna; Reason paying homage to Faith, Religion blessing the Arts, Pagan Art handing a compass to Christian Art. All this is summarized twice in an inscription in stone «LEO XIII PICTURIS EXCOLUIT A.D. MDCCCLXXXIII».

At the end of his days, the Pope enjoyed spending every day a few hours in the Vatican Gardens, the last property left of the former Papal States; but no coat of arms recalls that it was Leo XIII who had the small Chinese pavilion built on the side of a small hill. A portrait of the Pope can be seen in the Lourdes Grotto, which was presented to the Pope in 1902 by French Catholics; it is a little further down the garden. Pope Pecci also enjoyed spending some of his time near the Torre Leonina where today the offices of the director of *Radio Vaticana* are situated.

Leo XIII preserved another, far more important monument, or more accurately, fragments of a monument: Pius IX wanted to erect it on the Gianicolo in front of the Church of San Pietro in Montorio, to commemorate the First Vatican Council. It was a statue of St. Peter with an appropriate bas-relief, and it was moved by Leo XIII into the Cortile della Pigna. In 1936, Pius XI had it removed from there, and today fragments can be seen all over the lawns of the Vatican Gardens, or placed on the walls of the small palace of the Archeological Directorate. Two small plaques with rather melancholic inscriptions recall the project of

Pius IX and the initiative of his successor: ≪INIURIA TEMPORUM PROHIBITUS≫ – injustice of the times forbade it – , because the erection of the monument had been lately frustrated; and ≪TUTIORE IN LOCO INTRA VATICANI SEPTA ERIGI IUSSIT ANNO CHR. MDCCCLXXXV≫, adding that Leo XIII had to have it moved inside the Vatican in 1885.

Coming down the Vatican Hill, we can see the arms of Leo XIII once again on the modern Palazzo dei Tribunali, where it reminds us that the Pope had the *Seminario Minore Romano* moved into the Vatican and had it quartered for a short time in the adjoining Palazzo di S. Marta.

Another example of the arms of Leo XIII can be seen painted on the painted ceiling of what used to be the dining room of the Chamberlain of the Pope. This room is today the *salon d'honneur* of the *Sezione Straordinaria* of the *Amministrazione del Patrimonio della Sede Apostolica* near the Cortile di San Damaso.

Before we end our heraldic excursion, let us go for a moment to the first floor of the Apostolic Palace. Here, in the Cappella Paolina, where the Pope had some restoration work carried out, we can see the heraldic 'pine proper' from his armorial bearings on the ballustrade of the small platform which overhangs the altar and on a wall painted on an imitation damascene tapestry.

Finally, let us go down from the Sala Regia to St. Peter's Basilica, not to see Pope Pecci's tomb, because that is in the Lateran Basilica, but to take a look at his coat of arms on the organ of the Choir Chapel and on a stained glass window in a door near the sacristy.

The arms of Leo XIII used to be in the centre of the multi-coloured floor of the porch in the

The Cross *Pro Ecclesia et Pontifice* was instituted by Leo XIII in 1888.

La Croce *Pro Ecclesia et Pontifice*, istituita da Leone XIII nel 1888.

Das Kreuz *Pro Ecclesia et Pontifice* wurde in 1888 von Leo XIII gestiftet.

Basilica. On the eve of the Second Vatican Council the floor was renovated and Pope Leo's arms were replaced by a version of rather stylised armorial bearings of John XXIII. The arms of Leo XIII were moved to a small place on the floor on the extreme right, but sadly they lost all their colouring during the move.

Three items from the dinner service of Pope St. Pius X, decorated with the papal coat of arms.

Tre pezzi del servizio da tavola di Papa S.Pio X, decorati col suo stemma.

Drei Teile des Tafelgeschirrs von Papst St. Pius X, die mit seinem Wappen verziert sind.

XVI

S.PIUS X (1903)
TO
BENEDICT XV (1922)

S.PIUS X (1903–1914)   BENEDICT XV (1914–1922)

Pius X, Giuseppe Sarto (1903–1914), was the son of a humble village postman and a seamstress from Riese in Upper Venetia, and he had obviously no family coat of arms.

When Pope Leo XIII appointed him Bishop of Mantua, Giuseppe Sarto adopted as his coat of arms a field *azure* and as his charges a three-tined anchor pale-wise above waves of the sea all proper and in chief a star of six points gold.

When he was appointed Patriarch of Venice and a cardinal in 1893, he added to his coat of arms a chief with the winged lion of St.Mark. After his election to the papacy in 1903, Pius X retained the same arms: *"d'azzurro all'ancora di tre uncini di nero cordata di rosso, posta in banda, pescante in un mare ondato al naturale e accostata al capo da una stella di sei punte d'oro. Al capo di Venezia: d'argento al leone alato e nimbato passante al naturale, reggente nella destra un libro aperto recante la leggenda:* PAX TIBI MARCE EVANGELISTA MEUS".

In his arms with the black anchor interlaced with a cord *gules* on a field *azure* and in chief a six-pointed gold star, he retained the 'chief of Venice', the Lion of St. Mark passant proper holding with his right paw an open book with the words: "PAX TIBI MARCE EVANGELISTA MEUS".

St. Pius X (1903–1914)
S. Pio X (1903–1914)
St. Pius X (1903–1914)
GIUSEPPE SARTO.

203

Pius X was well intentioned when he retained the chief of Venice in his pontifical arms, but, like four of his predecessors who misguidedly added the arms of the Religious Order to which they had belonged to their personal arms, so this saintly Pope set a precedent which was subsequently followed by John XXIII and John Paul I.

Heraldically it was wrong for the Universal Pastor to have retained a diocesan chief in his pontifical coat of arms. When the Pope published his pontifical arms just prior to the coronation, there were some objections in Rome.

Letting their imagination run wild, some artists changed the charges and colours of the blazon. Count Pasini-Frassoni, who was one of the leading heralds at the time of Pius X, publicly deplored such liberties, stating that these liberal interpretations were serious breaches of heraldic art and science. He complained that: ''people continue to place the anchor 'in banda', giving as a reason that there is so little space between the sea and the star. They do not seem to consider for a moment that the anchor symbolises not only hope but also strength. And yet, continuing to depict the anchor as they do, they represent a very unstable and wavering force''!

In spite of such strong words from the leading herald of the time, even the *Annuario Pontificio* stubbornly persisted in reproducing the Pope's anchor 'in banda', and that is also how the armorial bearings of Pius X can be found in the Vatican.

The 'chief of Venice' has been the subject of much disagreement between heraldic specialists. It is expected to be *gules* because it symbolises the historical and ancient standard

Opposite: the ceiling of the anteroom of the present-day apartment of the Secretary of State is decorated with the coat of arms of St. Pius X.

Lato opposto: il soffitto dell'anticamera dell'odierno appartamento del Segretario di Stato è ornato dallo stemma di S.Pio X.

Gegenüber: die Decke des Vorzimmers des heutigen Apartments des Staatssekretärs ist mit dem Wappen von St. Pius X geschmückt.

The arms of Popes John XXIII and John Paul I. The chief of Venice: "silver, a lion proper passant, winged and nimbed."

Gli stemmi dei Papi Giovanni XXIII e Giovanni Paolo I. Al capo, di Venezia: "d'argento, al leone passante alato e nimbato, al naturale".

Die Wappen der Päpste Johannes XXIII und Johannes Paulus I. "Im silbernen Schildhaupt von Venedig: ein beflügelter Löwe in natürlicher Tinktur mit Nimbus".

flown by the *Serenissima* – the ancient maritime Republic of Venice. But the Holy Father preferred a silver field for the chief because he wanted to emphasize that it was the religious emblem of St. Mark's Lion and not the insignia of the Venetian Republic he had adopted for his armorial bearings.

In the history of the papacy there have been many pontiffs who had their origin in Venice or who had been Patriarchs of the ancient Republic: Gregory XII, Angelo Correr (1406–1415), born in Venice and after a period as Latin Patriarch of Constantinople, was Cardinal Priest of S.Marco in Venice; Eugene IV, Gabriele Condulmer (1431–1447), was born in Venice of wealthy patrician parents; Paul II, Pietro Barbo (1464–1471), was born in Venice and built the Palazzo S.Marco, (now the Palazzo Venezia), as his main residence in Rome. Alexander VIII, Pietro Ottoboni (1689–1691), was also born in Venice of an noble family; Clement XIII, Carlo della Torre Rezzonico (1758–1769), born into one of the richest and most influential noble families of the Venetian Republic; he was a judge of the Rota for Venice and a cardinal, and after he settled the long-standing dispute between Venice and the Empire over the patriarchate of Aquilea, the Republic of Venice withdrew all anti-papal legislation when he was elected pope. None of these eminent sons of the illustrious Republic of Venice adopted the arms or charges of the Venetian arms for his personal armorial bearings or augmented his pontifical arms with the chief of Venice.

It was left to three Popes of the twentieth century – St. Pius X, who was Patriarch of Venice for ten years before his election to the papacy, John XXIII, who was Patriarch for five years, and John Paul I, Patriarch for nine – to commemorate the fact by augmenting their arms with the chief of Venice.

Unfortunately, this heraldic 'novelty' did not end there: having changed the field of the chief from *gules* (the heraldically correct standard of the Serenissima), they had to make a further modification which in heraldry is looked on with as much scorn: they blazoned the lion gold, thus placing metal upon metal. This was true heraldic heresy! To avoid any further disputes among heraldic scholars, the blazon of the lion was described "proper", which, by a stretch of the imagination is not unrealistic considering the natural colouring of a lion. Furthermore, in the Venetian standard the lion was armed with a sabre; this was removed to emphasize the peaceful character of the lion, being the symbolic animal of the evangelist St. Mark.

The inscription in the open book which the lion holds with his paw refers to a legendary event in the life of St. Mark: disembarking on an island in the Venetian Lagoon during his apostolic mission, an angel is said to have greeted him with the words: "PEACE BE WITH YOU MARK, MY EVANGELIST". The Republican Government of Venice, inspired by this legend, included the lion with the open book and the inscription in its own coat of arms.

As I have said about Pope St. Pius V, the holiness of individual pontiffs does neither express itself in glorious new buildings, nor in patronage of the arts. This also applied to Pope St. Pius X: there are few coats of arms of this saintly Pope in the Vatican. This is not only due to their lack of any desire to set up monuments to themselves to withstand the ravages of time, but often the pontificates of such saintly popes is shorter than those of others.

Above: a lion winged, nimbed and armed. Below: the correct lion of Popes Pius X, John XXIII and John Paul I: only winged and nimbed.

In alto: un leone alato, nimbato e armato. In basso: il leone corretto dei Papi Pio X, Giovanni XXIII e Giovanni Paolo I: solo alato e nimbato.

Oben: ein beflügelter Löwe mit Nimbus und bewaffnet. Unten: der korrekte Löwe der Päpste Pius X, Johannes XXIII und Johannes Paulus I: nur beflügelt und mit Nimbus.

The arms of Pius X reproduced here are above the entrance of the former building of the Pinacoteca along the main road of the Museums. Only few examples of the arms can be found.

Lo stemma di Pio X qui riprodotto si vede su un ingresso dell'antica sede della Pinacoteca lungo lo stradone dei Musei. Ne esistono pochi esemplari.

Das Wappen von Pius X, das man hier sieht, ist über dem Eingang der ehemaligen Pinacoteca entlang der Museumsstrasse. Es gibt nur wenige Beispiele von diesem Wappen.

Compared with the pontificate of Pius IX which lasted thirty-two years, and that of Leo XIII of twenty-five years, the eleven year period St. Pius X occupied the See of St. Peter appears short. However, some major works were carried out during his pontificate: the private apartments of Pius X's predecessors were on the second floor of the Apostolic Palace; he moved his private apartments to the third floor and allocated the apartments on the first floor to the Papal Secretary of State. This is the reason the ornate armorial bearings of Pius X can be seen in the stucco work and painted on the ceiling of the enormous rectangular reception room on the first floor which leads to the apartment of the Cardinal Secretary of State.

On the second floor, Pius X had a chapel built in the so-called Countess Matilda apartments, which Gregory XIII had built in this wing of the Apostolic Palace at the end of the sixteenth century and which had been restored in the following century by Urban VIII. Some frescos by Francesco Romanelli recalling the main events of the life of that famous benefactress of the Holy See, can still be seen there. The ashes of the Countess Matilda were transferred by Pope Urban VIII into the Vatican Basilica.

If we look at the ceiling of the chapel we can only see the dragon of Gregory XIII and the angel of Pius VI; there is no sign of the coat of arms of Pius X. However, three examples of this can be seen above the entrance door of the Scala which bears his name and which leads from the area of the Vatican Post Office and the offices of the Poliglotta Printing House to the Cortile di San Damaso. There is no coat of arms on the façade of the Poliglotta building, merely a Latin inscription which states that the See of St. Peter is presently occupied by Pope Pius X.

208

There are also coats of arms on the Palazzo del Belvedere where many Vatican employees live, and at the entrance to the vault in the Choir of the parish church of St. Anna dei Palafrenieri, which he had restored.

Along the Grottone, the tunnel along which today motorcars make their way from the Cortile del Belvedere to the Cortile di San Damaso, there is on the right hand side another, rather mysterious, tunnel which is closed off by iron railings that bear the coat of arms of Pius X. This tunnel was excavated underneath the galleries in the Vatican Gardens on the instruction of Pius X to make it unnecessary to cross Italian territory. Before the Lateran Treaty of 1929, the Italian frontier surrounded the Vatican Basilica, leaving the road that pilgrims and visitors used to get to the Vatican Museums in Italian territory. A very pleasing example of the arms of Pius X can be seen above one of the doors which until the pontificate of Pius XI used to lead into the Pinacoteca transferred there from the Sala Bologna on the third floor of the Apostolic Palace.

Heraldically, it is interesting to note that the chief of Venice in the Pope's coat of arms on both the iron gates which close the tunnel is wrong: once again the Lion of St. Mark appears to have fallen under the belligerent spell of the Venetian Republic, and the sabre which this peace-loving Pope removed, had been put back.

There are two more examples of the armorial bearings of Pope St. Pius X: on the occasion of his fiftieth anniversary as a priest, his coat of arms was inlaid in the centre of the marble floor of the Chapel of St. Petronilla. Finally, it appears on the Pope's tomb in the left aisle opposite the tomb of Innocent VIII.

Benedict XV (1914–1922)
Benedetto XV (1914–1922)
Benedikt XV (1914–1922)
GIACOMO DELLA CHIESA.

209

An important event in 1917: Benedict XV consecrating Mons. Eugenio Pacelli, the future Pope Pius XII, titular Archbishop of Sardes.

Un avvenimento importante nel 1917: Benedetto XV consacra Mons. Eugenio Pacelli, più tardi Papa Pio XII, Arcivescovo titolare di Sardi.

Ein wichtiges Ereignis in 1917: Benedikt XV weiht Mons. Eugenio Pacelli, den zukünftigen Papst Pius XII zum Titular Erzbischof von Sardes.

There are very few heraldic mementoes of Benedict XV, Giacomo della Chiesa (1914–1922). The First World War made any building programmes impossible, and the few years left to him after 1918 were occupied with using what limited influence he had to bringing a more lasting and just peace to the world.

The arms of the Della Chiesa family, an ancient noble family of Genoa, are canting arms; since the sixteenth century they always had a church in their armorial bearings, but Benedict XV added the demi-eagle in chief. His blazon reads: "Party bendwise *azure* and gold, a church silver roofed *gules* and a chief gold with a demi-eagle *sable*".

Benedict XV was the last pontiff to exercise the office of Grand Master of the Equestrian Order of the Holy Sepulchre of Jerusalem. He was also closely associated with the Sovereign Military Order of Malta. In 1915, after having been Pope for a year, he expressed the wish to place his pontifical arms on a cross of Malta as, for example, his predecessor Clement VII (1523–1534) had done, commemorating the fact that he had belonged to the Order of St. John. Others maintain that he wanted to place the cross of Malta in chief of his pontifical arms. In any case, he was informed that it was much too late to alter his pontifical arms, which had already been published and appeared in carvings and paintings.

There are many examples of living and dead cardinals, patriarchs, archbishops and prelates who have placed their armorial bearings on the cross of the Order of Malta or on that of the Order of the Holy Sepulchre of Jerusalem; there are those who have placed their arms on the cross of secular but strictly Catholic Orders of Knighthood, a privilege reserved for Bailiffs of such Chivalric Orders; however, Clement VII appears to have been the only Pope who retained his chivalric cross behind his pontifical arms. One must be grateful to those who advised Benedict XV against having the cross of Malta in chief or behind his arms. We have already seen the over-loading of pontifical armorial bearings with the arms of such Religious Orders, as the Dominicans, the Franciscans, the Benedictines and Camaldolese. Augmentations with chivalric crosses in chief or in

The canting arms which refer to the family name of Benedict XV: a church surmounted by an eagle.

Lo stemma parlante, allusivo cioè al nome di famiglia di Benedetto XV: una chiesa sormontata di un'aquila.

Das 'sprechende' Wappen, das sich auf den Familiennamen von Benedikt XV bezieht: eine Kirche die von einem Adler überragt ist.

211

The Monument of Benedict XV. The Pope pleads with the Mother of God for peace for mankind which suffers from the perils of the First World War.

Il Monumento di Benedetto XV. Dalla Madre di Dio il Papa implora la pace per l'umanità travolta dalla prima guerra mondiale.

Das Grabmal von Benedikt XV. Der Papst fleht die Gottesmutter um Frieden für die Menschheit an, die unter den Untaten des ersten Weltkriegs leidet.

saltire might not only have caused heraldic confusion but serious disagreements between Orders of Chivalry as most popes had attained the elevated rank of Bailiff in several Orders of Knighthood while they were cardinals.

The arms of Benedict XV can be seen on his elegant tomb in the left aisle of St. Peter's Basilica, erected there by Pietro Canonica, and other examples are in the Vatican Gardens on the shrine of the Madonna della Guardia, presented to him by the people of Genoa, his native town, on the Holy Water stoup in the Pauline Chapel and on the floor of the Sala Ducale; there the painter Silvio Galimberti commemorated in two rather mediocre frescos two major events during Benedict XV's pontificate: the promulgation of the Code of Canon Law, and the founding of the Sacred Congregation for the Oriental Churches.

XVII

PIUS XI (1922–1939)

A coat of arms we come across quite frequently in the Vatican is that of Pius XI, Achille Ratti (1922–1939) from Milan. He signed the Lateran Treaty in 1929 and became the ingenious builder of the STATO DELLA CITTÀ DEL VATICANO – the Vatican City State.

The coat of arms of the De Ratis family appeared for the first time in Tortona in the thirteenth century. It was later adopted, with some variations, by the families of Ratti from Genoa and Opizzoni from Milan who added to their coat of arms three roundels surmounted by an eagle and the motto "OMNIA CUM TEMPORE" – "everything comes with time".

With a clear allusion to his surname 'Ratti', the future Pius XI chose his own motto: "RAPTIM TRANSIT" – everything happens quickly – which has the opposite meaning to the ancient motto but proved to be prophetic; it certainly applies to his own phenomenally rapid advancement: Bishop in 1918, Cardinal in 1921 and Pope in 1922.

The blazon of the armorial bearings of Pope Ratti are: "Troncato; al primo d'oro alla aquila spiegata di nero, imbeccata e armata del campo; al secondo d'argento a tre palle die rosso 2:1"; – silver three roundels *gules* and a chief gold with an eagle *sable* beaked and armed gold".

After the signing of the Lateran Treaty and for many months to come, the Città del Vaticano looked like an enormous building site. Many ancient buildings were demolished,

Pius XI (1922–1939)
Pio XI (1922–1939)
Pius XI (1922–1939)
ACHILLE RATTI.

213

The most significant diplomatic achievement during the pontificate of Pius XI were the negotiations and signing of the Lateran Treaty which established the Vatican City as an independent State. Left: the treaty was signed by the Secretary of State, Cardinal Pietro Gasparri and the Italian Prime Minister, Benito Mussolini, on 11 February 1929.

La più importante realizzazione diplomatica del pontificato di Pio XI fu il negoziato e la firma del Trattato Lateranense che segnò l'inizio dello Stato della Città del Vaticano come stato indipendente. A sinistra: il Trattato fu firmato dal Segretario di Stato, Cardinale Pietro Gasparri, e dal Primo Ministro Italiano, Benito Mussolini, l'11 Febbrario 1929.

Die bedeutentste Errungenschaft während des Pontifikats von Pius XI waren die Verhandlungen und die Ratifizierung des Lateran Vertrags, der die Vatikanstadt als einen unabhängigen Staat gründete. Links: der Vertrag wurde von dem päpstlichen Staatssekretären, Kardinal Pietro Gasparri und dem italienischen Premier Minister, Benito Mussolini, unterschrieben.

214

among them the small palace of the Archpriest of the Basilica, the small church of St. Marta, and the Monastery di Santo Stefano degli Abissini. And while this was going on, far humbler and much more functional buildings were being erected. However small the Vatican State was in size, modern administrative building were an absolutely necessary; so a number to the charming and pleasing buildings had to be sacrificed.

On 1 November 1931, Pius XI was welcomed at the entrance of the Pontifical Mint by Marquis Camillo Serafini, the first Governor of the Vatican City. We shall now follow the Holy Father's walk on that historic day, guided by heraldic signposts.

Let us begin our heraldic excursion from outside the City because the first and quite monumental coat of arms is in the Piazza del Risorgimento. We can see it on the corner of the walls surrounding the Vatican City; the height of the walls was increased in 1932.

To enter the Vatican, we go from here to the Porta di Sant'Anna. Here at the entrance, the heraldic representations leave something to be desired: they should have been more accurate and atractive. The eagles of Pius XI on both sides of the entrance are majestic; indeed they are quite overpowering! However the roundels have been placed horizontally under each eagle instead of in the correct triangular arrangement. But let us be charitable to the designers and consider the armorial 'mobili as an artistic or heraldic licence.

Having gone through the entrance we are now in the Vatican City State and stand right in front of the Church of Saint Anna, which has been converted into a parish church and stands right next to modern and functional buildings.

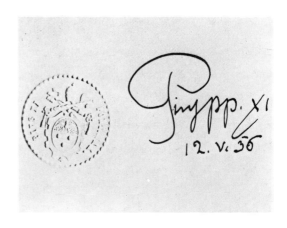

A good example of the seal and the signature of Pius XI. The Pope disliked illegible signatures which he referred to as 'delinquent signatures'.

Un bell'esemplare dell'emblema e della firma di Pio XI. Il Papa non poteva soffrire le firme illeggibili, che chiamava 'firme delinquenti'.

Ein gutes Beispiel des Siegels und der Unterschrift von Pius XI. Der Papst hatte eine Abneigung gegen unleserliche Unterschriften, die er als 'pflichtvergessen' beschrieb.

215

The arms of Pope Ratti on the Government Palace.

Lo stemma di Papa Ratti sul Palazzo del Governatorato.

Das Wappen von Papst Ratti auf dem Gouverneurspalast.

On our right, at the corner of the Via del Pellegrino, we can again see the arms of Pius XI. Following the road, we enter a part of the Vatican none of our previous excursions has taken us to: every building is modern here and adorned with, or surmounted by, the arms of Pope Ratti.

We see the arms first on our left on the rear façade of the Annona, an enormous food-store for those who live in the Vatican; on our right we see the arms at the entrance of the laboratory for the restoration of tapestries, entrusted to the the Franciscan Missionary Sisters of Mary. We now walk past the buildings of L'Osservatore Romano, the newspaper of the Holy See, and we arrive at an enormous building with an equally majestic pontifical coat of arms. At the entrance is an inscription in large letters which leaves us in no doubt where we are; it is in Latin, and even accomplished scholars will be forgiven if they find it difficult to translate, though in its originality it is worthy of Cicero: "*machinas electricas et vaporarias, alternis vel geminatis etiam viribus actas*"; what it means is 'electricity'. On entering, we find ourselves in the central power station, in front of gigantic generators which supply the whole Vatican City with electricity for light and heat.

Let us retrace our steps and go to the quarters of the Pontifical Swiss Guard. Here we see Pope Ratti's coat of arms adorning the small palace which is their headquarters. We find the Pope's arms again in the inside courtyard together with the arms of the Medici Pope Clement VII, who erected a monument in honour of those guardsmen who gave their lives to defend the Pope during the sacking of Rome in 1527.

We now walk towards the Cortile del Belvedere, but before we make the climb up to the Grottone, let us stop for a moment in front of a gate which is surmounted by Pope Ratti's coat of arms and where there is an inscription which must strike the reader as rather mysteriously prophetic considering the time its was placed there: ''RAEDIS PONTIFICUM SERVANDIS'' and rather significantly '' PER CUSTODIRE LE VETTURE DEI PAPI'' – to take care of the motorcars of the popes – .

Beside the motorcar used by Pius XI, flying the yellow and white standard of the Supreme and Sovereign Pontiff, this garage housed only the old statecoach of Pius IX and the carriage of Cardinal Bonaparte, decorated with the Imperial Eagle.

Today, all the ''*raedae*'' have been moved to a very large under-ground car park, that was built under the garden of the Pinacoteca.

But all this is just a foretaste of things to come. We have to go to the principal buildings of the Pontifical State. First we see the Palazzo del Governatorato, the Palace of the Governor of the City State, which was built near St. Peter's Basilica. Here we find ourselves inundated with an abundance of heraldic symbols and messages. All four sides of the massive cornice of this large building is one gigantic frieze of alternating eagles and enormous roundels.

Should curiosity move us to enter the building, an inscription under a bust of Pius XI by the sculptor Roscioli gives us the history of the building. It was originally planned to house the Seminario Minore of the diocese of Rome: it explains the enormous chapel that was built there, which is quite out of proportion to the piety, however commendable, of the small number of government officials and clerics working in the Governor's Palace. It also explains the many coats of arms which adorn the interior and exterior of the chapel.

The arms of Pius XI on other buildings which were erected after the reconciliation between Church and State.

Lo stemma di Pio XI su altri edifici costruiti dopo la Conciliazione.

Das Wappen von Pius XI auf anderen Gebäuden, die nach der Versöhnung zwischen Kirche und Staat gebaut worden sind.

217

The coat of arms of Pius XI on the floor of the
Sala del Concistoro.

Lo stemma di Pio XI sul pavimento della Sala
del Concistoro.

Das Wappen von Pius XI auf dem Boden im Sala
del Concistoro.

Like all countries, the Vatican City State has
its own railway; it is very short and there is
little rail traffic to be seen. Nevertheless, we
can hardly miss the railway station with its
monumental coat of arms, held by two
herculean supporters. Two bas-reliefs depict,
on the one side, the chariot of fire of the
prophet Elijah, and on the other, the fishing
boat of St. Peter. I suppose those two modes of
transport were the only ones the artists found
suitable to demonstrate the progress transport
had made in the age of locomotion!

But let us continue with our heraldic
excursion. Though even the smallest countries
may have a railway station, there are few which
can lay claim to a research studio for mosaics;
nevertheless, there is one in the Vatican. That
also was built by Pius XI as we can see from the
coats of arms on the outside of the doors. We
see the Pope's coat of arms again on the façade
of the Palazzo dei Tribunali, which houses the
ecclesiastical courts of law and justice, and the
adjacent small palace of St.Marta, the residence
of two senior Curial Cardinals; another coat of
arms is on the plinth of a most elegant fountain
which delights us with its cheerful sound.

Pius XI wanted his small State to be modern
and enjoy the most up-to-date technology. On
12 February 1931, in the ninth year of his
pontificate and on a historic day in mass
communication, the Supreme Pontiff addressed
the whole world when he inaugurated the
Vatican Radio Station. This powerful station
was built with the help of Guglielmo Marconi,
and the aerials which transmit the voice of the
Holy Father himself, rise from the green lawns
of the Vatican Gardens.

Walking on, in the direction of the Tower of
Leo IV, the arms of Pius XI can once again be
seen on another building which, incidentally,
is graced by another delightful fountain: it is

218

the Ethiopian College, the only college to enjoy the most ancient privilege of being inside the Pontifical City.

Pius XI was the real architect of many of the buildings that the young State needed to carry out its governmental and administrative functions. Nevertheless, he did not neglect those hallowed buildings which his predecessors had erected for the benefit of the human spirit: the Vatican Library and the Museums. During the First World War, from 1914 until 1918, Benedict XV had appointed him Prefect of the Vatican Library; that is the reason we see the coat of arms of Pius XI, alternating with that of Leo XIII, on the glass door to the entrance of the Library, at the bottom of the staircase and in the Sala di Consultazione. But the arms of Pius XI literally dominate the new entrance to the Museums that are along the Vatican Avenue. At the end of 1931 the Pontiff inaugurated the new entrance which was designed by the architect Momo who had also built that avant-garde spiral heraldic staircase. The new building for the Pinacoteca, also adorned with the arms of Pius XI, was designed by the Milanese architect Beltrami, and the Pope opened it on 27 October 1932.

Though very conscious of the need to preserve the cultural heritage of the Vatican, Pius XI was also determined to establish an institution which would demonstrate to the world that the Church had a definite role as protectress of ever-advancing human knowledge, and on 29 October 1936 by a Papal Brief *motu proprio* Pius XI founded the *Pontificia Accademia delle Scienze* – today one of the leading and most highly esteemed Academies of Science in the World – which he housed in the Casina di Pio IV in the Vatican Gardens, and which for that reason has been adorned with the armorial bearings of Pius XI.

The eagle and the roundels adorn the cornices of the Government Palace.

Il fregio con l'aquila e le palle che orna il cornicione del Palazzo del Governatorato.

Der Adler und die heraldischen Medaillons schmücken das Gesims des Gouverneurspalasts.

219

The Pope attends the inauguration of the spiral staircase in the Vatican Museums. Dug deep into the hill, the staircase has alongside the bronze railings the coats of arms of popes from the Renaissance onwards.

Il Pontefice presenzia all'inaugurazione dello scalone elicoidale dei Musei Vaticani. Scavata nella collina la scala porta nel parapetto in bronzo gli stemmi dei pontefici dal Rinascimento in poi.

Der Papst nimmt an der Einweihung der grossen Wendeltreppe im Vatikanischen Museum teil, die tief aus dem Hügel ausgegraben worden war. Entlang des bronzenen Treppengeländers sind die Wappen von Päpsten seit der Renaissance.

NICHOLAS V (1447-1455)

PIUS II (1458-1464)

SIXTUS IV (1471-1484)

ALEXANDER VI (1492-1503)

JULIUS II (1503-1513)

221

LEO X (1513-1521)

PAUL III (1534-1549)

PIUS IV (1559-1565)

S. PIUS V (1566-1572)

GREGORY XIII (1572-1585)

SIXTUS V (1585-1590)

PAUL V (1605-1621)

URBAN VIII (1623-1644)

BENEDICT XIV (1740-1758)

PIUS VI (1775-1799)

PIUS VII (1800-1823)

GREGORY XVI (1831-1846)

223

COLOUR PLATES

XVII

Left to right, top: Arms of Innocent XI; Basilica Vaticana. Arms of Innocent XII; Basilica Vaticana. Below: Arms of Clement XI; Cortile del Belvedere. Arms of Innocent XIII; 'Grotte' della Basilica Vaticana.

Da sinistra a destra, in alto: Stemma di Innocenzo XI; Basilica Vaticana. Stemma di Innocenzo XII; Basilica Vaticana. In basso: Stemma di Clemente XI; Cortile del Belvedere. Stemma di Innocenzo XIII; 'Grotte' della Basilica Vaticana.

Links nach rechts, oben: Wappen des Innozenz XI; Basilica Vaticana. Wappen des Innozenz XII; Basilica Vaticana. Unten: Wappen des Klemens XI; Cortile del Belvedere. Wappen des Innozenz XIII; 'Grotte' della Basilica Vaticana.

XVIII

Left to right, top: Arms of Benedict XIII; Cortile del Belvedere. Arms of Benedict XIV; Basilica Vaticana. Below: Arms of Clement XIII; Cortile del Belvedere. Arms of Pius VI; Sala del Concistoro.

Da sinistra a destra, in alto: Stemma di Benedetto XIII; Cortile del Belvedere. Stemma di Benedetto XIV; Basilica Vaticana. In basso: Stemma di Clemente XIII; Cortile del Belvedere. Stemma di Pio VI; Sala del Concistoro.

Links nach rechts, oben: Wappen des Benedikt XIII; Cortile del Belvedere. Wappen des Benedikt XIV; Basilica Vaticana. Unten: Wappen des Klemens XIII; Cortile del Belvedere. Wappen des Pius VI; Sala del Concistoro.

XIX

Arms of Pius IX; ceiling in the Sala del Trono.

Stemma di Pio IX; soffitto della Sala del Trono.

Wappen von Pius IX; Decke des Sala del Trono.

XX

Left to right, top: Arms of Leo XII; Basilica Vaticana. Arms of Pius VIII; Basilica Vaticana. Below: Arms of St. Pius X; Basilica Vaticana. Arms of Pius XI; Sala del Concistoro.

Da sinistra a destra, in alto: Stemma di Leone XII; Basilica Vaticana. Stemma di Pio VIII; Basilica Vaticana. In basso: Stemma di S. Pio X; Basilica Vaticana. Stemma di Pio XI; Sala del Concistoro.

Links nach rechts, oben: Wappen des Leo XII; Basilica Vaticana. Wappen des Pius VIII; Basilica Vaticana. Unten: Wappen des Hl. Pius X; Basilica Vaticana. Wappen des Pius XI; Sala del Concistoro.

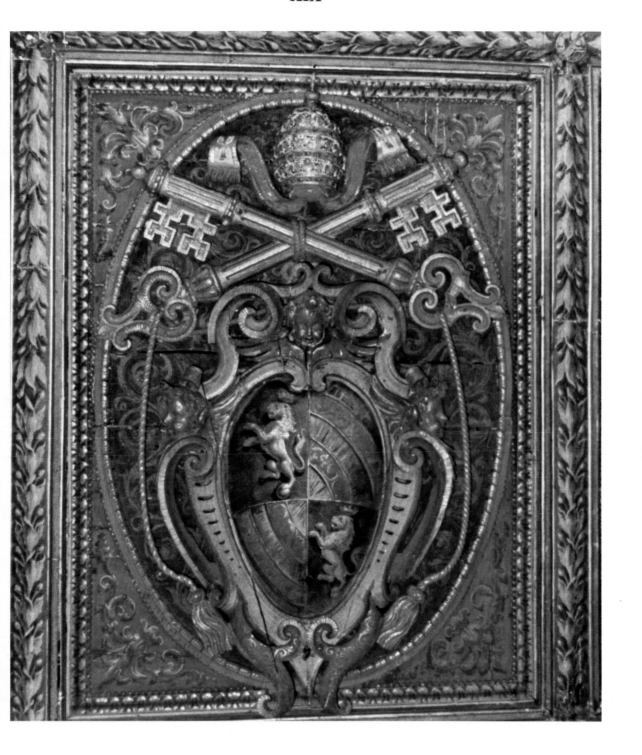

COLOUR PLATES

XXI

Top: Arms of Leo XIII; window on a landing in the Apostolic Palace.

In alto: Lo stemma di Leone XIII; finestra dello scalone del Palazzo Apostolico.

Oben: Wappen des Leo XIII; Fenster an einem Treppenabsatz im Palazzo Apostolico.

Below – in basso – unten: Biblioteca Vaticana: *"Jeu d'Armoiries des Souverains et Estats d'Europe"*, C. O. Finé, 1669. (Arms of Clement IX; Stemma di Clemente IX; Wappen des Klemens IX).

XXII

Arms of Pius XII; stained glass window, Cortile del Belvedere.

Stemma di Pio XII; finestra a vetri istoriati, Cortile del Belvedere.

Wappen von Pius XII; gemaltes Fenster, Cortile del Belvedere.

XXIII

Arms of John XXIII; anteroom of the Cardinal Secretary of State.

Stemma di Giovanni XXIII; anticamera del Cardinale Segretario di Stato.

Wappen des Johannes XXIII; Vorzimmer des Kardinal-Staatssekretärs.

XXIV

Papal coats of arms: Paul VI, John Paul I and John Paul II.

Stemmi Pontifici: Paolo VI, Giovanni Paolo I e Giovanni Paolo II.

Wappen der Päpste Paulus VI, Johannes Paulus I und Johannes Paulus II.

Other examples of the Pope's coat of arms can be found on the floor of the Sala del Concistoro, in the Vatican Basilica in the central nave and in the apse which he had restored, at the top of the Scala Regia, and wherever other minor renovation was done in St. Peter's Basilica. Finally, his coat of arms can be seen on his statue in the right aisle, opposite the monument of his successor, Pius XII, in the Chapel of St. Sebastian.

Pius XI has been the only Pope in history to have two monuments: the first one was sculpted by Pietro Canonica, who perhaps had lost some of his artistic genius since sculpting the statue of Benedict XV. Pope Paul VI had it moved to the Lateran where it seems to look better in the new environment. Paul VI commissioned a new monument for Pius XI from the architect Francesco Nagni, which took the place of the old one. That statue is also surmounted by the armorial eagle of that great Pope from Milan.

One of the last photographs taken of Pius XI (at the inauguration of the Academy of Sciences).

Una delle ultime foto di Pio XI (all'inaugurazione dell'Academia delle Scienze).

Eine der letzten Fotografien, die von Pius XI aufgenommen worden sind (Einweihung der Akademie der Wissenschaften).

XVIII

PIUS XII (1939–1958)

Although Pius XII, Eugenio Pacelli (1939–1958), the Pope of the Second World War, reigned for almost twenty years, he had neither the time nor inclination to promote building projects. We therefore do not need to prepare ourselves for a long heraldic excursion; a short walk in the Vatican City will be sufficient to see the occasional dove with an olive twig in its beak, the main heraldic charge from his coat of arms.

The blazon of his armorial bearings published on his election to the papacy was: *"d'azzuro alla colomba con testa rivolta imbeccante un ramoscello d'ulivo posto in sbarra, posante su un monte di tre pezzi all'italiana: il tutto d'argento. Il monte, fondato su una fascia abbassata e ristretta di verde e questa posta su di un mare al naturale ondato d'argento"*; *"azure*, on a mount of three *coupeaux argent* in Italian fashion, issuant from a *champagne vert* with waves of the sea proper a dove reguardant holding in the beak an olive branch, all silver". [Many heralds give the colour of the olive branch as vert].

But the dove has not always been sitting restfully on the mountain; Cardinal Pacelli's blazon had been: *"azure*, on a mount of three *coupeaux* in Italian fashion in base *argent* a silver dove rising reguardant holding in the beak an olive branch *vert*, a rainbow *haussé* in bend sinister proper with the motto OPUS IUSTITIAE PAX". The dove was flying in a blue sky which was crossed by a rainbow. When Cardinal Pacelli was elected to the papacy, it

Pius XII (1939–1958)
Pio XII (1939–1958)
Pius XII (1939–1958)
EUGENIO PACELLI.

Opposite: The Lateran Treaty (page 214) was ratified by Pope Pius XI and Victor Emanuel III, King of Italy.

Lato opposto: Il Trattato Lateranense (pagina 214) fu ratificato dal Papa Pio XI e dal Re d'Italia Vittorio Emanuele III.

Gegenüber: Der Lateran Vertrag (Seite 214) wurde von Papst Pius XI und König Viktor Emanuel III von Italien ratifiziert.

227

The modernisation of the offices of the Secretariat of State is due to Pius XII. The offices are situated on the third Loggia of the Apostolic Palace.

A Pio XII si deve l'ammodernamento degli uffici della Segreteria di Stato che si aprono lungo la terza loggia del Palazzo Apostolico.

Die Modernisierung der Büroräume des Staatssekretariats ist Pius XII zu verdanken. Die Amtszimmer sind in der dritten Loggia des Apostolischen Palasts.

seemed more in keeping with the stability of the Pontifical Magisterium that the dove should fold its wings and settle on the peak of the three mountains which now rose from a green carpet, perhaps a green island, on the waters of the sea.

The original armorial bearings of the Pacelli family had been *"azure,* upon a mount of three *coupeaux argent* issuing from a *champagne vert,* a silver dove *contournée,* holding in the beak an olive branch *vert".* This blazon was later changed to *"azure,* upon a mount *argent* issuant from water in base proper a silver dove holding in its beak an olive branch *vert".*

From a heraldic point of view the final change from the arms Eugenio Pacelli bore as Cardinal to those he adopted as Pope may be arguable; however, symbolically the result is satisfying because it represents the peaceful will and endeavours of the Pope whom St. Malachy describes in his prophecies as *Pastor Angelicus,* the angelic shepherd. The motto of the Pope: OPUS IUSTITIAE PAX, appears to be similarly contradictory for one who laboured in a world whose motto was INJUSTICE AND WAR!

The building work commissioned by Pius XII was practical and functional. He had the offices of the Papal Secretariat of State completely rebuilt and more lifts installed from the Cortile di S. Damaso to the Belvedere.

The Papal Secretariat had been housed on the third floor of the Apostolic Palace since 1870, and as its work and activities had grown massively with the continual increase in importance of the Church's government, those narrow and rather temporary rooms had become totally unsuited for the work that had to be carried out there. The entrance to the Papal Secretariat of State in particular left

The arms of Pius XII.
Lo stemma di Pio XII.
Das Wappen von Pius XII.

229

Eugenio Cardinal Pacelli, Secretary of State of Pius XI, (1930–1939).

Eugenio Cardinale Pacelli, Segretario di Stato di Pio XI, (1930–1939).

Eugenio Kardinal Pacelli, Staatssekretär von Pius XI, (1930–1939).

much to be desired: there was a small, rather unsightly door at the top of a dark narrow staircase leading into an equally dark and narrow corridor along which there were a few small rooms for the vastly increasing number of visitors to the Papal Secretariat.

Pius XII had a spacious and dignified lobby built in front of the big loggia with panoramic windows which allow the visitor to admire a stunning view of Rome and beyond as far as the mountains of Sabina. It is a view nobody should miss before admiring the spacious antechamber with the frescos of the two hemispheres of the earth, each star on these frescos indicating the Apostolic Nunciature and Delegations throughout the world. Only a few people notice the multi-coloured stained glass window and the fresco depicting the arms of Pius XII, and almost nobody sees that the handle to the entrance door is in the shape of a mount, surmounted by a dove. These are items which escape those who do not look at their surroudings with a heraldic eye.

As so often happens in the Vatican, when renovations are carried out, unexpected treasures come to light; on the walls of the Loggetta or glass gallery, known as the Manica Lunga, and long sleeve, which faces the Cortile del Maresciallo, some frescos were discovered, the colours of which were remarkably well preserved.

The Loggetta dates from the pontificate of Leo X and formed part of the apartment of Cardinal Bibbiena. It had been designed and built by Raphael who gave to his assistants his own drawings and cartoons to carry out the painting of the walls. A small Latin inscription has been placed there to tell the visitor of the accidental discovery of these beautiful frescos.

The extensive reconstruction continued with the building of a terrace in the extension of the Manica Lunga and the complete rebuilding of almost the entire floor of offices.

The most important plan was to build a superstructure and an additional floor above the third one; it was to accommodate additional offices of the Papal Secretariat of the State and to house cardinals who would come to Rome during the *Sede Vacante* to elect a new pope. Unfortunately Pius XII's latter intentions were never realised, for when the conclaves that elected his successor assembled, all the cardinals stayed elsewhere. As in the Loggetta, we find no coat of arms of Pius XII in this part of the building, which I described earlier as 'practical and functional' and which enabled the Holy See and particularly the Papal Secretariat of State to meet the ever-increasing workload and accommodate the staff needed to carry it out.

However, the name PIUS XII PONT. MAX. can be seen carved prominently on the uppermost part of the Borgia Tower, where Pius XII had two floors added and which can be clearly seen from the Cortile del Belvedere; the Pope's name can also be seen carved above the names of Leo X and Julius II which were sculpted on the balconies of the Borgia Apartments and the Stanze of Raphael.

Pius XII had also ordered the extensions of lifts from the Cortile del Belvedere, a fact commemorated by a long inscription composed by Cardinal Bacci, whose inexhaustible knowledge of ancient and modern Latin was phenomenal. Waiting for one of the two lifts, we have ample time to reflect on the most useful *"anabathrum electride actum"* – the raised chair driven by electricity – and compare it with the *"scansorio pegmati"* – the

The Medal *'Sede Vacante'* (1939) of Cardinal Pacelli, Camerlengo of the Holy Roman Church.

La medaglia *'Sede Vacante'* (1939) del Cardinale Pacelli, Camerlengo di Santa Romana Chiesa.

Die Medaille *'Sede Vacante'* (1939) von Kardinal Pacelli, Camerlengo der Heiligen Römischen Kirche.

231

The library vestibule, Sala degli Scrittori. On the walls hang portraits of cardinals who were librarians. Inlaid in the marble floor are the arms of Pius XII.

Il vestibolo della Biblioteca, Sala degli Scrittori. Alle pareti sono appesi ritratti di cardinali bibliotecari. Nel pavimento di marmo è intarsiato lo stemma di Pio XII.

Das Vestibül der Bibliothek, Sala degli Scrittori. An den Wänden hängen Gemälde von Kardinälen, die Bibliothekare waren. In den Marmorboden ist das Wappen von Pius XII eingelegt.

scaffolding which had to be climbed – in olden days.

On the opposite wall are two stained glass windows with the coat of arms of Pius XII, and there are two further examples: one on the third floor by the lift and one on the floor where the rooms for the lift operators are situated, near the Cortile di S. Damaso.

Pius XII also had a small lift installed in the Borgia Tower, and above the Borgia Apartment are some rooms that are laid out in a similar manner to those for the Secretariat of State, where we find the *Consilium pro publicis Ecclesiae negotiis* – the Council for the Public Affairs of the Church. If you walk up the stairs of the Borgia Tower to the Cortile del Belvedere you can see a commemorative inscription under the dove of Pius XII, and on the upper floors where the lifts stop, the door lintels are decorated with the arms of Pius XII carved in stone.

The armorial bearings of Pius XII are almost totally absent elsewhere in the Vatican City, apart from a few places where similar renovations were carried out, for example on the third floor of the Apostolic Palace, on the floor and on the cornices of the large rectangular room of the Pope's private apartment which is directly above his private library. Sadly, they cannot even be found in the area of the extensive excavations which were initiated by him under the *Confessione* in the Vatican Basilica, probably one of the most memorable undertakings during his pontificate.

However, his coat of arms can be seen on the slightly higher level of the Grottoes, the restoration of which coincided with the excavations. On the sides of the famous marble statue of the Apostle Peter, to which a never-ending queue of pilgrims pays homage, and also on the tomb of the Pope we can see two doves on their mountains rising from the rear walls.

In the Basilica it is possible to find some circular ventilation grids with the arms of Pius XII, which have been let into the marble floor to allow fresh air into Grottoes underneath. His coat of arms is also on one of the two organs, while the second, the more recent, bears the arms of John XXIII.

Finally we stand in front of his monument: it is situated in the right aisle in the Chapel of St. Sebastian and faces that of his predecessor Pius XI. The statue of Pius XII is by Francesco Messina; he sculpted the Pope with that tormented figure, angles hold the golden dove, who so desperately wanted peace and bring life, but instead faced the horrors of the Second World War and its aftermath. Above this tormented figure, angles hold the golden dove, as if to set free this heraldic bird of the *Pastor Angelicus*.

The Medal *'Anno I'* of Pius XII.
La medaglia *'Anno I'* di Pio XII.
Die Medaille *'Anno I '* von Pius XII.

233

The Arms of John XXIII: two of the lions which John XXIII bore in chief, that were rejected by the Pontiff, and (above) the final version which he accepted. (See page 239 and compare the lion whom Pope Roncalli accepted with his arms as Patriarch of Venice).

Lo stemma di Giovanni XXIII: i due leoni del capo che furono scartati dal'Pontefice e (in alto) il terzo che fu accettato. (Vedi pagina 239 e paragonare il leone accettato da Papa Roncalli con quello che aveva come Patriarca di Venezia).

Das Wappen von Johannes XXIII: zwei der Löwen, die Johannes XXIII im Schildhaupt führte, die er abgelehnt hat und (oben) der dritte Entwurf, den er angenommen hatte. (Vergleichen Sie den Löwen, den Papst Roncalli angenommen hat mit dem, den er als Patriarch von Venedig führte, auf Seite 239).

XIX

JOHN XXIII (1958–1963)
TO
PAUL VI (1963–1978)

John XXIII, Angelo Giuseppe Roncalli (1958–1963), affectionately known simply as ''Papa Giovanni'', has distinguished himself in so many fields that it may seem almost trivial to discuss his coat of arms at great length. However, it is not known to many that he personally took a great interest in heraldry as a relaxing recreation. Together with friends who shared his hobby, he became a proficient amateur heraldist, whose counsel was sought by those who needed advice on adopting a coat of arms when they became bishops. Indeed, less than one month before his death, in the evening of 4 May 1963, John XXIII wrote a small treatise on his pontifical coat of arms for the author, which is appended in facsimile to this chapter.

To Angelo Giuseppe Roncalli heraldry was a living art form which should always have something to say about the bearer of a coat of arms. Having been the third of thirteen children in a family of frugal peasant farmers, he had no family coat of arms and adopted one when Pius XI appointed him archbishop. He designed his coat of arms himself. Apart from the traditional Roncalli Tower which he used as the main heraldic charge, he placed a *fleur-de-lis* on either side of the tower. There have been many explanations given why he chose two *fleurs-de-lis*. Having already expressed his deep affection for his native city by adopting the tower, he took the *fleurs-de-lis* which are present in the coat of arms of the Cathedral

John XXIII (1958–1963)
Giovanni XXIII (1958–1963)
Johannes XXIII (1958–1963)
ANGELO GIUSEPPE RONCALLI.

Above: Archbishop Roncalli, Apostolic Nuncio in France with his secretary Mons.Bruno Heim. Below: the arms of Nuncio Mons. Roncalli.

In alto: l'Arcivescovo Roncalli, Nunzio Apostolico in Francia col suo segretario Mons.Bruno Heim. In basso: lo stemma del Nunzio Mons. Roncalli.

Oben: Erzbischof Roncalli, Apostolischer Nuntius in Frankreich mit seinem Sekretär Mons. Bruno Heim. Unten: das Wappen von Nuntius Mons. Roncalli.

Chapter of Bergamo of which he had been appointed Honorary Canon. Together with roses they form the iconographic symbolism of St. Alexander the Martyr, the principal Patron Saint of the city and diocese of Bergamo. Angelo Giuseppe Roncalli's roots were very deep in that city.

In December 1944 Archbishop Roncalli was appointed Apostolic Nuncio to Paris. Immediately speculation arose about the *fleurs-de-lis* in his coat of arms and many saw in them an allusion to France. The new Apostolic Nuncio unhesitatingly replied with his outstandingly characteristic goodness of heart which lovingly embraced all God's children, a quality which later conquered the hearts of the world, that one *fleur-de-lis* would remind him of Bergamo, the other of France.

Nuncio Roncalli received many requests from newly created Nuncios for guidance with their coats of arms. In 1949 his old friend Archbishop Gustavo Testa from Bergamo, the recently appointed Apostolic Delegate to Jerusalem, wrote several times, asking for a design for a suitable coat of arms. At the top of his letter, Archbishop Testa drew an empty shield, surmounted by the archiepiscopal cross and hat, and he asked in most humorous terms for a design for a coat of arms, saying of himself: ''. . . . it is unheard of that a *quasi-Patriarch* of Jerusalem should not have a coat of arms!''.

It is only fair to add that he received at least five designs from ''Caro Don Angelo'' and later from Mons. Heim, who was then Nuncio Roncalli's Secretary and an accomplished heraldist, but he adopted none of them.

After Nuncio Roncalli had been created a cardinal and Patriarch of Venice he wrote to his

236

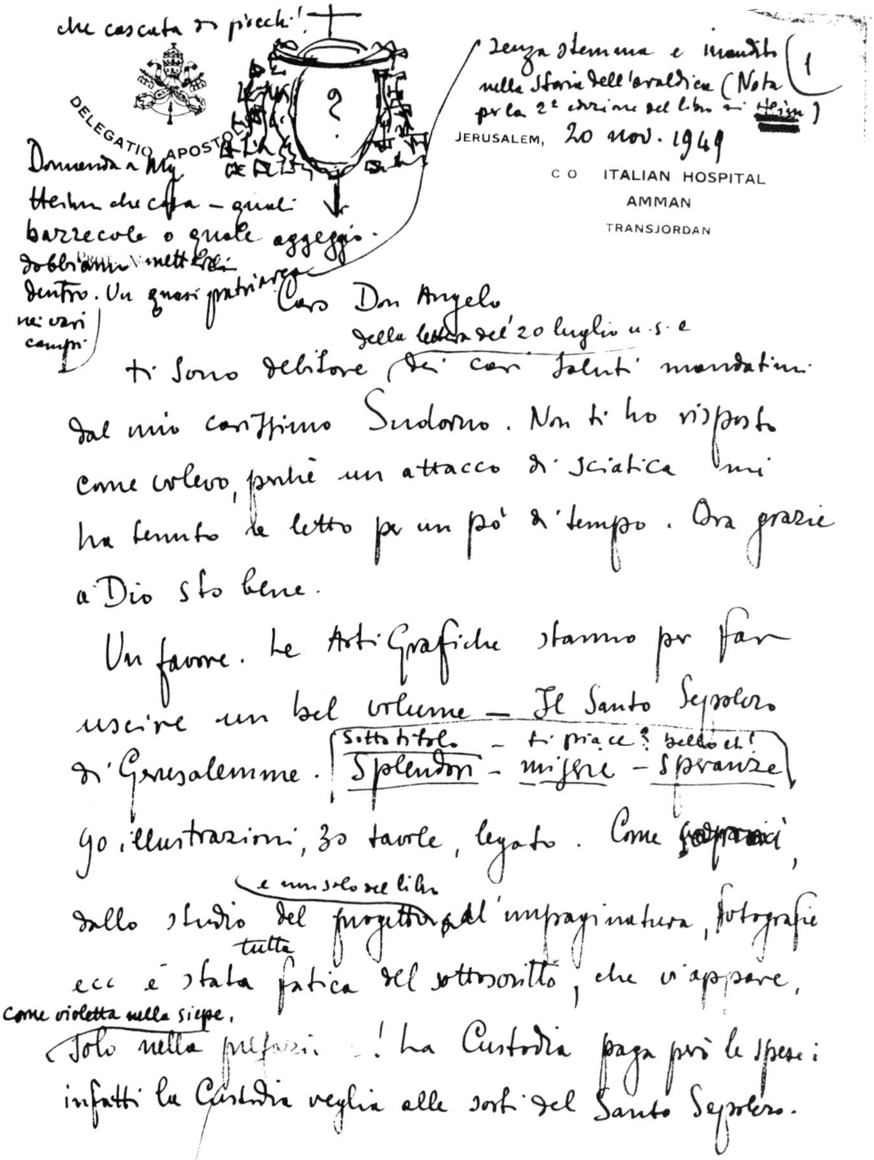

che cascata di picchi!

Senza stemma e mantello nella storia dell'araldica (Nota per la 2a edizione del libro di Heim)

DELEGATIO APOSTOLICA

JERUSALEM, 20 nov. 1949

C O ITALIAN HOSPITAL
AMMAN
TRANSJORDAN

Domanda a Mgr Heim che cosa — quali barzecole o quale aggeggio dobbiamo mettere dentro. Un quasi patriarca nei vari campi.

Caro Don Angelo

ti sono debitore della lettera del 20 luglio u.s. e dei cari saluti mandatimi dal mio carissimo Sindaco. Non ti ho risposto come volevo, perchè un attacco di sciatica mi ha tenuto a letto per un po' di tempo. Ora grazie a Dio sto bene.

Un favore. Le Arti Grafiche stanno per far uscire un bel volume — Il Santo Sepolcro di Gerusalemme. [Sotto titolo — ti piace? bello eh!] Splendori — miserie — speranze, 90 illustrazioni, 30 tavole, legato. Come ~~[illegible]~~, dallo studio del progetto (e non solo del libro) all'impaginatura, fotografie ecc è stata tutta fatica del sottoscritto, che vi appare, come violetta nella siepe, solo nella prefazione! La Custodia paga però le spese: infatti la Custodia veglia alle sorti del Santo Sepolcro.

Letter from the Apostolic Delegate Mons. Testa in Jerusalem, asking his friend Nuncio Mons. Roncalli in Paris to design a coat of arms for him.

Lettera del Delegato Apostolico a Gerusalemme Mons. Testa richiendente al suo amico Mons. Roncalli, Nunzio a Parigi, di disegnarli uno stemma.

Brief des Apostolischen Delegaten Mons. Testa in Jerusalem, in dem er seinen Freund Mons. Roncalli, Apostolischer Nuntius in Paris, bittet, ihm ein Wappen zu entwerfen.

Venezia 25.III.959

Sono confuso del ritardo a ri
spondere ai suoi duplicati com
plimenti, ma ella mi può com
patire, e sa anche che io
Le sono sempre affezion
to e fedele. Anche fra lo
sterminio assestato alla mia
nuova funzione non potei
ricorrere immediatamente
alle sue indicazioni, per
chè urgeva di far presto.
Ella però vede che ho te
nuto come base la sua
firma: e il resto fu com
binato abbastanza bene.
Certo, così come è, fu ben
tosto: e piace.

Letter from Cardinal Roncalli, Patriarch of Venice, to Mons. Heim, explaining why he could not consult his former secretary before designing his patriarchal coat of arms himself.

Lettera del Cardinale Roncalli, Patriarca di Venezia, a Mons. Heim, in cui spiega il motivo per cui non potè consultare il suo antico segretario prima di disegnare egli stesso il proprio stemma patriarcale.

Brief von Kardinal Roncalli, Patriarch von Venedig, an Mons. Heim, in dem er erklärt, warum er seinen ehemaligen Sekretär nicht um Rat fragen konnte und sein Patriarchenwappen selbst entworfen hätte.

former Secretary Mons. Bruno Heim with whom he had often collaborated on heraldic projects that pressure of time had not allowed prior consultation about his patriarchal coat of arms.

This is particularly interesting because when Cardinal Roncalli became Pope, he insisted not only on retaining the chief of Venice with the Lion of St. Mark, but, as Mons. Heim illustrated in his *"HERALDRY IN THE CATHOLIC CHURCH"*, Pope John was adamant in having the Lion of St. Mark depicted in a particular way. When Mons. Heim submitted paintings of his designs for the pontifical arms, the Pope commented on one that the lion looked too fierce for the jolly person he was; on another that the lion was too lean and thin. Besides, he also wanted the lion to look people in the eye. He then gave to Mons. Heim an example of how he wanted the Lion of St. Mark to be represented. The example was in fact the lion which Cardinal Roncalli had sent Mons. Heim in July 1953 with the letter in which he explained that time had been so pressing that he himself had had to design the Lion of the chief of Venice which he was to adopt. But all his suggestions were made with such loving guidance and tact that Mons. Heim was not even aware of the fact that in the end he had merely reproduced Pope John's own design. The saintly Pope's care not to hurt the Monsignor's feelings came to light only twenty-five years later.

The blazon of the pontifical arms of John XXIII is "di rosso alla fascia d'argento, alla torre al naturale, traversante sul tutto accostata da due gigli d'argento e al Capo patriarcale di S. Marco: d'argento al leone passante alato e nimbato al naturale, reggente nella destra un libro aperto recante la leggenda: PAX TIBI MARCE EVANGELISTA MEUS.

240

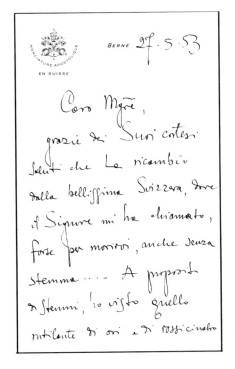

Letter from Mons. Testa, Apostolic Nuncio in Germany, to Mons. Heim, expressing sadness that he has not adopted a coat of arms.

Lettera di Mons. Testa, Nunzio in Germania, a Mons. Heim, in cui esprime dispiacere per non aver adottato un proprio stemma.

Der Brief von Nuntius Testa in Deutschland an Mons. Heim, in dem er traurig mitteilt, dass er sich noch nicht für ein Wappen entschlossen hat.

Allow me to digress once more and recall another heraldic event which took place here in the Vatican but which is not recorded by a monument or even by a simple coat of arms. I mentioned earlier the many letters from Archbishop Testa to Archbishop Roncalli. After Pius XII had created Archbishop Roncalli Cardinal Patriarch of Venice, Mons. Testa, now Apostolic Nuncio in Switzerland, wrote to Mons. Heim:

"I have just seen that splendid coat of arms, full of gold and purple, of the new Patriarch of Venice. What a heraldic masterpiece! God has called me to this wonderful Switzerland probably to die without a coat of arms of my own".

Opposite: John XXIII blessing *Urbi et Orbi* with his coat of arms on a tapestry.

Lato opposto: Giovanni XXIII mentre da la benedizione *Urbi et Orbi* col suo stemma sul drapo.

Gegenüber: Johannes XXIII gibt den Segen *Urbi et Orbi*; sein Wappen ist auf einem dekorativen Wandteppich.

Above: the seal of Pope John XXIII.
In alto: il sigillo di Papa Giovanni XXIII.
Oben: das Siegel des Papstes Johannes XXIII.

In December 1959 John XXIII created his life-long friend from Bergamo a cardinal. The Editor of the *Annuario Pontificio* was most anxious to have Cardinal Testa's coat of arms for the 1960 edition which was ready for printing, and he requested the Cardinal's coat of arms without delay. There was no time for further consultations with his friend.

As a result Cardinal Testa adopted the most unconventual coat of arms ever to have been borne by a cardinal: in the empty shield he wrote the words SOLA GRATIA TUA, and he chose the motto ET PATRIA ET COR. He then wrote a note which he sent to the Pope, enclosing his coat of arms and explaining to the Holy Father that he had taken the opportunity of using his coat of arms and motto to send a message to his dear friend the Supreme Pontiff, and he rendered his own (Italian) translation from the Latin:

"In the shield it says: 'I AM A CARDINAL BECAUSE OF YOU ALONE" and in my motto: "BECAUSE I AM FROM BERGAMO AND A FRIEND".

It is only because this has been a contemporary event, and because John XXIII, to whom heraldry was alive and an art form for communication, sent the note to his former Secretary who has so carefully preserved it, that we can witness that a coat of arms is not always an object of pomposity but can tell us much about the bearer. It also proves that heraldry does not lack humour.

The coat of arms of John XXIII was reproduced by Giacomo Manzù on the floor of the porch of the Vatican Basilica. The shape and colour the artist had given to the lion are a little perplexing, and the rest of the coat of arms is in a similar style: a rendering which tends to horrify any heraldic scholar. Why was it put there in the first place? The answer can be found in the date which accompanies it, 11 October 1962, the day of the solemn opening of the Second Vatican Council. On the eve of this most important event, when the bishops from all over the world would gather here, it was felt that the floor of the porch needed cleaning, and above all restoring where the endless shuffle of pilgrims' feet had worn it down. The last time the floor had been restored was under Leo XIII (1878–1903), when two coats of arms of Pope Clement X (1670–1676) had been left, flanking a multi-coloured coat of arms of Leo XIII. Since the cleaning and renovation of the floor in 1962 the multi-coloured arms of John XXIII have been flanked on their left by that of Leo XIII and on their right by the arms of Clement X.

It is useless to look for the arms of John XXIII on his tomb in the Basilica. It is the only papal tomb without the pontifical arms on it.

Could it have been pure ignorance on the part of that modern artist or a self-inflated sense of doing something 'unique'?

All attempts to persuade Emilio Greco, the sculptor who had been commissioned to create the tomb for John XXIII – even by the highest official from the Administration of the Fabric of St. Peter's Basilica – were in vain.

Scholars of heraldry will for ever ask the question how such a *'muratore'* – a stonemason – could flout the requests of the experts responsible for the Fabric of the Vatican Basilica!

Tapestry from the apartments of Pope John XXIII with his coat of arms.

Tappezzeria degli appartamenti di Papa Giovanni XXIII col suo stemma.

Damast Wandbehängung vom Apartment des Papstes Johannes XXIII mit seinem Wappen.

Opposite: The arms of John XXIII; anteroom of the Secretary of State.

Lato opposto: lo stemma di Giovanni XXIII; anticamera del Segretario di Stato.

Gegenüber: Das Wappen von Johannes XXIII; Vorzimmer des Staatssekretärs.

Pope John spent frequently some time at night writing down some thoughts on a special theme. On 4 May 1963, one month exactly before he died, he wrote some reflections on his pontifical coat of arms. He mentioned that the French people had always asked him if the two *fleurs-de-lis* had a connection with France, and his reply that one *fleur-de-lis* would always remind him of his native Bergamo, the other of France.

Papa Giovanni soleva dedicare ogni sera un pò di tempo, per scrivere alcuni pensieri su qualche tema particolare. Il 4 Maggio 1963, un mese esatto prima di morire, scrisse questa riflessione sul suo stemma

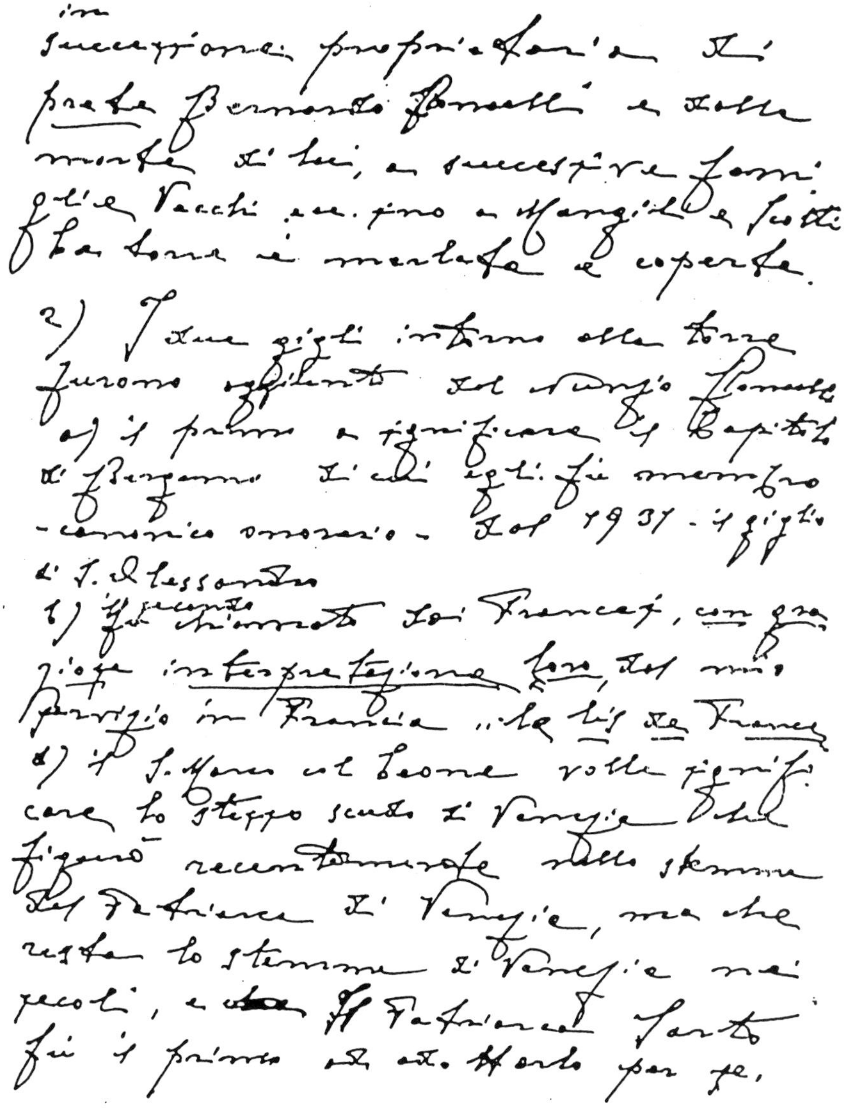

[handwritten note, in Italian]

im
successione proprietaria di
prete Bernardo Fornelli e dalla
morte di lui, a successive formi-
glie Vacchi ecc. fino a Mangili e sotti
la torre e merlata e coperte.

2) I due gigli intorno alle torre
furono aggiunti dal servizio Fornelli
a) il primo a significare il Capitol
di Bergamo di cui egli fu membro
-canonico onorario - dal 19 31 - i gigli
di S. Alessandro
b) il secondo dai Francesi, con gra-
ziosa interpretazione loro, del mio
servizio in Francia "le lis de France
c) il S. Marco col leone volle significare lo stesso scudo di Venezia che
figurò recentemente nella stemma
del Patriarca di Venezia, ma che
resta lo stemma di Venezia nei
secoli, e che il Patriarca Sarto
fu i primo a ... farlo per se.

---

pontificio. Ricordando che i francesi gli avevano sempre chiesto se i due gigli avessero alcuna relazione con la Francia, egli risponde che uno gli ricorda la sua Bergamo natìa, l'altro la Francia.

Papst Johannes verbrachte oft einige Zeit am Abend, Gedanken über ein gewisses Thema niederzuschreiben.Am 4.Mai 1963, genau ein Monat vor seinem Tod, schrieb er diese kurze These über sein päpstliches Wappen. Er sagte, dass die Franzosen ihn immer gefragt hätten, ob die beiden *fleurs-de-lis* eine Beziehung zu Frankreich hätten, und seine Antwort, dass eine ihn an seinen Geburtsort Bergamo, die andere an Frankreich erinnern würde.

The Tower of St. John.
La Torre di San Giovanni.
Der St. Johannesturm.

John XXIII has his coat of arms on one of the two organs on the left side of the apse. It is not difficult to read the name 'Giovanni XXIII' in the Cortile di S. Damaso at the entrance of the lifts and on the adjacent doors, and also in the Vatican Gardens by the Grotto of Lourdes, where an inscription reminds us that the altar came from the Grotto of Masabielle and was a present offered to the Holy Father by the Bishop, Mons.Théas. To see the coat of arms of John XXIII again, we have to go further along and up to that imposing tower which after considerable restoration and renovation has been given the name Torre S. Giovanni.

Had this unforgettable Pope lived a few years longer, he would have liked to have gone there to pray and to admire *pulcherrimum almae Urbis prospectum*, the most beautiful view of that wonderful City as an inscription states, also noting that the restoration work was carried out in the fourth year of a pontificate which so sadly ended in the fifth.

But the work remained and it was the Tower of St. John which welcomed the Patriarch Athenagoras in October 1967, and later became the home for two months of the former Patriarch of Hungary, Cardinal Mindszenty after His Eminence left his fifteen years refuge in the American embassy in Budapest and went into exile to the Vatican.

Above the entrance door to the tower Patriarch Athenagoras, the illustrious guest of Paul VI, was able to see another tower in miniature: that of his 'brother' the Patriarch of the West in whose pontificate the brotherhood awoke from a long sleep.

Remaining in the Vatican Gardens, we can see Pope John's coat of arms once more, above the entrance of the old pontifical mint which,

246

after having been used for a while as an electrical power station, became a storage hall for carpets, armchairs, prie-dieu and surplus furniture from the Floreria Apostolica.

Before leaving the Vatican through the Gate of St. Anna, we see on our left the building that houses the post office where those beautiful postage stamps originate that are collected by philatelists all over the world. The rapid growth of the international postal traffic caused new problems to the Vatican State. During the pontificate of John XXIII, an additional floor had to be built onto the small palace which houses the post office. Pope Roncalli's coat of arms now surmounts the small palace with an inscription which itself seems to revive the custom of ancient Rome, the *"imperatoria brevitas"*, the imperial brevity of announcements: *"Pius XI aedificavit Joannes XXIII altius eduxit"* – "Pius XI built it, John XXIII raised it higher".

We now reach the pontificate of Paul VI, Giovanni Battista Montini (1963–1978). Pope Montini's name immediately suggests what one of the heraldic charges in his coat of arms will be, the others, the *fleurs-de-lis*, he inherited from his family. After the conclave of 1963 they seemed to give credence to the adherents of the prophecies of St. Malachy

The arms of John XXIII on the Palace of the Vatican Post Office.

Lo stemma di Giovanni XXIII sul palazzo delle poste vaticane.

Das Wappen von Johannes XXIII über the Palast des vatikanischen Postamts.

The coat of arms of John XXIII on the monumental organ on the left side of the aisle in St. Peter's Basilica.

Lo stemma di Giovanni XXIII sul monumentale organo a sinistra dell'abside nella Basilica di S. Pietro.

Das Wappen von Johannes XXIII an der imposanten Orgel im linken Seitenschiff der St. Peter Basilika.

The arms of Pope Roncalli above the entrance of the Tower of St. John.

Lo stemma di Papa Roncalli sulla porta d'ingresso della torre San Giovanni.

Das Wappen von Papst Roncalli über dem Eingangstor des St. Johannesturms.

Popes John XXIII and Paul VI wearing their coats of arms embroidered on both falls of the stole.

I Papi Giovanni XXIII e Paolo VI coi loro stemmi ricamati sui due lati della stola.

Die Päpste Johannes XXIII und Paulus VI tragen ihre Wappen auf beiden Seiten der Stolen gestickt.

which had foretold that John XXIII would be *"pastor et nauta"*, the shepherd and the sailor, a description which would have fitted far better John's immediate successor, that intrepid globe-trotter Paul VI, to whom Malachy gave the attribute *"flos florum"*, usually referring in the past to the *fleur-de-lis*. True, among the eighty cardinals who attended the conclave – the largest number ever – Cardinal Archbishop Montini of Milan was the only cardinal to have *fleurs-de-lis* in his coat of arms.

249

The traditional arms (above) and a modern version (below) of Paul VI.

Lo stemma tradizionale (in alto) e moderno (in basso) di Paolo VI.

Das traditionelle Wappen (oben) und eine moderne Ausführung (unten) von Paulus VI.

Heraldic *mobili* of Paul VI: *monti* and *fleurs-de-lis*.

Mobili di Paolo VI: monti e gigli.

Heraldische *mobili* von Paulus VI: *monti* und *fleurs-de-lis*.

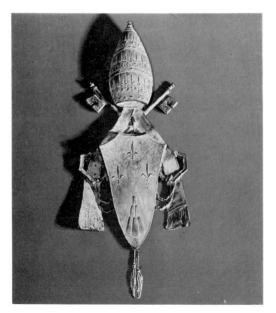

Paul VI (1963–1978)
Paolo VI (1963–1978)
Paulus VI (1963–1978
GIOVANNI BATTISTA MONTINI.

The blazon of Paul VI is *"di rosso, al monte di sei pezzi all'italiana, uscente dalla punta dello scudo accompagnato in capo di tre gigli posati 1 e 2, il tutto d'argento"*; gules, issuant from the base a mount of six *coupeaux* in Italian fashion and in chief three *fleurs-de-lis* one and two *argent*.

His coat of arms can be seen in St. Peter's Basilica on the floor in front of the chapel of Michelangelo's Pietà; Paul VI had the Pietà restored after a mentally deranged person had mutilated it. We find the Pope's arms in the Aula della Benedizione, the enormous hall above the portico of the Basilica and where newly elected popes step onto the balcony for the first time and give their Blessing *"Urbi et Orbi"*. The Montini arms are also in the Sala del Concistoro and in several rooms on the second floor of the Apostolic Palace which were modernised during his pontificate.

Finally we see them in that majestic hall built for the Synod of Bishops, instituted by Paul VI during the Vatican Council, and also in the grandiose Aula for public audiences, designed and built by the architect Pier Luigi Nervi, between the Ospizio di S. Marta and the Palazzo del S. Uffizio.

Sadly there are no *monte all'italiana* or *fleurs-de-lis* to remind us of Pope Montini in the Vatican Gardens at the rear of the Pinacoteca where now the Archeological, the Paleochristian, the Ethnological and the Missionary Museums are housed.

Above: the seal of Paul VI. Below: Vatican postage stamps; the cancellation also includes heraldry.

In alto: il sigillo di Paolo VI. In basso: francobolli del Vaticano; anche l'obliterazione include l'araldica.

Oben: das Siegel von Paulus VI. Unten: vatikanische Briefmarken; auch der Entwertungsstempel ist heraldisch.

PAX TIBI MARCE EVANGE LISTA MEUS

XX

JOHN PAUL I (1978)
TO
JOHN PAUL II (1978– GLORIOSAMENTE REGNANTE)

We have now arrived at the end of our heraldic excursions in the Vatican through fifty-eight pontificates, from Eugene IV (1431) to John Paul II, who ascended the See of St. Peter in 1978 and who is at the time of writing this chapter in the eighth year of his pontificate.

The successor to Paul VI was John Paul I, Albino Luciani who reigned from 26 August to 28 September 1978. His pontificate of thirty-three days was too short to leave behind many heraldic mementoes. His coat of arms appeared on the tickets for audiences. His successor, John Paul II, commemorated the short pontificate of Pope Luciani when he ordered the striking of a Pontifical Medal which bears his portrait and his armorial bearings. He also had the arms of John Paul I placed in the Cortile della Pigna, where during his short reign the work continued on the underground galleries for the Secret Archives of the Vatican. The work had been started in the pontificate of Paul VI at the initiative of Antonio Cardinal Samorè, who in 1974 had become Librarian and Archivist of the Holy Roman Church.

That coat of arms of John Paul I will keep his memory alive. The blazon of his coat of arms is: "*d'azzurro al monte di sei pezzi d'argento all'italiana uscente dalla punta dello scudo, accompagnato in capo da tre stelle d'oro di cinque punte; al capo patriarcale di San Marco, che è d'argento al leone alato e nimbato passante al naturale reggente un libro aperto*

John Paul I (1978), ALBINO LUCIANI, and (opposite) his coat of arms.

Giovanni Paolo I (1978), ALBINO LUCIANI, e (lato opposto) suo stemma.

Johannes Paulus I (1978), ALBINO LUCIANI, und (gegenüber) sein Wappen.

A second design for the arms of John Paul I.

Un secondo disegno per lo stemma di Giovanni Paolo I.

Ein zweiter Entwurf für das Wappen von Johannes Paulus I.

The seal of John Paul I.
Il sigillo di Giovanni Paolo I.
Das Siegel von Johannes Paulus I.

recante la leggenda: PAX TIBI MARCE EVANGELISTA MEUS''; – *azure* from the base a mount of six *coupeaux argent* surmounted by three five-pointed stars gold; the patriarchal chief of San Marco, *argent* a winged and haloed lion passant proper holding an open book with the motto PAX TIBI MARCE EVANGELISTA MEUS.

One day after the election to the papacy the Holy Father personally telephoned Mons. Heim in London to discuss his pontifical arms. Pope Luciani knew exactly what he wanted: he wished to retain the partriarchal chief of San Marco as a special sign of his esteem and affection for the late John XXIII and to remember the happy days he had spent as

254

Cardinal Karol Wojtyla pays homage to the newly elected Pope John Paul I, who only reigned for one month.

Il Cardinale Karol Wojtyla rende omaggio al neo-eletto Papa Giovanni Paolo I, che regnò per un solo mese.

Kardinal Karol Wojtyla huldigt dem neu gewählten Papst Johannes Paulus I, der nur einen Monat regierte.

Partriarch of Venice. Although before he had been elevated to the patriarchal see, he had adopted for his . blazon some mountains to remind him of his birthplace Canale d'Agordo, an upland village about 1,000 metres above sea level in the Dolomites; he told Archbishop Heim that he wished to adopt the six *coupeaux all'italiana* in silver from the arms of Paul VI whom he wanted to honour as well.

The three golden stars which occupy the centre of his coat of arms, were the subject of a fairly long discussion between the Holy Father and Archbishop Heim. At first Pope

Luciani wanted three six-pointed stars; he changed this on the same day to five-pointed stars as he felt that he should adopt three *stelle all'italiana* (five-pointed) rather than three *stelle di David* (six-pointed). When Mons.Heim asked the Pope whether the stars should perhaps represent some Marian symbolism, such as the name from the Litany of the Blessed Virgin, *Stella Matutina*, the Holy Father replied that the stars should stand for the motto that had sustained him all his life 'Faith, Hope and Charity'.

From the two designs which were sent to the Apostolic Palace by special messenger, John Paul I selected as his official coat of arms a traditional design which was published on the eve of his enthronement; however, he also wanted to make use of the second design on the first postage stamps that would be issued during his pontificate. However, the post-humously-issued stamps with the portrait of John Paul I and his coat of arms used the traditional design.

There remains John Paul II, Karol Wojtyla, Cardinal Archbishop of Krakow, who was elected by the conclave in October 1978 as successor to John Paul I, and who is truly *gloriosamente regnante*, gloriously reigning, at the time of publication of this book.

Above: the medal *'Sede Apostolica Iterum Vacante'* (1978). Below: the medal commemorating the short reign of John Paul I which his successor had struck posthumously.

In alto: la medaglia *'Sede Apostolica Iterum Vacante'* (1978). In basso: la medaglia commemorativa del breve pontificato di Giovanni Paolo I. Fu coniata a titolo postumo dal suo successore.

Oben: die Medaille *'Sede Apostolica Iterum Vacante'* (1978). Unten: die Gedenkmedaille an das kurze Pontifikat von Johannes Paulus I, die von seinem Nachfolger herausgegeben wurde.

The blazon of his coat of arms has caused some discussion, not to say controversy, because it did not conform with the heraldic practices of most countries. The blazon is: *"d'azzurro alla croce latina d'oro decentrata a destra e accompagnata nel cantone senestro della punta colla lettera 'M' (per Maria) d'oro"*; azure, a Latin Cross gold, slightly off centre to the dexter side and in the lower part on the sinister side the letter 'M' also gold.

Before I endeavour to explain the blazon, I should mention that the *Annuario Pontificio* gave the blazon of Cardinal Wojtyla differently: the field was *"d'azzurro del mare"* a dark blue, the Latin Cross was gold but the letter 'M' black, which made it hardly visible on the dark blue field.

There was no shortage of advisers who suggested that John Paul II should change his blazon completely. However, apart from the deeply spiritual symbolism of the Pontiff's heraldic charges, he made it absolutely clear that the arms he had proudly borne as Archbishop of Krakow were the arms he would bear as Universal Pastor. The only concession he made was that the letter 'M' should also be gold in future and the blue of the field lighter.

The blazon of the arms of John Paul II is first and foremost a visible sign of the homage he pays to the central mystery of Christianity: the Redemption. The Latin Cross, the principal heraldic charge and which is off-centre, takes on a different significance when seen together with the second heraldic charge, the letter 'M'. This majestic capital 'M' symbolises the presence of Mary at the foot of the cross and highlights her exceptional participation in the Redemption. The Pope's deep devotion to the Blessed Virgin Mary was also expressed in the motto of Cardinal Wojtyla: TOTUS TUUS.

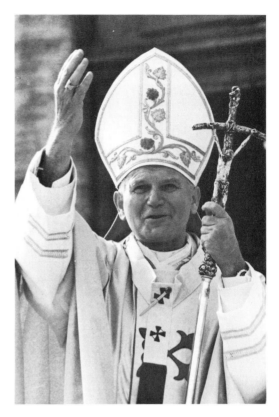

John Paul II (1978–) and his arms.
Giovanni Paolo II (1978–) e suo stemma.
Johannes Paulus II (1978–) und sein Wappen.
KAROL WOJTYLA

INIZIO DEL PONTIFICATO DI
S.S. GIOVANNI PAOLO II

Commemorative postage stamps to mark the beginning of the pontificate of Pope John Paul II. His Holiness ordered a similar set to be issued to remember the short reign of John Paul I.

Francobolli commemorativi dell'inizio del pontificato di Giovanni Paolo II. Sua Santità ordinò che ne fosse emesso uno simile per commemorare il breve pontificato di Giovanni Paolo I.

Gedenkbriefmarken zum Beginn des Pontifikats von Johannes Paulus II. Seine Heiligkeit ordnete an, einen ähnlichen Satz herauszubringen zur Erinnerung an das kurze Pontifikat von Johannes Paulus I.

The arms of Cardinal Wojtyla.
Lo stemma del Cardinale Wojtyla.
Das Wappen von Kardinal Wojtyla.

Although it did not take long for articles and chapters to appear in learned journals and books, trying to prove that the arms of John Paul II were typical Polish armorial bearings, and that only Poland and Switzerland allowed letters of the alphabet as heraldic charges, the fact remains that the coat of arms of this Polish Pope is far more expressive in its spiritual meaning than in heraldic conformity.

There has not been enough time to see the arms of John Paul II in many places in the Vatican; it has already been added to those of his two predecessors in the Cortile della Pigna. The works begun in the pontificate of Paul VI

The Pontifical Ecclesiastical Academy. Founded in 1701 by Clement XI as 'The Pontifical Academy for Noble Ecclesiastics', one of its requirements for admission was, until the reform by Pius XI in 1937, that the candidate could prove noble descent. Above the balcony on the first floor, one can see two coats of arms, that of the reigning Pope and the arms of the Cardinal Secretary of State *pro tempore* and Protector of the Academy. At the time of writing this book, the arms of John Paul II and Cardinal Agostino Casaroli were displayed, (below).

La Pontificia Accademia Ecclesiastica. Fondata nel 1701 da Clemente XI come 'Pontificia Accademia dei Nobili Ecclesiastici'; uno dei requisiti per l'ammissione era, fino alla riforma di Pio XI nel 1937, quello che il candidato potesse provare una discendenza nobile. Sul balcone del primo piano si possono vedere due stemmi, quello del Pontefice regnante e quello del Segretario di Stato *pro tempore*, Protettore dell'Academia. Quando fu scritto questo libro gli stemmi erano quelli di Giovanni Paolo II e del Cardinale Agostino Casaroli, (in basso).

Die Pontifikale Geistliche Akademie. Gegründet in 1701 von Klemens XI als 'Pontifikale Akademie für Geistliche Adlige', eine der Bedingungen dort studieren zu dürfen war, dass der Kandidat Beweis adliger Abstammung prüfen konnte. Über dem Balkon auf der ersten Etage sieht man zwei Wappen; das des regierenden Papstes neben dem des päpstlichen Staatssekretärs *pro tempore*, dem Beschützer der Akademie. Zur Zeit des Schreibens dieses Buches, waren es die Wappen von Johannes Paulus II und Kardinal Agostino Casaroli, (unten).

were finally completed during the first years of his own pontificate, and on 18 October 1980 he inaugurated the underground galleries of the Secret Archives of the Vatican.

On 11 April 1986 John Paul II inaugurated the two new bronze doors of the Vatican Library and of the Secret Archives, sculpted by Gismondi. On both we can see the coat of arms

259

Left: the seal of John Paul II; right: an adaption of the papal arms for use on audience tickets.

A sinistra: il sigillo di Giovanni Paolo II; a destra: una adattazione dello stemma papale da usarsi nei biglietti d'udienza.

Links: das Siegel von Johannes Paulus II; rechts: eine Umbearbeitung des päpstlichen Wappens zum Gebrauch auf Audienzausweisen.

of John Paul II next to the arms of Cardinal Stickler, Librarian and Archivist of the Holy Roman Church.

As in the case of his two predecessors, his coat of arms adorns the two Papal Awards of merit, the Cross *pro Ecclesia et Pontifice* and the Medal *Benemerenti*. It is also on the reverse side of the Pontifical Medal *Anno I*, and it has appeared on numerous postage stamps. Several valuable *objets d'art* which have been presented to the Pontiff and which are in the Apostolic Palace, bear his coat of arms, but only from the dome of the Vatican Basilica, looking down to the gardens in front of the *Palazzo del Governatore della Città del Vaticano*, we can see a flower bed which, so much more vividly and beautifully than stone or metal can do, shows the art which is so unique to our gardeners: a reproduction of the coat of arms of the reigning pontiff in glorious colours. They use flowers and foliage to create their masterpiece.

If coats of arms sculpted into stone or cast in metal challenge the centuries and provide

260

precious evidence to the historian, then flowers convey a different message: they show us that the papacy which is commemorated by heraldry in all its glory, is everlastingly alive.

Se gli stemmi scolpiti nella pietra sfidano i secoli e sono testimonianze preziose per lo storico, anche i fiori, però – queste cose così straordinariamente vive – possono essergli talvolta di aiuto. È forse troppo ardito considerarli un simbolo, e concludere che l'araldica pontificia, come il papato di cui vuol tramandare le glorie, è perennemente viva?

Wenn in Stein gemeisselte oder in Metall geschmiedete Wappen die Jahrhunderte überleben und den Historikern wertvollen Beweis liefern, haben die Wappen, die in Blumen den Vatikanischen Garten verzieren, eine andere Botschaft. Zeigen sie uns nicht dass das Papsttum, das von der Heraldik für alle Zeiten geehrt ist, nicht auch für alle Zeiten lebt?

APPENDIX

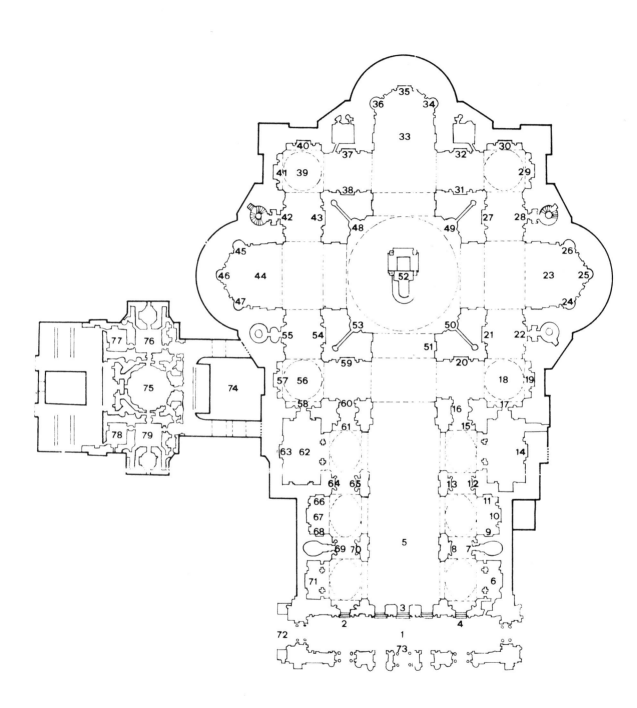

264

265

1 Vorhalle	41 Säulenaltar
2 Totentür	42 Monument Alexanders VII.
3 Hauptportal (Filarete)	43 Herz Jesu-Altar
4 Heilige Pforte	44 Linkes Querschiff
5 Kirchenschiff	45 Altar des hl. Thomas
6 Pietà-Kapelle	46 Altar des hl. Joseph
7 Monument Leos XII.	47 Altar der Kreuzigung
8 Monument Christinas	des hl. Petrus
von Schweden	48 Statue der hl. Veronika
9 Monument Pius' XI.	49 Statue der hl. Helena
10 Kapelle des hl. Sebastian	50 Statue des hl. Longinus
11 Monument Pius XII.	51 Statue des hl. Petrus
12 Monument Innozenz' XII.	52 Konfessio und Papstaltar
13 Monument der Gräfin Mathilde	53 Statue des hl. Andreas
14 Sakramentskapelle	(Eingang der Grotten)
15 Monument Gregors XIII.	54 Altar der Lüge
16 Monument Gregors XIV.	55 Monument Pius' VIII.
17 Monument Gregors XVI.	(Sakristei-Tür)
18 Gregorianische Kapelle	56 Klementinische Kapelle
19 Altar der Muttergottes	57 Altar des hl. Gregors
als Helferin	58 Monument Pius' VII.
20 Altar des hl. Hieronymus	59 Altar der Verklärung
21 Altar des hl. Basilius	60 Monument Leos XI.
22 Monument Benedikts XIV.	61 Monument Innozenz' XI.
23 Rechtes Querschiff	62 Chorkapelle
24 Altar des hl. Wenzeslaus	63 Altar der Unbefleckten
25 Altar der hl. Processus	Empfängnis
und Martinianus	64 Monument Pius' X.
26 Altar des hl. Erasmus	65 Monument Innozenz' VIII.
27 Schiff-Altar	66 Monument Johannes' XXIII.
28 Monument Klemens' XIII.	67 Kapelle des Tempelgangs
29 Altar des Erzengels Michael	Mariae
30 Altar der hl. Petronilla	68 Monument Benedikts XV.
31 Altar des hl. Petrus,	69 Monument
der Tabitha erweckt	M. Clementina Sobieskis
32 Monument Klemens' X.	(Eingang zur Kuppel)
33 Apsis	70 Stuart-Monument
34 Monument Urbans VIII.	71 Baptisterium
35 Thron des hl. Petrus	72 Glocken-Bogen
36 Monument Pauls III.	73 Schiff-Mosaik
37 Monument Alexanders VIII.	74 Braschi-Platz
38 Altar des hl. Petrus,	75 Sakristei
der den Lahmen heilt	76 Sakristei der Pfründner
39 Säulenkapelle	77 Schatzkammer
40 Altare des hl. Leos des Großen	78 Kapitelsaal
	79 Kanoniker-Sakristei

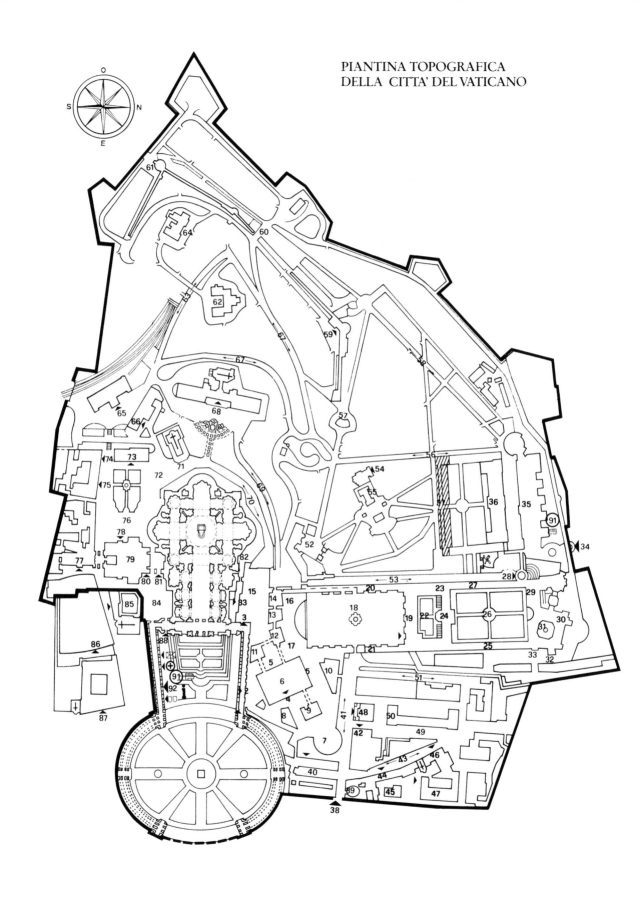

PIANTINA TOPOGRAFICA
DELLA CITTA' DEL VATICANO

LEGENDA

1 Portone di Bronzo
2 Scala di Pio IX
3 Scala Regia
4 Scala Nobile
5 Logge
6 Cortile di S. Damaso
7 Torrione di Niccolò V
8 Cortile del Maggiordomo
9 Cortile di Sisto V
10 Cortile del Triangolo
11 Cortile del Maresciallo
12 Cortile dei Pappagalli
13 Cortile Borgia
14 Cortile della Sentinella
15 Cappella Sistina
16 Torre Borgia
17 Appartamento Borgia
Stanze di Raffaello (II piano)
18 Cortile del Belvedere
19 Biblioteca Apostolica
(Salone di Sisto V)
20 Biblioteca Apostolica
(Museo Sacro)
Galleria delle Carte
Geografiche (II piano)
21 Galleria Lapidaria
22 Cortile della Biblioteca
23 Torre dei Venti
24 Braccio Nuovo del Museo
Chiaramonti
25 Museo Chiaramonti
26 Cortile della Pigna
27 Biblioteca Apostolica
(Museo Profano)
Galleria dei Candelabri e
degli Arazzi (II piano)
28 I Quattro Cancelli

29 Museo Gregoriano Egizio
Museo Gregoriano Etrusco
(II piano)
30 Museo Pio-Clementino
31 Cortile Ottagono
32 Scala del Bramante
33 Fontana della Galea
34 Musei Vaticani: Ingresso
35 Musei Gregoriano-Profano,
Pio-Cristiano e Missionario-
Etnologico
36 Pinacoteca
37 Museo Storico
38 Ingresso di Sant'Anna
39 Chiesa parrocchiale di
Sant'Anna
40 Cortile della Guardia Svizzera
41 Via del Belvedere
42 Tipografia Poliglotta Vaticana
43 Via del Pellegrino
44 Laboratorio Restauro Arazzi
45 Servizio Assistenziale del
Santo Padre
46 Tipografia «L'Osservatore
Romano»
47 Residenza del corpo
del servizio di vigilanza
48 Posta centrale
49 Farmacia
50 Palazzo del Belvedere
51 Via Pio X
52 Fontana del Sacramento
53 Stradone dei Giardini
54 Pontificia Accademia delle
Scienze
55 Casina di Pio IV
56 Viale del Giardino Quadrato
57 Fontana dell'Aquilone
58 Viale Centrale del Bosco
59 Direzione Radio Vaticana
60 Grotta di Lourdes
61 Torre S. Giovanni

62 Collegio Etiopico
63 Viale del Collegio Etiopico
64 Centro trasmittente
«Marconi»
65 Stazione ferroviaria
66 Studio del mosaico
67 Viale dell'Osservatorio
68 Palazzo del Governatorato
69 Via del Governatorato
70 Via delle Fondamenta
71 Chiesa di S. Stefano
72 Largo S. Stefano
73 Palazzo del Tribunale
e Ufficio Centrale di Vigilanza
74 Residenza dell'Arciprete
75 Palazzo S. Carlo
76 Piazza S. Marta
77 Ospizio di S. Marta
78 Uff. Rev. Fabbrica S. Pietro
79 Sacrestia, Canonica, Museo
Storico Artistico (Tesoro)
80 Ufficio Parrocchiale
81 Ufficio Scavi
82 Uscita Grotte
83 Centro diffusione oggetti
religiosi
84 Piazza Protomartiri Romani
85 Collegio e Camposanto
Teutonico
86 Aula Paolo VI
87 Palazzo Santo Uffizio
88 Arco delle Campane

✉ Ufficio Postale

✚ Posto di Soccorso S.M.O.M.

91 Autobus Musei Vaticani

✕ Posto di ristoro

□□ Toilette

92 Ufficio Informazioni Pellegrini
e Turisti

THE INDEX

The Index contains no reference to names in the Author's Preface and Acknowledgements. Specific heraldic charges, tinctures and terminology used in the blazons described in this work can be found in any book on basic heraldry; unless a particular blazon has been subject to controversy, the charges are not listed in the Index.

Popes are listed under their adopted names, but a cross-reference is given under their family name. For reasons of consistency, Basilicas, Chapels and many Churches are listed under their Italian names.

Coats of arms of popes reproduced in colour are given after the Pope's name: COL. PL.

Quirinal, see: *Palazzo del Quirinale*